KT-195-636

AQA computing

Exclusively endorsed by AQA

A2

Kevin Bond
Sylvia Langfield

ɔrnes

Text © Kevin Bond and Sylvia Langfield 2009
Original illustrations © Nelson Thornes Ltd 2009

Published in 2009 by:
Nelson Thornes Ltd
Delta Place
27 Bath Road
CHELTENHAM
GL53 7TH
United Kingdom

10 11 12 13 / 10 9 8 7 6 5 4 3

A catalogue record for this book is available from the British Library

ISBN 978 0 7487 8298 7

Cover photograph by Alamy
Illustrations by Angela Knowles and Fakenham Photosetting
Page make-up by Fakenham Photosetting
Printed and bound in China by 1010 Printing International Ltd

Acknowledgements

The authors and publishers wish to thank the following for permission to use copyright material:

Figure 1.1.1 Getty/Steve Cole; Figure 1.1.2 Enigma machine, Bletchley Park www.bletchleypark.org.uk/content/enigmasim.rhtm; Figure 1.1.5 London Underground map No. 09/E/1472/P, Pulse Creative Limited; Figure 1.1.7 Alamy/ (a) Richard Cooke, (b) Arco Images, (c) Fabrice Bettex, (d) blickwinkel, (e)Martin Harvey, (f) David Cook; Figure 1.1.9 AA Media Ltd; Figure 1.4.4–5 Turing machine screenshots reproduced by kind permission from SwissEduc www.swisseduc.ch/compscience/karatojava/turingkara/screenshots.html; Figure 2.2.1 Frances Topp; Figure 2.4.1 Alamy/Eye Candy Images; Figure 2.4.8 Jupiter Images/Tetra; Figure 2.5.1 AA Media Ltd; Figure 2.5.18–19 Algorithmics adapted from *Algorithmics: The Spirit of Computing* by David Harel, Yishai Feldman 2004; Figure 3.1.11 European Space Agency; Figure 5.2.1 IBM; Figures 5.3.1–5.3.10 MySQL products reproduced by kind permission from Sun Microsystems, Inc.; Figure 6.2.15 IANA; Figures 6.2.19, 6.3.5, 6.3.6, 6.3.8–10, 6.3.14, 7.5.1–5 Microsoft product screen shot(s) reprinted with permission from Microsoft Corporation; Figures 6.3.13, 7.2.5, 7.6.1–2 OpenGL (Open Graphics Library) www.opengl.org managed by the Khronos Group www.khronos.org; Figure 7.1.1 iStockphoto; Figure 7.1.3 Activity for Systems Development reproduced by kind permission from CS Inside, Department of Computing Science, Glasgow University, http://csi.dcs.gla.ac.uk; Figure 7.1.15 AA Media Ltd. Figure 7.2.2 Michael McElwee; Figure 7.6.1 Kevin Chandler; Figure 7.6.2 Dave Hayden, Aylesbury Grammar School.

Every effort has been made to contact the copyright holders and we apologise if any have been overlooked. Should copyright have been unwittingly infringed in this book, the owners should contact the publishers, who will make the corrections at reprint.

Contents

Introduction

Nelson Thornes has worked in partnership with AQA to ensure this book and the accompanying online resources offer you the best support for your A2 course.

All resources have been approved by senior AQA examiners so you can feel assured that they closely match the specification for this subject and provide you with everything you need to prepare successfully for your exams.

These print and online resources together **unlock blended learning**; this means that the links between the activities in the book and the activities online blend together to maximise your understanding of a topic and help you achieve your potential.

These online resources are available on kerboodle! which can be accessed via the internet at **www.kerboodle.com/live**, anytime, anywhere. If your school or college subscribes to this service you will be provided with your own personal login details. Once logged in, access your course and locate the required activity.

For more information and help visit **www.kerboodle.com**

Icons in this book indicate where there is material online related to that topic. The following icons are used:

Learning activity

These resources include a variety of interactive and non-interactive activities to support your learning:

- Animations
- Presentations
- Simple interactive activities
- Worksheet activities
- Glossary

Progress tracking

These resources include a variety of tests that you can use to check your knowledge on particular topics (Test yourself) and a range of resources that enable you to analyse and understand examination questions (On your marks...).

Research support

These resources include WebQuests, in which you are assigned a task and provided with a range of web links to use as source material for research. These are designed as extension resources to stretch you and broaden your learning, in order for you to attain the highest possible marks in your exams.

Study skills

These resources are designed to help students develop skills that are key to this course, for example, in identifying computing problems and solutions and for their coursework. These resources include text and image analysis tools, discussion tools, a study kit to guide your coursework and video and audio interviews.

Practical

This icon signals where there is a relevant practical activity to be undertaken on a computer. Where indicated, support is provided online.

Weblinks

Our online resources feature a list of recommended weblinks, split by chapter. This will give you a head start, helping you to navigate to the best websites that will aid your learning and understanding of the topics in your course.

How to use this book

This book covers the specification for your course and is arranged in a sequence approved by AQA. The main text of the book will cover Units 3 and 4 of the AQA A Level Computing specification. These units account for 30% and 20%, respectively, of the overall A Level mark.

Unit 3 directly relates to COMP3 of the AQA specification, and therefore covers Problem solving, Programming, Operating systems, Databases and Networking. Through this unit, you will build on the topics covered during AS study, focusing on computational thinking, examining the strengths and limitations of computers in terms of what can be computed, developing your programming knowledge and skills and enhancing your understanding of problem solving. Through this unit, you will also look closely at communication and networking. On completion of this unit, you should have acquired the vital knowledge and skills necessary to complete your A Level coursework.

Unit 4 has been designed to provide step-by-step guidance in the completion of your A Level coursework. Within this project, you will need to demonstrate that you fully comprehend the concepts covered in your AS study, and within COMP3 of your A2 study, and that you have acquired the necessary skills and knowledge to produce a computer-based programmed solution to a problem. By working through this unit you will build a comprehensive A Level Computing project that will be truly representative of your full potential.

Unit openers give you a summary of the content you will be covering and give a brief context for each topic/section.

The features in this book include:

Learning objectives

At the beginning of each section you will find a list of learning objectives that contain targets linked to the requirements of the specification. The relevant specification reference is also provided.

Key terms

Terms that you will need to be able to define and understand are highlighted in bold blue type within the text, e.g. **Attribute**. You can look up these terms in the glossary.

Case studies

Real-life examples to illustrate a point.

Did you know?

Interesting facts to bring learning to life.

Remember

Key points and common errors.

Activities

Classroom-based tasks to help you apply knowledge and understand key concepts.

Questions

Short questions that test your understanding of the subject and allow you to apply the knowledge and skills you have acquired to different scenarios.

AQA Examiner's tip

Hints from AQA examiners to help you with your studies and to prepare you for your exam.

AQA Examination-style questions

Questions in the style that you can expect in your exam. These are supplied free at: **www.nelsonthornes. com/aqagce/computing.htm**

AQA examination questions are reproduced by permission of the Assessment and Qualifications Alliance.

Nelson Thornes is responsible for the solution(s) given and they may not constitute the only possible solution(s).

Web links for this book

As Nelson Thornes is not responsible for third party content online, there may be some changes to this material that are beyond our control. In order for us to ensure that the links referred to in the book are as up-to-date and stable as possible, the websites are usually homepages with supporting instructions on how to reach the relevant pages if necessary.

Please let us know at **kerboodle@nelsonthornes.com.** if you find a link that doesn't work and we will do our best to redirect the link, or to find an alternative site.

Introduction to this book

The next twenty years will be the most exciting and momentous of times for anyone involved in studying Computing or Computer science. Computing is a relatively young subject with many great problem-solving challenges facing it currently. Today it stands at the crossroads of a revolution in thinking as did Physics at the beginning of the twentieth century. What has heralded this revolution? The answer is the realisation that computation is not just something that computers do but something that nature does and does in a way that is only just being recognised. 'In DNA, nature has placed an information process at the foundations of life,' claims Nobel Laureate David Baltimore. Coded within DNA in an alphabet of inheritance are the instructions for the creation of life forms as well as the data that represents the forms of life to be produced.

Computer scientists concern themselves with representations of information in patterns of symbols, known as data or data representations, the most appropriate representation for this data, and the methods or sets of instructions to transform this data into new representations to provide new information. These methods or sets of instructions must also be represented by patterns of symbols called procedural representations. There are only two essentials of computation therefore:

- a series of representations
- a set of instructions for transforming each representation to the next in the series.

We draw the conclusion from this that the computer is not essential! The computer is one of many possible media in which computations can happen. What you are embarking on by studying from this book is an understanding of the principles on which computation is based. Computing is a principles-based discipline and it exists in a principles-based framework, unlike ICT, which exists in a technology-based framework. If you want only to acquire skills in using office tools created by computer scientists then studying ICT would be a better option. If you want to be at the forefront of twenty-first-century thought and science then study Computing.

Computation is at the heart of the quest to unravel the secrets of life, to understand more about the human brain, the natural sciences and economic systems. This quest began back in 1936 when Alan Turing discussed what is meant by computation in his famous paper on computable numbers. Turing used an imagined machine that has come to be called a Turing machine (this was before the advent of the electronic digital computer) to reason about the act of computation. At the present time, computer scientists use electronic computers as tools to study computation. However, in the future, computer scientists may very well use nature itself, in the form of DNA computers, to study the limits and complexities of computations.

Computer scientists are very much interested in computational procedures for solving problems, such as the mapping of the human genome. These procedures are called algorithms. Algorithms are at the heart of computing. In this book, you will learn to write simple algorithms to describe and control what computers can do. You will also learn about the limitations of algorithms for, despite the awesome power of computers, at present computing machines cannot be controlled to do many things that humans can do easily, such as object recognition. This is one of the great challenges facing computer scientists today. If you are reading this book as you are about to embark on the learning adventure that is Computing, then consider where you might be in ten years time – a fully qualified computer scientist? Will you be one of those computer scientists contributing to the solution of one or more of the great challenges of computer science in the twenty-first century? If on the other hand, your future career takes a different route, then rest assured you will have acquired a good grounding in how to think computationally and to solve problems in a logical manner. Thinking computationally is considered an important life skill underpinning many careers. By the way, if you are also considering studying maths, try to take the Decision maths or Discrete maths option. You will find these subjects very useful to your future studies in Computing. Good luck in your studies!

Problem solving, programming, operating systems, databases and networking

Introduction

Sections in this unit:

There is something much deeper to computing than simply programming, abstractions, logic gate circuits and networks. That is what you are going to explore in this unit. Unit 1 began by explaining what is meant by computation. The subject of computer science or computing is not the study of phenomena surrounding computers. The subject is more fundamental than this. Hence the subject's wider applicability in fields such as biology and physics. What happens in cell structures of living organisms is a form of computation. The language of computing is a language that people working in other fields need to acquire in order to understand and advance their own fields. This is not because the computer is a tool that they use to carry out their work. It is because computation is the principle on which much of what is observed is explained. For example, the copying of DNA is a computational process that relies on a principle of computation that code can be treated as data and data can be treated as code.

This unit focuses on what it means to think computationally. This means to think recursively, to reformulate a seemingly difficult problem into one that we know how to solve. Allocating fish to fish tanks so that predators are not together with fish that they like to eat, reduces to a similar representation for the problem of allocating mobile phone frequencies to mobile phone cells, i.e. a graph representation; hence, the study of graphs in this unit. Computational thinking means choosing an appropriate representation or modelling the relevant aspects of a problem to make it tractable or amenable to solution; hence, the study of information hiding, abstraction applied to large complex systems and data structures in this unit. Tractability is an important field of study in computing. Algorithms can be classified theoretically according to how long they would take to process input. You will study the complexity of algorithms so that you can understand that computation has limits. For example, computer scientists have defined a class of problems abbreviated 'NP' (for nondeterministic polynomial), whose members share the feature that finding solutions can take centuries on the fastest supercomputers, but verifying solutions takes only a fraction of a second. This class includes over 3000 common problems from science, engineering and commerce – problems such as finding optimal routes, producing a school timetable and scheduling airline flights. No fast algorithm is known that will solve any of these. However, it is known that a fast algorithm for any one can be converted to a fast algorithm for any other. They are all equally hard (or equally easy). If anyone finds a fast solution for any one, everyone benefits. For this reason, the Clay Mathematics Institute is offering a $1 million prize to anyone who can solve the 'NP' problem. This discovery of computer science helps us understand why intractable computational problems are encountered in so many fields, and it has helped computer scientists find heuristics (tricks) for producing approximate solutions that solve these problems most of the time in a reasonable time period.

You will consider the question of what it means to compute by studying a Turing Machine, a theoretical machine that predates the invention of the digital computer. Computer scientists construct theoretical models of computer systems so that reliable predictions can be made of how these will behave – in just the same way that engineers use theoretical models of structures to predict how buildings, airplanes and cars will behave. Computer scientists also have to deal with design, social, legal and ethical issues related to the explosion in communication systems such as MP3 file-sharing systems, privacy and security of electronic data, electronic voting systems, verification and security. This unit addresses these from the point of view of a computer scientist.

Computational thinking takes a particular approach to solving problems and designing systems. The approach is to distinguish the principles from practices. In Unit 2 you studied the Internet. Computer scientists view the Internet as a system for moving data (communication), a set of protocols (coordination), an information retrieval system (recollection) and a set of software layers (design). The principles are communication, coordination, recollection and design. In this unit you will study information retrieval and design.

The overall message that this unit attempts to convey is that computational principles exist independently of computers and therefore are not subject to change as the technology of computers changes. However, to be a computing professional you must not only know the principles but you must also be competent in the core practices. The four core practices of computing professionals are programming, systems, modelling and innovating. To be a complete computing professional, you should know the principles and be competent in the four practices. Unit 4 will give you grounding in the core practices via the computing project.

1.1 Information hiding and abstraction

People who are employed in the defence industries in the UK are granted access to information on a need-to-know basis because of the nature of their work. Employees are required to sign the Official Secrets Act. Defence industries exist because, even in the 21st century, countries need to be able to have the potential to resist attacks that threaten their very existence. In the Internet Age, threats do not come just from military action but can arise from cyber attacks where the very means to govern, control defences and conduct economic affairs can be frustrated by an attack on the very computers on which so much of these now depend. Access to information must be restricted for security reasons.

However, the systems that are produced must be usable by people, so what exactly is it that needs to be hidden or kept secret? It is the internal design of such systems – how they operate – that is kept secret for a very obvious reason. If the design of a system is revealed, then this information could be used to defeat the system. In Fig. 1.1.1 messages are encrypted and decrypted by the black-box devices at each end of the communications link. The internal design of these devices is a secret, which makes it harder to unscramble the encrypted messages.

During the Second World War, the German armed forces communicated secretly using a system of messages encrypted with Enigma machines. The Allies were greatly aided in their attempts to decrypt these secret messages by the capture of an Enigma machine. They were able to reverse-engineer the captured Enigma machine and to confirm how the plain text messages were converted into encrypted messages. This greatly assisted the construction of computer programs for the Colossus computer to decrypt future intercepted encrypted messages. The Colossus machine was an electronic computing device used by British code breakers to read encrypted German messages during the Second World War. The instructions for these programs were placed in the computing machine by actually rewiring the machine's control store.

Activity

Ask your teacher to arrange a visit to Bletchley Park.

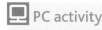

PC activity

Use the World Wide Web to research the cyber attacks on Estonia and Georgia.

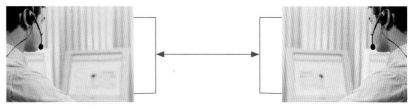

Fig. 1.1.1 *Secure communications achieved by a device at each end of the communications link*

Information hiding and interfaces

Fig. 1.1.2 shows an Enigma machine simulator. Its internal design is a complex system of rotors and wiring hidden behind a nearly standard qwerty keyboard. This keyboard is the **interface** between the user and the internal operation of the machine. The operator does not need to know how the operation of the machine is achieved only how to control it.

Fig. 1.1.2 *Enigma machine simulator*

Interfaces are important for another reason. By hiding the complexities of the machine behind a well-designed interface, users are able to learn how to use a machine with the minimum of training. The design of the motor car is a classic example. Motor cars present a standard interface (pedals, gear shift, instrument gauges, light switches) on which people can be trained and licensed without needing to know anything about the internal design and operation of the internal combustion engine, transmission systems and gearboxes. What is more, a licensed driver does not need to learn a completely different way of driving every time they drive a new model, accepting that there are slight differences between manual and automatic transmissions.

The same applies to software or hardware systems in computing. A user familiar with the Windows operating system can successfully use this operating system on a range of computers with different processors, different amounts of RAM, etc. If we consider each computer as a separate object, the user controls each through an identical interface, even though behind this common interface the objects are different. This is a very important principle: two objects having different implementations can have identical interfaces.

Interfaces are fundamental in object-oriented systems. Objects are known only through their interfaces. There is no way to know anything about an object or to ask it to do anything without going through its interface. An object's interface says nothing about its implementation – different objects are free to implement requests differently. That means two objects having completely different implementations can have identical interfaces.

Fig. 1.1.3 illustrates this for a computer game involving different species of snake. The user's request to the snake objects A and B is 'kill mouse'. If snake A is implemented as a python and snake B as a viper, the request is implemented differently in each case:

- The python will attempt to squeeze the mouse to death.
- The viper will attempt to poison the mouse to death.

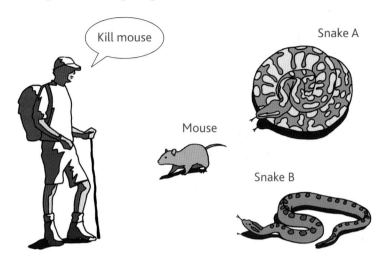

Fig. 1.1.3 *Snake objects that interpret the message 'kill mouse' differently*

In software, snakes A and B declare that they can carry out an operation *Kill* that takes one parameter, *animal*, and returns one value, *Done*. This is known as the operation's signature. The set of all signatures defined by an object's operations is called the interface to the object. An object's interface characterises the complete set of requests that can be sent to the object.

For the scenario in Fig. 1.1.3, the parameter *animal* has value *mouse* and if snake A succeeds in killing the mouse, it returns *Done* set equal to *True* while snake B returns *False*.

Questions

1. What is meant by information hiding?
2. What is meant by the term 'interface'?
3. Give two reasons why interfaces are important.

Information hiding and design

The principle of information hiding allows the division of any piece of equipment, software or hardware into separate parts. For example, a car is a complex piece of equipment. In order to make the design, manufacturing and maintenance of a car manageable, a car is divided into parts with particular interfaces hiding design decisions. Some car parts or components are engine, gearbox, transmission (transfers power from engine to wheels), lights and pedals.

Did you know?

There is a very important difference between abstraction in computing and abstraction in maths and the sciences. Computing typically deals with two levels of abstraction at a time, whilst maths and the sciences deal with only one level of abstraction at a time. For example, the layered structure of operating system code supports a piece of code in one layer calling a routine in the layer below. For an application programmer, the interface between the two layers is called an Application Programming Interface (API). Each layer represents a level of abstraction. In maths, 'let x represent the number of apples sold in one transaction' is a single level of abstraction.

Did you know?

David Parnas first introduced the concept of information hiding around 1972. He argued that the primary criteria for system modularisation should concern the hiding of critical design decisions. In his seminal paper 'On the Criteria to Be Used in Decomposing Systems into Modules', published in 1972, he stressed hiding 'difficult design decisions or design decisions which are likely to change'. Hiding information in that manner isolates clients from requiring intimate knowledge of the design to use a module, and from the effects of changing those decisions.

This division into separate components or modules allows the car manufacturer to offer different options. For example, a particular model may be offered with different engine capacities: 1.8 litres, 2.5 litres, 3 litres. All three engines fit the same transmission, the same engine mounts and the same controls. This is possible because all three engines provide the same interface to the other parts or modules that they connect to.

Engineers design the car by dividing the task up into pieces of work which are assigned to teams. Each team then designs their component to a particular standard or interface. This allows each team to be flexible in the design of the component while ensuring that all of the components will fit together.

Information hiding provides flexibility of software design. A well-designed computer program has a solution in which the source code has been decomposed into modules using the principle of information hiding. When a programmer is working on one module, he or she does not need to know the detail contained in other modules, only what other modules can do for the programmer. Also, changes are much easier to make with this approach, because typically the changes are local to a module rather than global changes across all modules.

Questions

4 Explain the principle of information hiding in the context of car manufacture and maintenance.

5 Explain how information hiding can be applied to software development.

6 State six reasons why information hiding is useful.

Abstraction

The human brain is an exceptional piece of biological machinery capable of recognising objects even when most of their detail has been removed. This is illustrated in Fig. 1.1.4, which are abstractions of real objects.

Fig. 1.1.4 *Outline of an Alsatian dog*

Humans deal with abstractions all the time, because they are useful in everyday problem solving. For example, travelling from Marylebone to Russell Square by London Underground involves taking the Bakerloo line from Marylebone as far as Piccadilly Circus then changing to the Piccadilly line and travelling as far as Russell Square (Fig. 1.1.5). It is not necessary to include more details than these to succeed in reaching the desired destination. In fact, this example of Harry Beck's London Underground map is itself an abstraction. Unnecessary details have been removed and the layout of the stations adjusted to make the map easy to use. Ease of use is a very good reason to work with an abstraction rather than the real thing. **Abstraction** means omitting unnecessary details. Abstraction as a skill is drawing out the essence of a problem, solving it and then seeing what other problems can be solved using the same techniques.

■ Key terms

Abstraction: representation that is arrived at by removing unnecessary details.

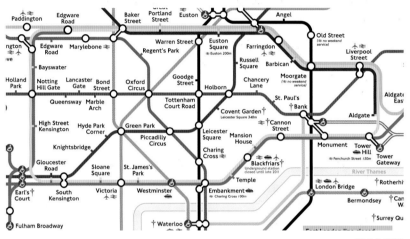

Fig. 1.1.5 *Henry Beck's map of the London Underground*   09/E/1472/P

The human brain versus the computer

When computer systems are supplied with images of objects they often struggle to recognise these objects. For example, a computer system tasked with differentiating between cat and dog images performs very badly, as it struggles to cope with the variations in cat and dog species. It is very difficult to program a computer system with the essence of cats and dogs. A rule-based approach in which a computer system is programmed with the essential details of cats and dogs, i.e. an abstraction of cats and dogs, does not work very well. A statistical approach has better success. A computer program is used that learns from seeing a large number of different cat and dog images. With sufficient training, a computer system using this program can draw conclusions with reasonable success when presented with cat and dog images it has not seen before.

However, a human will still perform better than a computer, especially when lighting conditions and background vary in the images. The current state of computing science means that a computer system presented with an image such as Nu bleu IV (1952) by Henri Matisse would struggle to recognise the human form that this abstraction represents.

Why are computers so poor at recognising objects and interpreting abstractions compared with the human brain? After all, computers are good at sorting lists of words into alphabetical order. The reason that computers are good at this is because sorting can be done through a

■ Did you know?

Nu bleu IV (1952) can be found at http://www.ocaiw.com/galleria_maestri/image.php?id=530&id_img=2078&catalog=pitt&lang=en&letter=M&start=1&name=Henri+Matisse.

series of logical steps or rules and computers are very good at following rules very quickly. However, codifying object recognition in a series of rules is extremely difficult. There will always be some special case that is not catered for. It is clear that the human brain must use a different mechanism for object recognition.

Kinds of abstraction used in computation

Abstraction is also very useful when computations need to be performed. There are two kinds of abstraction used in computations: generalisation or categorisation, and representation.

Questions

7 Explain what is meant by abstraction.

8 Explain the role of abstraction in solving a problem of your choosing.

Generalisation

Fig. 1.1.6 illustrates what is meant by abstraction by generalisation or classification. Rising up the hierarchy, we go from specific examples of animals to categories they belong to. The relationship is classified as 'is a kind of'. For example, *Rover* is a kind of *Alsatian*, which is a kind of *dog*, etc. All Alsatian dogs have characteristics in common. Similarly, all types of dog have *dog* characteristics in common. This grouping together by identifying common characteristics is a feature of generalisation.

Fig. 1.1.7 illustrates a simple program design example of abstraction of the generalisation kind. We start at the top of the diagram with an abstract description of the problem to be solved, CalculateSumOfTwoNumbers, and then descend through successive refinements until we arrive at the detail of the solution. In this approach, the detail is not considered until absolutely essential. This is also an example of decomposition where a problem is progressively decomposed into more and more detailed modules.

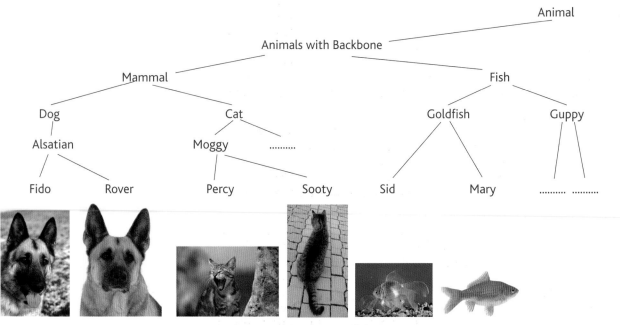

Fig. 1.1.6 *An example of abstraction by classification*

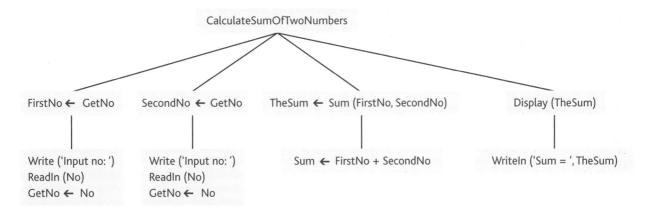

Fig. 1.1.7 *Top-down structured design as an example of abstraction*

Questions

9 Show how abstraction by generalisation would help in the design of a program to convert a temperature reading in degrees Fahrenheit to degrees Celsius (Hint: take 32 away and multiply by 5/9).

10 Using sufficient details to illustrate generalisation, draw a part of a classification chart for plants.

Pigeonhole principle

Generalisation can be applied to problem solving by identifying a principle that is shared among solutions to different problems. One example of this is the pigeonhole principle, which states that, given two natural numbers n and m with $n > m$, if n items are put into m pigeonholes, then at least one pigeonhole must contain more than one item.

A simple application of this principle is a situation where there are six people who want to play football ($n = 6$ objects) but there are only five teams available that they can play for ($m = 5$ holes). This would not be a problem except that each of the six refuses to play on a team with any of the other five. To prove that there is no way for all six people to play football together, the pigeonhole principle says that it is impossible to allocate six people among five teams without putting two of the people on the same team. Since they refuse to play on the same team, at most five of the people will be able to play.

Why is this principle applicable to more than just the football team problem? The reason is that when unnecessary details of specific problems are ignored, the problems reduce to the common problem of fitting n items into m holes. For example, there must be at least two people in London with the same number of hairs on their head. Is this true or false?

We will use the pigeonhole principle to answer this as follows. A typical head of hair has around 150 000 hairs; it is reasonable to assume that no one has more than 1 000 000 hairs on his or her head ($m = 1\,000\,000$ holes) but there are more than 1 000 000 people in London (n is bigger than 1 million objects). If we assign a pigeonhole for each number of hairs on a head and assign people to the pigeonhole with their number of hairs on it, there must be at least two people with the same number of hairs on their head.

Activity

Explain using the pigeonhole principle why a lossless compression algorithm that makes at least one input file smaller will make some other input file larger.

PC activity

Use the World Wide Web to research collisions in the technique known as hashing and explain why this is an example of the pigeonhole principle.

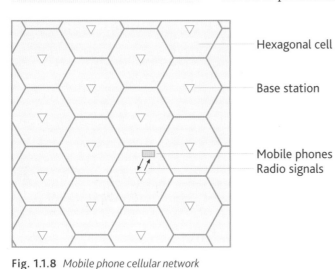

                                          Hexagonal cell

                                          Base station

                                          Mobile phones
                                          Radio signals

Fig. 1.1.8 *Mobile phone cellular network*

Questions

11 If there are n persons (where $n > 1$) who can shake hands with one another, explain using the pigeonhole principle why there is always a pair of persons who shake hands with the same number of people. Here the holes correspond to the number of hands shaken.

12 Assume that in a box there are 10 black socks and 12 blue socks and you need to get one pair of socks of the same colour. Supposing you can take socks out of the box only once and only without looking. How many socks do you have to pull out together? Use the pigeonhole principle.

Data representation

Representation abstraction is applied to problem solving. It is also known as problem abstraction or reduction. Details are removed until it becomes possible to represent the problem in a way that is possible to solve. For example, mobile phone networks consist of a series of base stations, each of which provides coverage over a limited range for mobile phones as shown in Fig. 1.1.8. A mobile phone signal is not strong enough to reach across the country. Instead, a mobile phone communicates with its nearest base station, usually mounted on a mast. The nearest base station then relays the signal to a base station in a neighbouring cell, which in turn passes the signal onto another base station. The mobile phone company needs to buy the radio frequencies used by its customers and base stations. These frequencies are very expensive, so the company needs to buy as few as possible and reuse them. The problem is that if mobile phones and base stations in neighbouring cells use the same broadcast frequency, calls will interfere with each other, resulting in poor communications.

Worked example

You are required to work out the minimum number of frequencies that a mobile phone company must buy in order to provide interference-free coverage of the area covered by phone masts located as indicated in Table 1 and Fig. 1.1.9.

Table 1 *Mobile phone masts problem*

Mobile phone mast	Location	Potential for interference
1	Stoke Mandeville Road	2, 3
2	Town Centre	1, 5
3	Turn Furlong	1, 4, 5
4	Tring Road	3, 5
5	Broughton	2, 3, 4

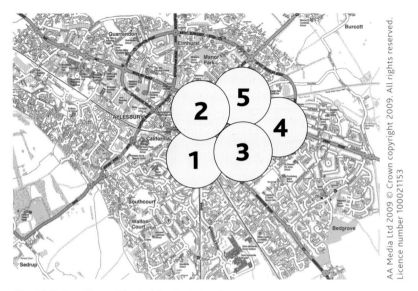

Fig. 1.1.9 *Locations of the mobile phone masts*

How could you represent the information from Fig. 1.1.9 and Table 1 to make it easier to understand? Remove unnecessary detail and represent it as a collection of circles (vertices) and connecting lines (edges) (see Fig. 1.1.10). Fig. 1.1.10 is known as a graph. This is a model of the mobile phone network shown in Fig. 1.1.9.

Next represent Fig. 1.1.10 in table form (Table 2). The first column is known as an adjacency list.

Table 2 *Adjacency list representation*

1–2, 3	Vertex 1 is connected to vertices 2 and 3
2–1, 5	Vertex 2 is connected to vertices 1 and 5
3–1, 4, 5	Vertex 3 is connected to vertices 1, 4 and 5
4–3, 5	Vertex 4 is connected to vertices 3 and 5
5–2, 3 and 4	Vertex 5 is connected to vertices 2, 3 and 4

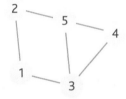

Fig. 1.1.10 *Abstract representation of mobile phone problem*

We now need to use the following algorithm to solve this problem:

```
Repeatedly
  Remove vertex with lowest connectivity wherever it appears
  in adjacency list
  Add this vertex and its list of connected vertices in the
  adjacency list to a record of those removed, held in order
Repeatedly
  Replace vertices in reverse order of removal, noting a
  legal colour each time
```

Figs 1.1.11 and 1.1.12 show the two stages of automation of this algorithm. We represent different frequencies by different colours. The solution shows that only three frequencies are required.

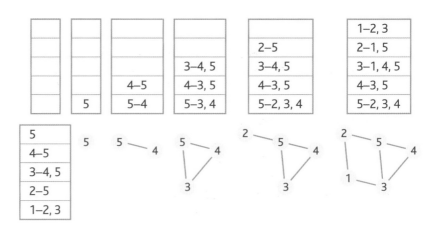

Fig. 1.1.11 *Automating the first stage of the algorithm for selecting frequencies by working from right to left*

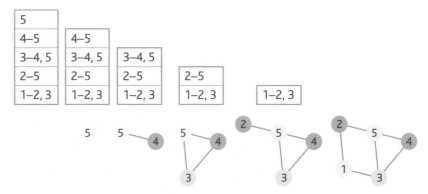

Fig. 1.1.12 *Automating the second stage of the algorithm for selecting frequencies*

Activity

Fig. 1.1.13 shows a map divided into numbered sections. Colour in this map following only two rules:

▪ No countries that share a border should be the same colour.

▪ As few colours as possible should be used.

Represent the map as a graph first and an adjacency list, then use the algorithm on page 11 to solve the problem.

The mobile phone problem solution and the map colouring problem solution have an abstract representation and an algorithm in common. The solutions to both problems may be automated by coding the common algorithm in a programming language and the common representation in the data structures supported by the programming language.

Abstraction in this context has enabled the essence of a problem to be identified then solved and the solution applied to other problems that share this essence.

Fig. 1.1.13 *Outline map*

Questions

13 Using a map of South America, draw a representation that would help in the task of colouring this map with the minimum number of colours and so that no two countries sharing a border would have the same colour.

14 Examination clash candidates A, B, C, D, E need to be assigned holding rooms so that the following rules are observed:

   A must not be in the same room as B and C.

   B must not be in the same room as D and E.

   C must not be in the same room as A and D.

   D must not be in the same room as E, B and C.

   E must not be in the same room as B and D.

  a Find a representation of this problem similar to that used for map colouring.

  b What is the minimum number of rooms that will be required?

In this topic you have covered:

- information hiding means hiding design details behind a standard interface
- information hiding allows different objects to have identical interfaces
- information hiding supports sharing of a common interface among many different objects, with the consequence that users of the objects do not need to be retrained when changing from using one object to using another
- information hiding means that a user needs to have no knowledge of the module's or object's internal design in order to use it
- information hiding means the internal design can be kept secret
- information hiding allows flexibility; one module may be replaced by another module with an identical interface but a different internal design or manner in which the module's function is carried out
- information hiding means changes are made easier because changes are local to modules
- abstraction means omitting unnecessary detail
- abstraction as a skill is the drawing out of the essence of a problem, solving it and then seeing what other problems can be solved using the same techniques
- there are two kinds of abstraction used in computations: generalisation or categorisation, and representation
- abstract generalisation enables problems to be solved by ignoring the details
- abstract generalisation enables problems to be solved by applying a general principle
- abstract representation enables the essence of a problem to be identified
- abstract representation shows the commonality between a range of different problems
- abstract representation supports a problem-solving technique in which problems are transformed into a common representation.

Key terms

Algorithm: a sequence of unambiguous instructions for solving a problem, i.e. for obtaining a required output for any legitimate input in a finite amount of time. It can be represented as a Turing machine program.

What is an algorithm?

An **algorithm** is a sequence of unambiguous instructions for solving a problem, i.e. for obtaining a required output for any legitimate input in a finite amount of time.

The word 'instructions' implies that there is something or someone capable of understanding and following the given instructions. We call this a computer. Before electronic computers, the word 'computer' meant a human being involved in performing numeric calculations, hence the concept of an algorithm is not dependent on hardware executing a computer program. Fig. 1.2.1 shows a computer executing an algorithm to transform input into output.

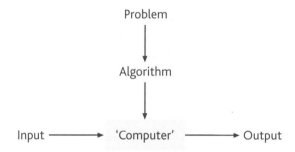

Fig. 1.2.1 *Input–computer–output problem solving*

In this chapter we will be interested mainly in answering the question, How long does it take for a machine to compute an output for a given input?

Algorithm essentials

Algorithms for the same problem can be based on very different ideas and can solve the problem with dramatically different speeds.

Consider the problem of summing the first n natural numbers, e.g. 1, 2, 3, …, 98, 99, 100, where $n = 100$.

One way this can be done is to add each number in turn to a running total: $1 + 2 = 3$, then $3 + 3 = 6$, then $7 + 5 = 12$, and so on. This algorithm can be expressed in the following pseudocode:

```
Algorithm SumNaturalNumbers(n)
//Implements sum of first n natural numbers
//Input: An integer n ≥ 1
//Output: Sum
Sum ← 0
For i ← 1 To n
 Do Sum ← Sum + i
Return Sum
```

// indicates a comment.

Tracing this algorithm for $n = 100$ produces the result Sum = 5050.

Another way that this can be done uses the formula Sum $= \frac{1}{2}n(n + 1)$:

```
Algorithm SumNaturalNumbersByFormula(n)
//Implements sum of first n natural numbers
//Input: An integer n ≥ 1
//Output: Sum
Sum ← n*(n + 1)/2
Return Sum
```

Tracing this algorithm for $n = 100$ produces the result Sum = 5050.

From these two different ways of solving the same problem, some observations may be made regarding algorithms in general:

■ Each step in any algorithm must be unambiguous.

■ The range of inputs for which an algorithm works has to be specified carefully.

■ Several algorithms for solving the same problem may exist.

■ Algorithms for the same problem can be based on very different ideas and can solve the problem with dramatically different speeds.

Table 1 shows the results when both algorithms are coded in a programming language and executed on an Intel Celeron processor operating at 1.50 GHz inside a laptop.

Key point

Algorithms for the same problem can be based on very different ideas and can solve the problem with dramatically different speeds.

Table 1 *Execution time of the two algorithms for summing the first n natural numbers*

n	Time (s)	
	SumNaturalNumbers(n)	SumNaturalNumbersByFormula(n)
2 000 000 000	9.05	Negligible
3 000 000 000	13.59	Negligible
4 000 000 000	17.98	Negligible

In the case of the SumNaturalNumbers(n) algorithm, the basic operation of addition dominates for even small values of n. In fact, there are n addition operations. Using this fact enables us to estimate the time for one addition operation:

$$\frac{1}{3}\left(\frac{9.05}{2\,000\,000\,000} + \frac{13.59}{3\,000\,000\,000} + \frac{17.98}{4\,000\,000\,000}\right) = 4.52 \times 10^{-9} \text{ seconds}$$

We can now estimate an execution time of this algorithm on the laptop for any value of n.

PC activity

Timing the execution of the program

Write separate programs for both algorithms in a programming language that you are familiar with. Use the programming language's support for capturing current time to output a measure of the execution time of each program for various values of n. Note that your program will need to handle very large integer values. See **www.nelsonthornes.com** for a solution in Delphi.

Why do we need to study algorithms?

Problem solving is an important human activity. Algorithms are considered to be procedural solutions to problems. What makes computer science different from other disciplines is its emphasis on precisely defined procedural solutions consisting of specific instructions for getting answers. Therefore, designing algorithms is a problem-solving activity that can be useful regardless of whether a computer is involved.

Also, computer programs would not exist without algorithms. Therefore a study of algorithms is considered to be a cornerstone of computer science. There may be more than one algorithm for solving a particular problem, as we have seen already, and algorithms for solving a particular problem may solve it with dramatically different speeds and with different memory requirements.

Algorithmic correctness

We must also ensure that an algorithm generates the correct output for all legitimate inputs, not just for some. Consider the crucial step in the SumNaturalNumbers(n) algorithm:

Sum ← Sum + i

for n = 1 then this step is executed just once, i.e.

Sum ← 0 + 1 = 1

and therefore SumNaturalNumbers(1) = 1. Next

SumNaturalNumbers(n+1) = SumNaturalNumbers(n) + (n + 1)

Setting n = 1 then,

SumNaturalNumbers(2) = SumNaturalNumbers(1) + (1 + 1)

Therefore

SumNaturalNumbers(2) = 1 + 2 = 3

But considering the For loop when n = 2, the loop terminates with

Sum ← 1 + 2

This gives the correct output. Therefore we may conclude that the algorithm is correct. However, correctness alone is not sufficient. We need also to consider how quickly an algorithm calculates its output and how much memory it consumes in the process.

Computational complexity

The **computational complexity of an algorithm** measures how economical the algorithm is with time and space.

The computational complexity of an algorithm depends on its time complexity and its space complexity. The **time complexity of an algorithm** indicates how fast the algorithm runs. The **space complexity of an algorithm** indicates how much memory the algorithm needs. Software devices such as personal digital assistants (PDAs) and mobile phones have limited memory for their data and their software. Therefore it is very important to develop programs with a small memory footprint.

Key terms

Computational complexity of an algorithm: measures how economical the algorithm is with time and space.

Time complexity of an algorithm: indicates how fast an algorithm runs.

Space complexity of an algorithm: indicates how much memory an algorithm needs.

However, there is extensive interest in time efficiency because there are still many problems for which exact solutions take longer in running time than a human lifespan for all but a very small range or size of input.

To some extent, there is a trade-off between time and space. Suppose the factors of every integer from 1 to 1000 are to be computed. Here is a simple algorithm for finding the factors of one integer n:

```
Algorithm FindFactors(n)
//Finds every factor of a given natural number, n
//Input: An integer n ≥ 2
//Output: Factors
While n > 1
  Do
    Factor ← LeastFactor(n)
    Output Factor
    n ← n Div Factor //Integer division
```

It uses this algorithm:

```
Algorithm LeastFactor(n)
//Finds smallestfactor of a given natural number, n
//Input: An integer n ≥ 2
//Output: Smallest factor
i ← 1
Repeat
  i ← i + 1
Until (n Mod i) = 0 //Integer remainder division
Return i
```

The algorithm FindFactors(n) will output the factors of n in increasing order. Now suppose this algorithm is used in a For loop to calculate the factors of every natural number between 2 and 1000 as follows:

```
For i ← 2 To 1000 Do FindFactors(n)
```

This is very efficient in terms of space since it uses only three variables i, n and Factor. However, it is very wasteful in terms of time. For example, to calculate the factors of the natural number 200, the algorithm calls LeastFactor(200). Its first output is 2. The algorithm continues by halving its argument n using n ← n Div Factor, which results in a new intermediate value of n of 100. LeastFactor(100) is then called. However, well before the For loop reached FindFactors(200), it would have calculated FindFactors(100), when n was 100. Thus, in calculating FindFactors(200), the algorithm repeats the calculation FindFactors(100) because it does not remember that it has found these factors already. In fact, for the number 10, this algorithm works out its factors 110 times in calculating the factors of each natural number in the range 10 to 1000.

It obviously makes sense to store the factors of the number 10 the first time and then refer to the stored values whenever the factors of 10 are needed again. In fact, it makes sense to store the factors for each value of n for future use when first calculated. A 1000 × 9 array is sufficient for this. Table 2 shows a sample from this array.

Table 2 *Sample of the factor array for values of* n *from 2 to 1000*

n	Factors								
55	5	11	1	1	1	1	1	1	1
56	2	2	2	7	1	1	1	1	1
57	3	19	1	1	1	1	1	1	1
58	3	29	1	1	1	1	1	1	1
59	59	1	1	1	1	1	1	1	1
60	2	2	3	5	1	1	1	1	1
61	61	1	1	1	1	1	1	1	1
62	2	31	1	1	1	1	1	1	1
63	3	3	7	1	1	1	1	1	1

The algorithm should now take less time but consume more space. This example illustrates a general principle that one can often improve time complexity of an algorithm at the expense of space complexity.

■ Measuring an input's size

Many algorithms run for longer on larger inputs. For example, it takes longer to reverse the elements of a list of 1000 numbers than a list of 10 numbers. Therefore it is logical to investigate an algorithm's time efficiency or time complexity as a function of some parameter n indicating the algorithm's input size. For the list of 1000 numbers, $n = 1000$. For the list of 10 numbers, $n = 10$.

Fig. 1.2.2 *Reversing elements of a list of 10 numbers*

Fig. 1.2.3 *Reversing a list of 1000 numbers*

■ Complexity of a problem

For some algorithms, defining what to use as a size measurement can be strongly influenced by the data making up the input and the algorithm. For example, if we use a brute-force algorithm to test for the presence of a particular value in a list of integers such as in Fig. 1.2.2, we need to consider three separate cases:

▨ **Worst-case complexity** is the complexity computed when we just happen to choose an input that requires the longest time or greatest workload. For example, if we search for the value 90, every number in the list must be examined.

▨ **Best-case complexity** is the complexity computed when we choose an input that requires the shortest time or smallest workload. For example, if we search for the value 25, then only one comparison is required.

▨ **Average-case complexity** is the average complexity calculated by averaging the times for every possible input. For example, if we search in turn for 25, 4, 47, 1, 10, 7, 2, 12, 13, 90, the average number of comparisons is $10/2 = 5$.

However, when comparing an algorithm for a particular task with a different algorithm for the same task, we compare the worst-case times in the knowledge that each represents the slowest case or upper limit.

The **complexity of a problem** is taken to be the worst-case complexity of the most efficient algorithm which solves the problem. The emphasis on problems is very important because computer scientists have discovered that problems can be classified according to their complexity. The discovery of a more efficient algorithm for a particular problem can then be applied to all other problems belonging to the same class of complexity.

▨ Units for measuring time

Using a standard unit of time measurement such as a second to estimate the running time of a program implementing the algorithm would not be sensible. The estimate would be dependent on the speed of the computer, the quality of the program implementing the algorithm, and the compiler used in generating the machine code. For example, in the section on algorithm essentials (page 16), the laptop's basic addition operation was timed at 4.52×10^{-9} seconds, but what if the algorithm was executed on a supercomputer? The basic addition operation would be at least 1000 times faster on the supercomputer. Table 1 timings would therefore be 1000 times smaller for the supercomputer. This makes comparing the efficiency of algorithms difficult because of factors that can vary from computer system to computer system.

An alternative approach is to count the number of times each of the algorithm's operations is executed. However, this can be quite demanding to do. Fortunately, this is seldom necessary. Instead, it is sufficient to identify the operation contributing the most to the total running time and to compute the number of times this operation is executed. This operation is called the **basic operation**.

Thus, the established method for the analysis of an algorithm's time efficiency is based on counting the number of times the algorithm's basic operation is executed on inputs of size n.

▨ Order of growth

If b_{op} is the execution time of an algorithm's basic operation on a particular computer and $C(n)$ is the number of times this operation needs to be executed for input n for this algorithm, then the estimated running time $T(n)$ of a program implementing this algorithm on this computer is given by the following formula:

▨ **Key terms**

Complexity of a problem: taken to be the worst-case complexity of the most efficient algorithm which solves the problem.

Basic operation: the operation contributing the most to the total running time.

$$T(n) = b_{op}C(n)$$

This formula will only give an estimate of the running time. But it allows us to answer the question, How much longer will the algorithm take to execute if its input size is doubled?

Suppose

$$C(n) = \tfrac{1}{2}n(n + 1) = \tfrac{1}{2}n^2 + \tfrac{1}{2}n$$

For all but very small values of n, this formula becomes

$$C(n) \approx \tfrac{1}{2}n^2$$

To understand why this is true, consider $n = 1000$, so $n^2 = 1\,000\,000$. Ignoring the n term introduces an error of only 1000 in $1\,000\,000$, which is 0.1%. Therefore, doubling the size of the input quadruples the execution time as follows:

$$\frac{T(2n)}{T(n)} = \frac{b_{op}C(2n)}{b_{op}C(n)} \approx \frac{\tfrac{1}{2}(2n)^2}{\tfrac{1}{2}n^2} = \frac{4n^2}{n^2} = 4$$

Note that the question has been answered without needing to know the value of b_{op}. It cancelled out in the ratio, as did the multiplicative constant $\tfrac{1}{2}$. It is for these reasons that time efficiency analysis ignores multiplicative constants and concentrates on the count's **order of growth** for large inputs. Order of growth assesses by what factor execution time increases when the size of the input is increased.

In the example, if the input size doubles, the algorithm takes four times longer to execute. The order of growth is therefore quadratic, i.e. varies as the square power. We say that the algorithm is $O(n^2)$. This is a consequence of the fact that the number of times that the basic operation needs to be executed, $C(n)$, is proportional to the square of the input size, n, for all but very small values of n. Table 3 shows values of n^2 for corresponding values of n. Doubling n always quadruples n^2. Notice how n^2 changes when n increases from 1000 to 2000 to 4000 to 8000.

■ Assessing order of growth

It is required to rearrange a line of discs consisting of an equal number of black and white discs so that the black discs end up on the right in one group and the white discs end up on the left in another group. For example, two black discs followed by two white discs become two white discs followed by two black discs, as shown in Fig. 1.2.4.

Here is a general algorithm for rearranging a line of discs containing an equal number of black and white discs for which the total number of discs ≥ 2:

Fig. 1.2.4 *Transforming an arrangement of two black and two white discs into two white and two black discs*

Table 3 *Table of n^2 values for values of n in the range 1000 to 10 000*

n	n^2
1000	1 000 000
2000	4 000 000
3000	9 000 000
4000	16 000 000
5000	25 000 000
6000	36 000 000
7000	49 000 000
8000	64 000 000
9000	81 000 000
10 000	100 000 000

■ **Key point**

$n^2 = n \times n$

$n^3 = n \times n \times n$

$n^4 = n \times n \times n \times n$

```
Algorithm RearrangeDiscs(LineOfDiscs, n)
//Rearranges a line of an equal number of black and white discs
//Inputs: Line of black and white discs
//        n, the total no of discs in line n ≥ 2
//Output: Rearranged line of discs
n ← n − 1
For NumberOfPairs ← n DownTo 1
  Do
    For j ← 1 To NumberOfPairs
      Do
          If LineOfDiscs[j] = black And LineOfDiscs[j + 1] =
          white
            Then Swap(LineOfDiscs[j], LineOfDiscs[j + 1])
```

Table 4 shows a trace of the execution of this algorithm.

Table 4 *Trace of execution of* RearrangeDiscs *algorithm*

n	NumberOfPairs	j	LineOfDiscs
4			●●○○
3	3	1, 2, 3	●○○●
3	2	1, 2	○○●●
3	1	1	○○●●

The basic operation for this algorithm is the comparison
If LineOfDiscs[j] = black And LineOfDiscs[j + 1] = white.

The number of comparisons is 3 when NumberOfPairs = 3, 2 when
NumberOfPairs = 2 and 1 when NumberOfPairs = 1. Therefore the
total number of comparisons is $1 + 2 + 3$ = the sum of the first $n − 1$
natural numbers. We know from earlier that the sum of the first k natural
numbers is $\frac{1}{2}k(k + 1)$, so we obtain the sum of the first $n − 1$ natural
numbers by writing $k = n − 1$, which gives $\frac{1}{2}n(n − 1)$. This result also
applies if n is 2, 3, 4, 5, 6 or any natural number greater than 6.

We can expand this formula to obtain

$$\frac{1}{2}n(n − 1) = \frac{n^2 − n}{2}$$

And for large n, we get

$$\frac{n^2 − n}{2} » n^2 = O(n^2)$$

This means that the order of growth of this algorithm is $O(n^2)$.

> **Activity**
>
> Try tracing the algorithm for
> $n = 4, 5$ and 6 to confirm that
> $\frac{1}{2}n(n − 1)$ applies.

Questions

1 Why are algorithms studied?

2 If $C(n)$ is the number of times an algorithm's basic operation needs to be
executed, say how much longer each of the following will take to run if
its input size is doubled: (a) $C(n) = \frac{1}{2}n$, (b) $C(n) = \frac{1}{4}n^3$, (c) $C(n) = 2^n$.

3 Why are the estimated running times of algorithms not measured in
seconds or milliseconds?

4 Explain how to estimate the running time of an algorithm.

5 What is meant by (a) the computational complexity of an algorithm and
(b) the computational complexity of a problem?

6   What is meant by (a) the time complexity of an algorithm and (b) the space complexity of an algorithm?

7   The following algorithm determines whether all the elements in a given array, A, of n elements are distinct. (a) By tracing this algorithm confirm that $C(n) = \frac{1}{2}n(n - 1)$. (b) How will $C(n)$ behave for large values of n?

```
Algorithm DistinctElements(A[1..n], n)
//Determines whether all elements in A are distinct
//Inputs: Array A and n, number of elements n ≥ 2
//Output: Returns "True" if all the elements are distinct
//        otherwise returns "False"
Result ← True
For i ← 1 To n – 1
  Do
        For j ← i + 1 To n
        Do
            If A[i] = A[j]
                Then Result ← False
Return Result
```

Table 5 *For small values of n, g appears to grow faster than f(n)*

n	f(n)	g(n)
0	1 000 000	1 000 000
1	1 000 012	1 000 012
2	1 000 032	1 000 044
3	1 000 066	1 000 096

Table 6 *Approximate values of function f and function g for larger values of n*

n	f(n)	g(n)
10^3	10^9	10^7
10^4	10^{12}	10^9
10^5	10^{15}	10^{11}
10^6	10^{18}	10^{13}

Key terms

Asymptotic behaviour of f: the behaviour of the function $f(n)$ for very large values of n.

Table 7 *Approximate values for f and g for even larger values of n*

n	f(n) ≈ n^3	g(n) ≈ $10n^2$
10^{10}	10^{30}	10^{21}
10^{20}	10^{60}	10^{41}
10^{30}	10^{90}	10^{61}
10^{40}	10^{120}	10^{81}

Asymptotic behaviour

Consider the following polynomials:

$$f(n) = n^3 + n^2 + 10n + 1\,000\,000$$
$$g(n) = 10n^2 + 2n + 1\,000\,000$$

A polynomial takes the form

$$p(n) = a_k n^k + a_{k-1} n^{k-1} + a_{k-2} n^{k-2} + \ldots + a_2 n^2 + a_1 n + a_0$$

where $a_k, a_{k-1}, a_{k-2}, a_2, a_1, a_0$ are constants called coefficients, n is a variable, n^k raises n to the power k, n^{k-1} raises n to the power $k-1$. For the case of $f(n)$ above, we can write

$$f(n) = a_3 n^3 + a_2 n^2 + a_1 n + a_0$$

where $k = 3$, therefore $a_3 = 1$, $a_2 = 1$, $a_1 = 10$ and $a_0 = 1\,000\,000$.

One way to assess how fast these functions grow is to try a few sample evaluations using a spreadsheet. Care should be exercised as choosing the wrong values of n can lead to misleading results (Table 5).

Looking at Table 5, it seems that function g grows faster than function f. But if n is chosen to be big enough, the value of function f easily dwarfs that of function g (Table 6).

In fact, for very large values of n, it is clear that the only term in function f that actually matters is n^3 and similarly the only term in function g that matters is $10n^2$.

The values that function f takes for very large values of n are said to define the **asymptotic behaviour of f**. We say that function f is of order n^3 because the asymptotic behaviour of f becomes increasingly indistinguishable from that of n^3 and we write $f = O(n^3)$. This means that the rate of growth of function f is ultimately the same as that of function n^3. Similarly, we say that function g is of order n^2 and write $g = O(n^2)$ to indicate that the rate of growth of function g (give or take a constant or two) is ultimately the same as that of function n^2. This is illustrated in Table 7.

For large values of n, it is the function's order of growth that counts. Table 8 contains values of a few functions particularly important for analysis of algorithms.

Table 8 *Values (some approximate) of several functions important for analysis of algorithms*

n	n^0	$\log_2 n$	n^1	$n \log_2 n$	n^2	n^3	2^n	$n!$
10^1	1	3.3	10^1	3.3×10^1	10^2	10^3	1.0×10^3	3.6×10^6
10^2	1	6.6	10^2	6.6×10^2	10^4	10^6	1.3×10^{30}	9.3×10^{157}
10^3	1	10	10^3	1.0×10^4	10^6	10^9	1.1×10^{301}	
10^4	1	13	10^4	1.3×10^5	10^8	10^{12}		
10^5	1	17	10^5	1.7×10^6	10^{10}	10^{15}		
10^6	1	20	10^6	2.0×10^7	10^{12}	10^{18}		

■ Big O notation

Given two functions f and g such that $g(n) \geq 0$ for all n, we write $f = O(g)$ – read as f is big o of g – if there exist constants $c, k > 0$ such that $f(n) \leq cg(n)$ for all $n > k$.

$O(g)$ represents the class of functions that grow no faster than g. Knowing which class an algorithm belongs to is particularly important when comparing two different algorithms that solve a particular problem. Quite clearly, an algorithm that grows at rate n^2, where n is the size of the input, cannot belong to the class $O(n)$, because this algorithm grows faster than the rate proportional to n.

Notice that the function g in the definition could easily be an overestimate. What we can say is that g grows at least as quickly as f and may indeed grow much more quickly. If we consider the functions in Table 8, we have

$f = O(\log_2 n)$
$f = O(n)$
$f = O(n\log_2 n)$
$f = O(n^2)$
$f = O(n^3)$
$f = O(2^n)$
$f = O(n!)$

■ Key terms

$O(g)$: called big O of g, represents the class of functions that grow no faster than g.

Order of complexity: of a problem is its big O complexity.

■ Order of complexity

The complexity of a problem is taken to be the growth rate of the most efficient algorithm which solves the problem. This complexity can be expressed by stating its order of growth in big O notation. It is known as the problem's **order of complexity**. Using Table 8, we can rank the orders of complexity as follows, with $n!$ greatest:

$O(n^0) << O(\log n) << O(n^1) << O(n\log n) << O(n^2) << \ldots$
$\ldots << O(n^k) << \ldots << O(2^n) << O(3^n) << \ldots << O(n!)$

Exponential time

Growth rates of the form 2^n, 3^n, ..., k^n, where k is a constant, are known as **exponential growth** rates and algorithms in this class are called **exponential time algorithms**.

Polynomial time

Growth rates of the form n^0, n^1, n^2, ..., n^k are known as **polynomial growth** rates and algorithms in this class are called **polynomial time algorithms**. It is very clear from Table 8 that exponential growth rates far exceed polynomial growth rates for large n. For example, when n increases by a factor of 10, n^2 increases by a factor of 100 whereas 2^n increases by a factor of approximately 10^{27}.

Linear time

A **linear time algorithm** is a polynomial time algorithm that executes in $O(n)$ time.

■ Questions

8 What is meant by the asymptotic behaviour of a function?

9 What is meant by big O notation?

10 Place the following in ascending order of complexity from the least complex to the most complex: $O(2^n)$, $O(n^3)$, $O(n)$, $O(n!)$, $O(n^2)$, $O(\log_2 n)$, $O(n\log_2 n)$.

11 Explain the following terms: (a) exponential growth, (b) polynomial growth, (c) polynomial time algorithm, (d) exponential time algorithm, (e) linear time algorithm.

In this topic you have covered:

- the meaning of the term 'algorithm'
- estimation of how long a machine will take to compute an output for a given input based on the basic operation of an algorithm
- time complexity of an algorithm as a function of the size of the input
- space complexity of an algorithm as a function of the size of the input
- meaning of complexity of a problem as the worst-case complexity of the most efficient algorithm which solves the problem
- big O notation and order of complexity
  $O(n^0) << O(\log n) << O(n^1) << O(n\log n) << O(n^2) << ...$
  $... << O(n^k) << ... << O(2^n) << O(3^n) << ... << O(n!)$
- growth rates of exponential time and polynomial time algorithms
- linear time algorithms are examples of polynomial time algorithms.

▮ Key point

As powerful as they are, FSMs cannot model English grammar.

▮ Key terms

State transition diagram: a directed graph whose nodes represent the states. An edge leading from state s to state t is called a transition and is labelled with a symbolic code, e.g. $a \mid b$. The a part of the label is called the transition's trigger and denotes the input symbol. The b part, which is optional, denotes the output symbol.

▮ Why finite state machines are useful

Many kinds of task can be modelled using a structure called a finite state machine.

Finite state machines (FSMs) are used extensively in applications in computer science. For example, finite state machines are the basis for

▥ Any kind of controller, e.g. traffic lights

▥ Specifying a language, e.g. given any string, an FSM determines if that string is in the language or not

▥ Programs for
– spell checking
– grammar checking
– indexing or searching large bodies of text
– recognising speech
– processing text containing mark-up languages such as XML and HTML

▥ Networking protocols that specify how computers communicate.

An FSM is used when searching for words in a large piece of text that match a given pattern such as br*v*, where the * can match any sequence of non-blank characters. The FSM would find matches, for example, in brave, bravo and brevity.

▮ State transition diagram

A **state transition diagram** (Fig. 1.3.1) is a directed graph whose nodes ⊙ (· could be s or t) represent the states. An edge or arc, such as the curved arrow from state s to state t is called a transition and is labelled with a symbolic code, e.g. $a \mid b$, where a and b are symbols. The a part of the label is called the transition's trigger and denotes the input symbol. The b part, which is optional, denotes the output symbol.

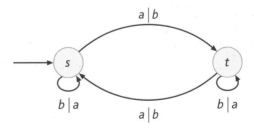

Fig. 1.3.1 *State transition diagram for an FSM with outputs*

🖥 PC activity

Use the finite state simulator to create an FSM with outputs for the state transition diagram shown in Fig. 1.3.1. Try various input strings consisting of different combinations of a's and b's.

Key terms

Finite state machine (FSM):
consists of a set of input symbols (input symbol alphabet) and if it produces output, a set of output symbols (output symbol alphabet), a finite set of states and a transition function that maps a state–symbol pair (current state and input symbol) to a state (next state) and possibly generates an output (output symbol) depending on the type of FSM.

Transition function: maps (input symbol, current state) to (output symbol, next state).

Transition table: tabulates the mappings (input symbol, current state) to (output symbol, next state).

Deterministic finite state machine: an FSM that has just one next state for each pair of state and input symbol.

Non-deterministic finite state machine: an FSM that may have several possible next states for each pair of state and input symbol.

Halting state: a state that has no outgoing transition.

A **finite state machine (FSM)** has a set of input symbols (input symbol alphabet) and if it produces output, a set of output symbols (output symbol alphabet). We will assume that the FSM in Fig. 1.3.1 has an input alphabet consisting of the symbols a and b and an output alphabet consisting of the symbols a and b. We can express this using set notation as follows:

input alphabet $= \{a, b\}$
output alphabet $= \{a, b\}$

{} enclose the symbols, which are members of the set. Using this input alphabet, input strings to this FSM can be any combination of a and b, such as *aabbaab, bbaa, ba, bbb*.

The FSM has a finite set of states, $\{s, t\}$. The FSM has a **transition function** that maps a state–symbol pair (current state and input symbol) to a state (next state) and possibly generates an output (output symbol) depending on the type of FSM. We can use a **transition table** (Table 1) to represent this transition function.

Table 1 *Transition table for the FSM in Fig. 1.3.1*

Current state	s	s	t	t
Input symbol	a	b	a	b
Next state	t	s	s	t
Output symbol	b	a	b	a

The FSM has one state that is designated as the start or initial state. This is indicated by the symbol $\rightarrow$ on the state transition diagram.

Starting in state s, the FSM takes input *aabba* and generates output *bbaab*. Satisfy yourself that the purpose of this FSM is to convert a's into b's and b's into a's.

To prevent ambiguity about the machine's next move, i.e. in order that its behaviour is **deterministic**, we require that each trigger has just one outgoing transition from a particular state. Fig. 1.3.2 shows a state transition diagram for which there is more than one outgoing transition for the same trigger. State s has two transitions labelled with the trigger a. This diagram describes an FSM which is **non-deterministic** because it contains an ambiguity. The FSM has two choices to exit state s when the input symbol is a.

AQA Examiner's tip

To avoid an FSM having to report an error, always ensure that for each state there is an outgoing transition for every symbol in the machine's input alphabet.

Key point

An FSM represents a system as a set of states, the transitions between the states along with the associated inputs and outputs drawn from the machine's alphabet of symbols. One state is designated the start state.

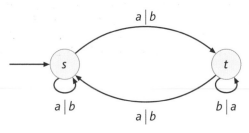

Fig. 1.3.2 *State transition diagram containing an ambiguity: state s has two outgoing transitions for trigger value a*

States that have no outgoing transitions are called **halting states**. If the FSM has not exhausted the input when it finds itself in a halting state, it will usually report an error. It will usually report an error if it is in a state with outgoing transitions, but none of them has a trigger which matches the current input symbol.

The FSM may be constructed to perform an action at the output stage instead of outputting a symbol:

(input symbol, current state) → (action, next state)

If a match is found for the pair (input symbol, current state) then an associated action function will be called and the current state will be set to the next state. Fig. 1.3.3 illustrates this for a digital watch with a button a which is pressed to switch state. The input symbol is replaced by a signal that signals the event pressing button a.

In Fig. 1.3.3 the input stage is a signal that signals an event – pressing button a – rather than a symbol.

An FSM can be designed so that if it cannot find a match for (input symbol, current state), it will search the table of transitions for transitions of the form (current state) → (action, next state)

In this way, transitions can be defined for a current state and any input symbol (Table 2). Any input symbol transitions must be searched after first searching for a specific (input symbol, current state) match.

It is possible to define a default transition as a catch-all case, to be used when
(input symbol, current state) → (action, next state)
　　　　(current state) → (action, next state)
produce no matches in the transition table. The action will call an exception handler.

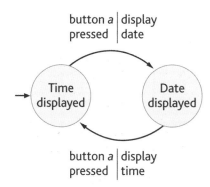

Fig. 1.3.3 *FSM for a digital watch that by pressing button a toggles between displaying the time and displaying the date*

Key point

The FSM may be constructed to perform an action at the output stage instead of outputting a symbol: (input symbol, current state) ⟶ (action, next state).

Key point

The input symbol may be replaced by a signal that signals an event.

Table 2 *Transition table for an FSM with input alphabet {a, b, c, d} incorporating a case for match any input which isn't a or b when in state t*

Current state	s	s	t	t	t
Input symbol	a	b	a	b	
Next state	t	s	s	t	s
Action	Action 1	Action 2	Action 3	Action 4	Action 5

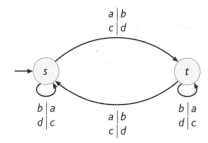

Fig. 1.3.4 *FSM with more than one label per transition*

It is possible to have more than one trigger from one state to another state, as shown in Fig. 1.3.4. If the FSM is in state s and the input symbol is c, the FSM outputs symbol d and moves to state t. Similarly, if while in state s the input symbol is a, the FSM outputs symbol b and moves to state t.

Questions

1 What is a finite state machine?

2 What is the output Y from the FSM shown in Fig. 1.3.5 when the input X is 001011? Assume that the bits are submitted to the FSM in the order of most significant bit through to least significant bit.

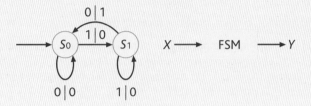

Fig. 1.3.5 *FSM with output for an alphabet of {0, 1}*

3 What is the output Y from the FSM shown in Fig. 1.3.6 when the input X is 00101100? Assume that the bits are submitted to the FSM in the order of most significant bit through to least significant bit. What is the final state of the machine when all the input has been processed?

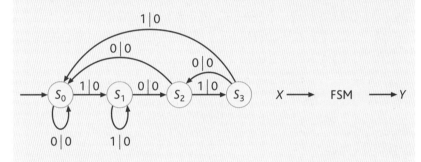

Fig. 1.3.6 *FSM with one input X and one output Y*

4 Table 3 shows the transition table for a finite state machine with outputs. The alphabet is {0, 1}. Draw the equivalent state transition diagram.

Table 3 *FSM with outputs, alphabet {0, 1}*

Current state	S_0	S_0	S_1	S_1
Input symbol	0	1	0	1
Next state	S_1	S_0	S_0	S_1
Output symbol	1	0	1	0

■ Types of FSM

FSMs may be classified into FSMs with output and FSMs without output. Then FSMs with output may be classified into Mealy machines and Moore machines. In Mealy machines, output is associated with a transition. In Moore machines, output is associated with a state.

An FSM without output is known as a finite state automaton (FSA), plural finite state automata, or a finite automaton. FSAs are restricted to decision problems, i.e. problems that are solved by answering YES or NO. Therefore FSAs do not write anything at all while processing input.

■ FSMs with output

FSMs with outputs are the most common controllers of machines we use in daily life, such as lifts, traffic lights and washing machines. In Fig. 1.3.7 the intersection of a main road with a pedestrian crossing is controlled by traffic lights and pedestrian lights. The traffic lights for cars have three possible values: Red (R), Amber (A) and Green (G). The pedestrian lights have three possible values: red (r), green (g) and flashing green (fg).

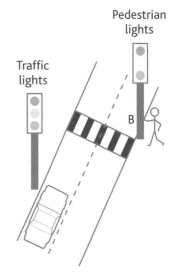

Fig. 1.3.7 *Pedestrian crossing and traffic lights*

FSMs include the following:

- ■ **Finite set of states**: Gr, Ar, Rg, RAfg (Table 4).
- ■ **Designated starting state**: Gr.
- ■ **Input alphabet**: B for 'button B pressed' and T for 'timer timed out'.
- ■ **Transition function** that assigns a next state to every state and input: if in state Gr and B occurs, then go to state Ar.
- ■ **Output function** that assigns to each state and input an output action: Green off, Amber on, start timer.

Table 4 *The possible combinations of traffic lights and pedestrian lights*

Traffic light	Pedestrian light	State codes
Green	red	Gr
Amber	red	Ar
Red	green	Rg
Red, Amber	flashing green	RAfg

Here are the outputs from the controller:

- ■ signals to the different-coloured lights to switch them on or off
- ■ a signal to start a timer when required.

Here are the inputs to the controller:

- ■ a signal when button B is pressed by a pedestrian
- ■ a signal indicating that the time interval set on the timer has elapsed (timer timed out).

The controller reacts to a pedestrian pressing button B only when it is in the Gr state. The traffic light system starts in the Gr state. Fig. 1.3.8 shows the finite state transition diagram for the controller.

This diagram consists of nodes representing states and labelled arcs representing transitions between the nodes. For a **Mealy machine**, output occurs on the transition, e.g. Green on, Amber off, green off, red on.

🖥 PC activity

Use the animation to see traffic lights cycling through the different states.

■ Key terms

Mealy machine: an FSM that determines its outputs from the present state and from the inputs.

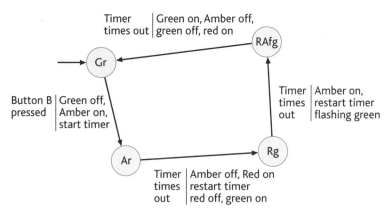

Fig. 1.3.8 *Mealy machine: state transition diagram with outputs for the pedestrian crossing system*

Satisfy yourself that this finite state transition diagram describes the given traffic light system.

In a **Moore machine** the transitions are labelled with the inputs only and the states are labelled with the outputs (Fig. 1.3.9), e.g. Green off, Red on, Amber on, red off, flashing green, timer restarted.

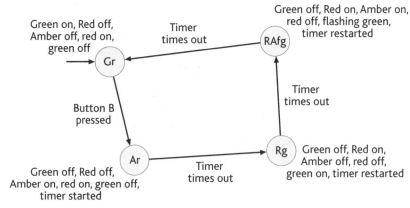

Fig. 1.3.9 *Moore machine equivalent of the traffic light system*

The current state of a Moore FSM is determined by the sequence of inputs that it has processed. In this way, this FSM can be said to remember the input sequence. It therefore possesses memory capability. In fact, a Moore machine models a RAM memory unit.

Questions

5 Distinguish between a Mealy FSM and a Moore FSM.

6 A traffic light system has two lights, red and green. The system starts with the red light on. After 30 seconds the red light goes out and the green light comes on. The green light goes off after 30 seconds and the red light comes on again. The cycle repeats indefinitely. Draw a finite state diagram for this FSM with outputs.

7 Fig. 1.3.10 is an FSM with an input alphabet of {0, 1} and an output alphabet of {0, 1, =, c}. It has four halting states: S_2, S_4, S_5, S_6. What is the machine's output for the inputs (a) 00, (b) 01, (c) 10, (d) 11?

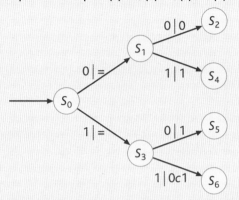

Fig. 1.3.10 *FSM with outputs*

8 What function is performed by the machine in Question 7?

Finite state automata

A **finite state automaton (FSA)**, or finite automaton, is an FSM that produces no output while processing the input. Finite state automata solve decision problems, i.e. problems where the outcome is either YES or NO. An FSA simply runs through the input sequence of symbols, one by one, changing states as a result of the current state and the current symbol from the input it sees. On reaching the end of the input, it stops and, depending on which state it stopped in, it outputs a YES or a NO. The states which cause the FSA to produce a YES response are called accepting states. All other states are, by default, states that cause the FSA to produce a NO response. Accepting states are indicated by putting two rings round them, like S_3 in Fig. 1.3.11. An FSA always has one or more accepting states.

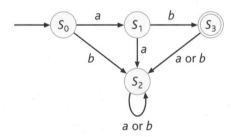

Fig. 1.3.11 *FSA with alphabet {a, b} and four states, S_0 (the starting state), S_1, S_2 and S_3 (the one accepting state)*

The machine described by the state transition diagram in Fig. 1.3.11 begins in the start state S_0 and moves to state S_1 if the first symbol in the input is *a*, or to state S_2 if the first symbol is *b*. From state S_1 the machine moves to the accepting state S_3 if the second symbol is *b*, or to state S_2 if the second symbol is *a*. The machine can leave the accepting state to go to state S_2 if there is further input, i.e. an *a* or *b*. From state S_2 there is no transition to another state. If the FSA is in state S_3 when the input is exhausted, the machine outputs YES. If the machine is in a state other than S_3 when the input is exhausted, the machine outputs NO.

This machine will respond YES only if the input string is *ab*. For strings such as *ba* or *abbbbba*, the machine responds NO. Check this for

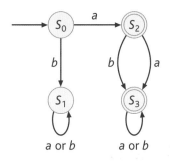

Fig. 1.3.12 *FSA with alphabet {a, b} and two accepting states, S₂ and S₃*

PC activity

Use the FSM simulator to implement the FSA described by Fig. 1.3.12. Try different combinations of *a*'s and *b*'s.

AQA Examiner's tip

If a particular outgoing transition has several triggers, then each trigger can be listed separated by commas, e.g. *a, c, e, f*. If trigger symbols are contiguous, then the following notation may be used: *a.z, A.Z.*

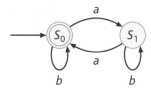

Fig. 1.3.13 *FSA with alphabet {a, b} that checks parity of input for an even or odd number of a's*

Did you know?

Several card tricks depend on parity.

yourself and confirm that the only input to cause the response YES is *ab*. Table 5 shows the equivalent transition table for the FSA described by Fig. 1.3.11.

Table 5 *Transition table that corresponds to Fig. 1.3.11*

Current state	S_0	S_0	S_1	S_1	S_2	S_2	S_3	S_3
Input symbol	a	b	a	b	a	b	a	b
Next state	S_1	S_2	S_2	S_3	S_2	S_2	S_2	S_2

FSAs are used as recognisers of valid strings or sentences in a language. A recogniser takes as input a string *x* and answers YES if *x* is a sentence of the language or NO otherwise.

Activity

The FSA in Fig. 1.3.12 recognises any string that starts with an *a* and is followed by zero or more *a* or *b*. For example, *abbbbaaabbbaabb* is a valid string, *baaabbbaa* is not. Check this for yourself.

FSAs may be used to answer questions about parity, i.e. evenness and oddness.

Activity

Fig. 1.3.13 shows an FSA that decides whether or not its input sequence of *a*'s and *b*'s contains an even number of *a*'s. Check that the response is YES if the input is *bbaaaabb* and NO if the input is *aababb*.

PC activity

Use the FSM simulator to implement the FSA described by Fig. 1.3.13. Try different combinations of *a*'s and *b*'s.

Activity

Lay out a 4 × 6 grid of cards, some face up, some face down. Now add to the end of each row of four cards and to the end of each column of six cards an extra card so that the grid is now a 5 × 7 grid. In each case the added card should be placed face down or face up so as to make the total number of face-down cards an even number in each row of five and in each column of seven. Now get someone to flip one of the cards while you are not looking. Examine the parity of each row to identify the row containing the flipped card. Now, focusing on this row, examine the columns to find the column with the flipped card. In each case the parity of evenness will be broken by the flipped card. Use this fact to identify the flipped card.

Deterministic and non-deterministic FSAs

All the FSAs considered so far are deterministic. In a deterministic FSA the trigger for each outgoing transition of a state must be unique, i.e. for each pair of state and input symbol there is just one next state. However, it can be more useful if an FSA behaves non-deterministically. In a non-deterministic FSA the triggers for outgoing transitions from a state do not have to be unique, i.e. for each pair of state and input symbol there may be several possible next states.

Fig. 1.3.14 is a state transition diagram for a non-deterministic machine. The machine recognises the patterns consisting of either *ab*, *aba*, *ababab* … or *abb*, *abbab*, *abbabab* …. The problem is that both potentially infinite patterns start with *ab*, so the machine must choose between state route 1347 and state route 126. The non-deterministic choice occurs at state 1, the start state, where an input *a* allows the machine to go either to state 2 or to state 3.

Non-deterministic FSAs turn out to be an excellent way to express pattern searches that occur in word processing and document searching. Any problem solved with a non-deterministic machine can also be solved with a deterministic machine, but many more states may be needed. The non-deterministic machine can be converted to a deterministic machine. The non-deterministic machine will transition along all transitions matching the input.

Key point

Deterministic FSAs are often called deterministic finite automata (DFAs); non-deterministic FSAs are often called non-deterministic finite automata (NFAs).

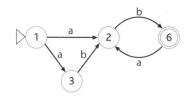

Fig. 1.3.14 *A non-deterministic FSA that accepts strings of the form* ababababab,… *or of the form* abb, abbab, abbabab,… *but no others.*

Activities

1 Convert the non-deterministic machine in Fig. 1.3.14 into a deterministic one.

2 Research the application of non-deterministic finite automata to pattern matching.

Questions

9 Explain the difference between an FSM with outputs and an FSA.

10 Draw the state transition diagram for a DFA for each of the following:
   a all strings over {a, b} that contain *bba* but not *aab*
   b all strings over {a, b} that contain neither *bab* nor *aab*
   c all strings over {a, b} that contain both *bab* and *aab*
   d all strings over {a, b} that contain an even number of *b*'s
   e all strings over {a, b} that contain an odd number of *b*'s and an even number of *a*'s.

11 Explain the difference between a deterministic FSA and a non-deterministic FSA.

12 Explain the role of an accepting state in an FSA.

13 State what strings the DFA in Fig. 1.3.15 accepts.

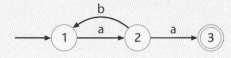

Fig. 1.3.15 *State diagram for Question 13*

 PC activity

Write your own DFA using the following specification. Create the DFA first as a state transition diagram then as a transition table.

Input: an input string x is terminated by the character #. A DFA D with start state S_0 and set of accepting states A.

Output: YES if D accepts x, NO otherwise.

The function Move(CurrentState, Ch) returns the state to which there is a transition from state CurrentState on input character Ch. The function NextCh returns the next character of the input string x.

Here is the algorithm:

```
CurrentState ← S₀
Ch ← NextCh
While Ch <> '#' Do
  CurrentState ← Move(CurrentState, Ch)
  Ch ← NextCh
EndWhile
If CurrentState In A
  Then Output 'YES'
  Else Output 'NO'
```

Test your program with one of the example DFAs given in the text and input x from the DFA's alphabet.

In this topic you have covered:

- FSMs can be used to control traffic lights, as recognisers that specify a language and check if a given string is in the language, to search for words in a large piece of text, and for parity checking

- an FSM has a set of input symbols (input symbol alphabet); if it produces output, it has a set of output symbols (output symbol alphabet)

- a deterministic FSM is an FSM that has just one next state for each pair of state and input symbol

- a non-deterministic FSM is an FSM that may have several possible next states for each pair of state and input symbol

- how to draw state transition diagrams consisting of nodes and labelled connected arcs with one node labelled the start state; an FSA has one or more accepting states

- how to draw state transition tables mapping current state–input symbol pairs to the next state

- how to draw a Mealy machine, which is an FSM where each transition is labelled with input symbol and output

- the difference between a Mealy machine and a Moore machine

- the difference between an FSM with outputs and an FSM without outputs (an FSA).

1.4 Turing machines

Key terms

Turing machine (TM): an FSM that controls one or more tapes, where at least one tape is of unbounded length (i.e. infinitely long).

Turing machine

Topic 1.2 gave an intuitive, non-rigorous definition of the term 'algorithm'. This topic will attempt to give a rigorous definition.

In the early 20th century, mathematicians wondered if there existed a process that could determine in a finite number of operations whether any mathematical statement was true or false. For example, is it true that $x^2 + y^2 + 1 = 0$ has roots which are whole numbers? This decision problem was named after the mathematician David Hilbert and was known as Hilbert's tenth problem. This challenge intrigued Alan Turing. In 1934 he set about devising an abstract model of computation that he hoped would enable an effective procedure to be found which would give a yes or no answer to Hilbert's tenth problem. Essentially, the effective procedure was an algorithm to solve this problem.

In order to devise his model, Turing had to define rigorously what he meant by an effective procedure. He based his definition on an analysis of how a human computer proceeds when executing an algorithm (Fig. 1.4.1).

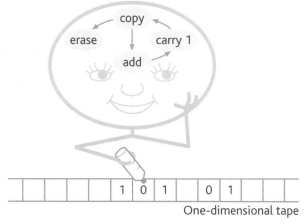

Fig. 1.4.1 *Turing's human computer*

In Turing's human computer, computing is normally done by writing certain symbols on paper. Turing imagined this paper to be divided into squares like a child's arithmetic book, as shown in Table 1. This shows a **Turing machine** that adds two binary numbers. The computer starts on the rightmost digit of the upper number, as indicated by the green outline. Check this computation and note the movement of the observation window, the red outline. The answer is given in the third row.

Table 1 *A section of a page of a child's arithmetic book: the observation window is called the read/write head*

			1	0	1	1	0
			0	1	0	0	1
			1	1	1	1	1

However, the two-dimensional character of paper is not essential and we can carry out computation with one-dimensional paper, i.e., on a

Key point

The definition of 'Turing machine' is amazingly robust. For example, a 2D or 3D tape does not increase computational power. Turing said, 'The two-dimensional character of paper is no essential of computation.'

Table 2 *Representing the natural numbers in unary (only one symbol, 1)*

n	Unary representation
1	1
2	11
3	111
4	1111
5	11111

Key point

To Turing, a computer program consisted of a precise set of instructions given to the human computer relating actions to observations. For example, if you read a 1 in the square you are scanning, replace it by a 0 and move one square to the left. Turing hypothesised that the notion of what is computable is equivalent to what his imaginary computer could do. For any computer so far built, he was right.

tape divided into squares (Fig. 1.4.2). Turing limited the number of different symbols which could be written on the tape. The effect of this restriction on the number of different symbols is not very serious. It is always possible to use sequences of symbols in place of single symbols, as shown in Table 2.

The behaviour of the human computer at any moment is determined by the symbols which he or she is observing and his 'state of mind' at the moment. The number of symbols or squares which the computer can observe at one moment is usually limited to one. If the human computer wishes to observe more, he or she must use successive observations. We will also suppose that the number of states of mind which need be taken into account is finite.

In a paper for the London Mathematical Society, published in 1937, Turing wrote:

> Let us imagine the operations performed by the computer to be split up into 'simple operations' which are so elementary that it is not easy to imagine them further divided. Every such operation consists of some change of the physical system consisting of the computer and his tape. We know the state of the system if we know the sequence of symbols on the tape, which of these are observed by the computer (possibly with a special order), and the state of mind of the computer. We may suppose that in a simple operation not more than one symbol is altered. ...

> Besides these changes of symbols, the simple operations must include changes of distribution of observed squares. ... Let us say that each of the new observed squares is within L squares of an immediately previously observed square.

(On computable numbers, with an application to the Entscheidungsproblem, Proceedings of the London Mathematical Society, Ser. 2, Vol. 42, 1937)

The simple operations must therefore include:

■ change of symbol on one of the observed squares

■ change of one of the squares observed to another square within L squares of one of the previously observed squares.

The most general single operation must therefore be taken to be one of the following:

■ a possible change of symbol together with a possible change of state of mind

■ a possible change of observed square, together with a possible change of state of mind.

Worked example _____

Construct a Turing machine that tests if a given character string consists of n zeros followed by n ones. For example, the tape could contain the valid string 0011 as shown in Fig. 1.4.2 sandwiched between the two instances of the delimiting symbol #. The observation window of this machine starts on the leftmost # symbol.

If the input string is valid, the Turing machine halts with only empty squares between the # symbols. If not valid, then the machine will either halt with symbols on the tape between the original two # symbols or it will report an error.

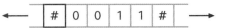

Fig. 1.4.2 *Turing machine: a one-dimensional tape containing a valid string between # symbols*

Fig. 1.4.3 shows the state transition diagram for this Turing machine. The labels on the transitions are defined in Tables 3 and 4. The Turing machine reads the symbol (the input) that the observation window is currently on and, if necessary, replaces this symbol with another (the output). The Turing machine may move the observation window one square to the left or one square to the right. To understand this Turing machine more easily, use the TuringKara simulator shown in Fig. 1.4.4.

Table 3 *Symbols used on the state transition diagram*

Symbol	Meaning
|	Separates input from output
□	Blank square
#	Delimiting symbol
→	Move the observation window one square to the right
←	Move the observation window one square to the left

Table 4 *Meaning of labels on some transitions*

Transition label	Meaning
1, 0 | ←	If observation window on a square containing a 0 or a 1, then move window one square to the left
#,□ | →	If observation window on a square containing a # or square is empty, then erase # then move window one square to the right
0 | □ →	If observation window on a square containing a 0, then erase 0 and move window one square to the right
1 | □ ←	If observation window on a square containing a 1, then erase 1 and move window one square to the left
0, #,□ | #	If observation window on a square containing a 0 or a # or is empty, then overwrite with a #

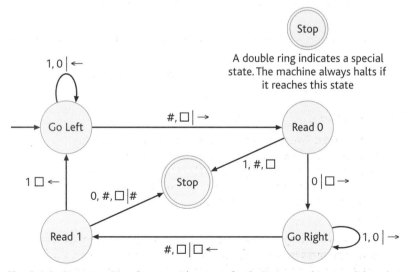

Fig. 1.4.3 *State transition diagram with outputs for the Turing machine to validate that a given string contains n zeros and n ones*

PC activity

Download Kara from **www.swisseduc.ch/compscience/ karatojava** and create the above state transition diagram and transition rules in TuringKara to observe this solution in action (Figs 1.4.4 and 1.4.5). Note that you will also need Java installed on the machine. Both can be installed and run from a memory stick. If you are using a PC at school or college, check with your teacher before you download the software.

As the Turing machine does not have internal memory to count the symbols, the state transition diagram describes a solution in which the zeros and ones are erased pairwise. The leftmost 0 is erased then the rightmost 1, and so on. If there are the same number of each, then the tape should end up with nothing between the two starting # symbols. If the number of zeros and the number of ones do not match, then the tape will not be blank between the two starting # symbols. The transition rules that achieve this solution are defined in Table 5.

Table 5 *Transition rules for the Turing machine which determines if a given character string consists of* n *zeros followed by* n *ones*

Current state	New state	Input	Output
Go Left	Go Left	1, 0	←
Go Left	Read 0	#, ☐	☐ →
Read 0	Go Right	0	☐ →
Read 0	Stop	1, #, ☐	
Go Right	Go Right	1, 0	→
Go Right	Read 1	#, ☐	←
Read 1	Go Left	1	☐ ←
Read 1	Stop	0, #, ☐	#

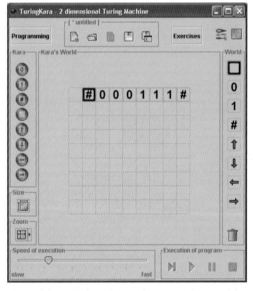

Fig. 1.4.4 *TuringKara's two-dimensional TM world view*

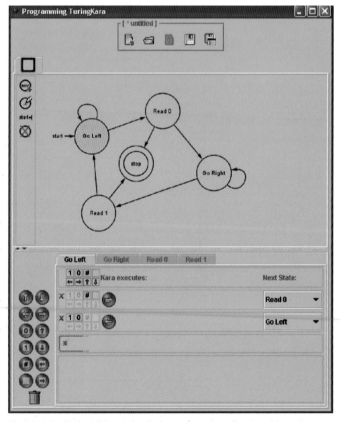

Fig. 1.4.5 *Screenshot to check character strings for matching* n *zeros followed by* n *ones*

In the standard Turing machine definition, each transition can have at most one write command followed optionally by a move command. In the TuringKara machine, each transition can have at most one write command followed by zero or more move commands. The TuringKara environment uses Turing machines which work on a two-dimensional sheet. Even though the sheet is irrelevant with regards to computability, it greatly simplifies the solutions of many problems. Note that in TuringKara, the world is not of unbounded size; it has a user-defined size. For most problems, this is not a restriction, as one can set the world size to suit the needs of the problem.

Performing a logical bitwise AND using a TuringKara machine

The task shown in Fig. 1.4.6 is a logical bitwise AND on two rows of binary numbers. These numbers are aligned vertically, as one would do on paper. A three-state Turing machine in the TuringKara simulator implements the AND operation. Solving the same problem on a one-dimensional tape would be significantly more complicated, as the read/write head of the tape would have to do far more movements.

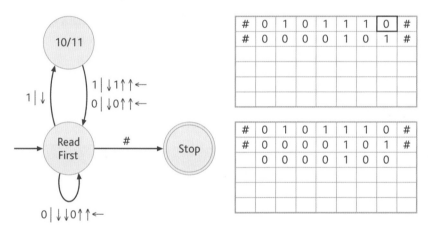

Fig. 1.4.6 *State diagram solution for a Turing machine that performs a logical bitwise AND on two binary numbers*

The read/write head (observation window shown as a red square) starts at the right-hand end of the first number in state Read First. If it reads a 0, then the machine knows that the output must be 0. It therefore moves the read/write head downwards two squares ($\downarrow\downarrow$), writes a 0 then moves upwards two squares ($\uparrow\uparrow$) and left one square ($\leftarrow$). If it reads a 1, then the output could be a 1 or a 0 depending on the corresponding value of the second binary number. The machine moves to state 10/11 and moves the read/write head down one square ($\downarrow$). Now, if the read/write head reads a 1, the machine moves down one square ($\downarrow$), writes a 1 then moves up two squares ($\uparrow\uparrow$) and to the left one square ($\leftarrow$), ending up back in state Read First. If it encounters a 0, the movement is the same but a 0 is written instead of a 1, the machine also ends up back in state Read First. In state Read First, the machine moves to the Stop state if it reads the # symbol.

Formal Turing machine

The TuringKara machine is very useful for gaining an understanding of Turing machines but it doesn't follow Turing's description of a Turing machine exactly. That is why it is easier to use.

PC activity

Program this problem in TuringKara and try the given problem.

Key point

Turing machines are usually interpreted either as computing some function, say the square of an integer, or as accepting a language, i.e. set of strings. A Turing machine to compute a function receives its (coded) input as the initial content of its tape or tapes, and produces its output as the final content of its tape or tapes, if it halts. If it doesn't halt on all inputs specified for the function, then no effective procedure exists that will calculate the output of the function for all inputs, i.e. no algorithm exists. The function is not computable.

A Turing machine as described by Turing is an automaton that has a set of possible states, one of which is the current state, a transition function (see next section), a set of halting states also known as stop states or accepting states, and a read/write head that allows input and storage to be combined in a single tape of cells. The tape has a definite left end but is infinite in the other direction, so it is impossible to run out of space to the right. The read/write head can move in both directions so that the tape cells can be visited in any order and multiple times. The Turing machine begins with its input written on the tape with typically one blank cell to the left. The read/write head is positioned over the leftmost symbol of the input. Any cells of the tape that do not have symbols written on them are considered to have a special blank symbol that we represent with □.

Transitions are based on the current state and the symbol under the read/write head. Each transition involves three things:

- a transition from the current state to the next state (the next state may be the same as the current state or a different state)
- the writing of a symbol to the current cell (it may be the same symbol or a different symbol)
- the direction to move the read/write head (one cell either right or left).

During execution, the Turing machine can move back and forth, rewriting cell symbols as much as necessary.

A Turing machine continues to execute until the transition function is not defined for the current state and tape symbol or if it tries to move off the left end of the tape. If the current state when the Turing machine stops is a stop state, then its output is valid, otherwise it is not. One state is designated the starting state.

Representing transition rules

Consider a Turing machine, M, which takes as input a unary number and calculates the result unary number $+ 1$. For example, if the unary number is 11 then this Turing machine calculates 111. For this calculation, the input would be set up on the Turing machine's tape as shown in Fig. 1.4.7(a) with the read/write head starting as shown by the position of the red rectangle. The Turing machine halts with this read/write head at the start of the result that is stored on the tape, as shown in Fig. 1.4.7(b).

Fig. 1.4.8 shows the state transition diagram for this Turing machine.

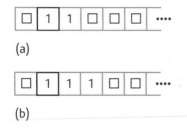

(a)

(b)

Fig. 1.4.7 *Turing machine tape showing (a) input and (b) output*

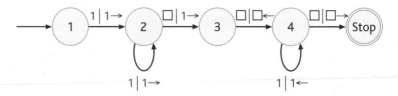

Fig. 1.4.8 *State transition diagram for a Turing machine that increments a unary number by one*

Transition rules

The transition rules for this Turing machine can be expressed in the form transition function (current state, input symbol) = (next state, output symbol, movement)

Using δ to represent the transition function, the transition rules are shown in Table 6.

Tracking an execution

To keep track of the work of a Turing machine, we will use a notation that represents the contents of the tape, the location of the read/write head and the current state. We consider the tape as broken into two parts:

- those cells to the left of the read/write head
- those cells under and to the right of the read/write head.

The notation is as follows:

(cells to the left, current state, cells under and to the right)

For example, the tape in Fig. 1.4.7(a) would be expressed as (□, 1, 11). Note blanks to the right of 11 are only shown when under the read/write head. The symbol under the read/write head will always be the first symbol in the third item of the notation.

(a)   (b)

Fig. 1.4.9 *Two positions of the read/write head during the execution of the Turing machine*

The tape in Fig. 1.4.9(a) is represented as (□1, 2, 1) and Fig. 1.4.9(b) as (□11, 3, 1).

Using this notation to represent the stages of execution of the Turing machine, *M*, we obtain Table 7.

Turing machines that calculate

It is important that a Turing machine that is used to calculate the value of functions leaves the answer on the tape. Convention requires that these Turing machines stop with their read/write head on the leftmost 1 symbol of the answer, as shown in Table 7. The reason for this is so that complex functions can be calculated by running a series of different Turing machines one after another, with the output of the previous machine as the input for the next machine.

If a function requires more than one input parameter, each of the parameters will be separated by a single blank symbol. The Turing machine will start with the read/write head on the leftmost symbol of the first input parameter for the function.

How programming language statements are represented in a Turing machine

Programming statements such as If Then and If Then Else allow choice of different actions depending on some condition. Each of the Turing machine transitions can be seen as a kind of If Then statement. Considering the value of the current state and current symbol, the transition function sets the next state for the Turing machine, which could

Table 6 *Transition function for the Turing machine that adds one to a unary number*

δ(1, 1) = (2, 1, →)	
δ(2, □) = (3, 1, →)	δ(2, 1) = (2, 1, →)
δ(3, □) = (4, □, ←)	
δ(4, □) = (Stop, □, →)	δ(4, 1) = (4, 1, ←)

Table 7 *Execution of M for unary input 11*

(□, 1, 11)
(□1, 2, 1)
(□11, 2, □)
(□111, 3, □)
(□11, 4, 1)
(□1, 4, 11)
(□, 4, 111)
(□, 4, □111)
(□, Stop, 111)

be the same as the current state. Some action is carried out in the process. For example, the transition δ(1, 1) = (2, □, →)] can be read as 'if we are in state 1 and the tape symbol is 1, go into state 2, write a □ symbol on the tape and move right'. Here it is expressed in Pascal:

```
If (State = 1) And (TapeSymbol = 1)
  Then
    Begin
      State := 2;
      Write('□');
      Move(Right);
    End;
```

Worked example

You will design a Turing machine to add two unary numbers. For example, if we wish to compute 2 + 3, we place unary numbers 11 and 111 on the tape, as shown in Fig. 1.4.10(a). The read/write head begins on the leftmost cell containing a 1 symbol. The answer is written to the tape as shown in Fig. 1.4.10(b). The procedure erases the first 1 and overwrites the □ between the first number and the second number.

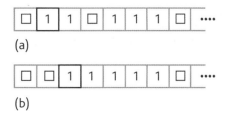

(a)

(b)

Fig. 1.4.10 *Tape storing two unary numbers to be added*

Begin by writing If statements in pseudocode to do just this. The tape starts in state 1.

```
If State = 1 And Symbol = '1'
  Then
    Write('□')
    Move(Right)
    State ← 2
EndIf
If State = 2 And Symbol = '1'
  Then Move(Right)
If State = 2 And Symbol = '□'
  Then
    Write('1')
    Move(Left)
    State ← 3
  EndIf
If State = 3 And Symbol = '1'
  Then Move(Left)
EndIf
If State = 3 And Symbol = '□'
  Then
    Move(Right)
    Stop
EndIf
```

The transition rules shown in Table 8 can now be constructed from this pseudocode.

Table 8 *Transition rules for addition of two unary numbers*

$\delta(1, 1) = (2, \square, \rightarrow)$	
$\delta(2, 1) = (2, 1, \rightarrow)$	$\delta(2, \square) = (3, 1, \leftarrow)$
$\delta(3, 1) = (3, 1, \leftarrow)$	$\delta(3, \square) = (\text{Stop}, \square, \rightarrow)$

Finally, the state transition diagram for these transition rules can be drawn (Fig. 1.4.11).

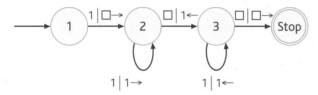

Fig. 1.4.11 *State transition diagram for a Turing machine that adds two unary numbers*

Questions

1 Show the state of the tape after the Turing machine is executed on a tape containing four 1s. The read/write head starts on the leftmost 1. The symbol → means move the read/write head one square to the right.

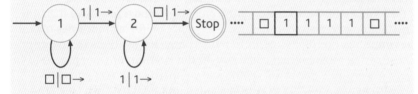

Fig. 1.4.12 *Diagram for Question 1*

2 The following Turing machines are expressed as sets of transition rules. Draw the state transition diagram for each. Assume that the starting state for each is state 1.

a $\delta(1, b) = (1, a, \rightarrow)$ $\delta(1, a) = (1, b, \rightarrow)$ $\delta(1, \square) = (\text{Stop}, \square, \leftarrow)$

b $\delta(1, 1) = (1, x, \rightarrow)$ $\delta(1, \square) = (2, x, \leftarrow)$ $\delta(2, x) = (3, 1, \rightarrow)$

    $\delta(3, 1) = (3, 1, \rightarrow)$ $\delta(3, \square) = (2, 1, \leftarrow)$ $\delta(2, 1) = (2, 1, \leftarrow)$

    $\delta(2, \square) = (\text{Stop}, \square, \leftarrow)$

3 Look at the Turing machines in Question 2 and explain what they do.

Rigorous definition of an algorithm

Now that we have an understanding of the operation of a Turing machine, we should explore why Turing machines are so important. It is sufficient to have just an intuitive understanding of what is meant by an algorithm and computability if we only want to show that some specific result can be computed by following a specific algorithm. However, this is not enough if we wish to show that a desired result is not computable, i.e. no algorithm exists. This requires us to assess whether something is computable by answering the question, Does a Turing machine exist for this computation which halts on every possible input allowed for this function when executed?

If such a Turing machine exists, then this Turing machine represents an algorithm that solves the problem. It represents this algorithm in its transition rules or instructions, i.e. its program. If a Turing machine exists, then the solution to the problem is computable. Putting it another way, a task is computable if and only if it can be computed by a Turing machine. Every algorithm can be represented as a Turing machine program. If a function is computable, then a Turing machine exists that computes the function. The algorithm that computes the function is coded in the transition rules or instructions for this Turing machine. This has become known as the Church–Turing thesis. The Church–Turing thesis states that if an algorithm exists, then there is an equivalent Turing machine for that algorithm.

Power of Turing machines

Turing devised a machine whose basic operations cannot be divided any further. A consequence of this is that all other types of computing machines can be reduced to an **equivalent Turing machine**. A conclusion that can be drawn from this is that no computing device that can be realised by controlling some physical process of the universe can be more **powerful** than a Turing machine. Effectively, this means that a Turing machine can do anything that a computer can do. Very importantly, a Turing machine provides a formal definition of the digital computer and that the two are equivalent in power.

Any program written to run on a Pentium or Core processor can be broken down into a sequence of the processor's most primitive machine instructions. In a similar manner, a sequence of Turing machines may be connected together to perform more complex operations matching those of any program that could run on the Pentium or Core processors. Very importantly, processors come and go, instruction sets and clock speeds change. If we are to reason about computability, then basing such reasoning on Pentium or Core processors would require the reasoning to be constantly re-evaluated. As Turing machines are independent of any real processor, it is possible to reason about computations with Turing machines and be confident that such reasoning will not need to be re-evaluated.

The busy beaver function

The function $B(n)$ is defined as calculating the largest number of ones an n-state Turing machine can write on an initially empty tape and still stop. Turing machines with n states which produce $B(n)$ marks are called busy beavers. The function $B(n)$ is well defined – we have just defined it – but non-computable. This is an example of the power of a Turing machine to decide what is computable.

We can create specific Turing machines that give an answer for each value of $n < 7$, i.e. the corresponding specific Turing machine stops, but we cannot produce a general Turing machine that produces an answer whatever the value of n. Unfortunately, $B(n)$ grows too fast to stop for every value of n. So it is impossible to find a Turing machine that will work with any n presented to it and that will stop every time. Fig. 1.4.13 shows a one-state Turing machine that implements $B(1)$. The stop state is omitted from the count of states because it is not a part of the busy beaver function. This Turing machine writes exactly one 1 to the tape, i.e. $B(1) = 1$.

Fig. 1.4.13 *A one-state Turing machine that implements B(1) not including the stop state in the count of states*

Fig. 1.4.14 shows a two-state Turing machine that implements $B(2)$. The stop state is omitted from the count of states because it is not a part of the busy beaver function. This Turing machine writes exactly four 1s to the tape, i.e. $B(2) = 4$.

The four-state busy beaver produces 13 marks on the one-dimensional tape. The five-state busy beaver produces at least 4098 and the six-state beaver at least 1.29×10^{865} marks.

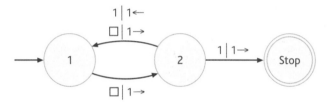

Fig. 1.4.14 *A two-state Turing machine that implements B(2) not including the stop state in the count of states*

■ Universal Turing machines

In a series of thought experiments, Turing imagined Turing machines for performing many different tasks and then a startling revelation occurred to him, a **universal Turing machine (UTM)**. A UTM, U, is a Turing machine that can execute other Turing machines by simulating the behaviour of any Turing machine. In a universal Turing machine that uses a single one-dimensional tape, the instructions of the Turing machine, M, being simulated are placed on the tape and followed by the data, D, to be processed by M. The read/write head must start on M and then move between M and D as M is executed. Naturally, U may be a lot slower than the Turing machine M that it simulates.

A UTM behaves as an **interpreter**. This is just what a PC does when it executes a Java applet or a Flash script.

Fig. 1.4.15(b) shows a more practical UTM that uses three tapes. Tape D stores exactly the same data as M's data tape D. Another tape stores the instructions for Turing machine M. A third tape acts as a temporary store. The Turing machine M that is being simulated is also shown in Fig. 1.4.15(a).

Did you know?

There is an ongoing competition to design the smallest possible UTM as measured by the product of the number of states and number of symbols in its alphabet. In his book *A New Kind of Science*, Stephen Wolfram announced his discovery of a 2-state, 5-symbol universal Turing machine. On 14 May 2007, Wolfram announced a $25,000 prize for the proof or disproof of the conjecture that a 2-state, 3-symbol Turing machine is universal. On 24 October 2007 the prize was won by Alex Smith, an undergraduate studying electronic and computer engineering at Birmingham University in the UK.

Key point

Programs and data can be treated as the same thing.

🖥 PC activity

This activity explores programs as data and programs as programs. Log on to www.nelsonthornes.com and launch Programs As Data animation.

Key terms

Principle of universality: a universal machine is a machine capable of simulating any other machine.

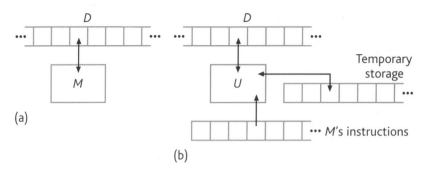

Fig. 1.4.15 *A three-tape UTM that simulates the Turing machine M acting on data D*

A consequence of a UTM is that programs and data are really the same thing. A program is just a sequence of symbols that looks like any other piece of input, but when fed to a UTM, this input wakes up and begins to compute. A computer downloads Java applets and e-mail viruses as data but can then proceed to execute them as programs. Nature also treats programs as data. DNA contains programs and data. Its programs carry out the task of replicating DNA by treating the DNA as data.

Another even more important consequence is that the world of computation is powered by UTMs. A single desktop computer can run a word processor, a spreadsheet, as well as new applications that have yet to be devised. This may seem completely natural, but most technology does not work this way at all. In most cases the device is the application and they are the same thing. If you own a radio and want to watch TV, you must buy a new device. You cannot download a new set of instructions to turn your radio into a TV. Desktop PCs are based on the computing **principle of universality**.

Case study

Computing with DNA

Download and read **www.usc.edu/dept/molecular-science/papers/fp-sciam98.pdf** (*Scientific American*, **279**(2): 54–61, August 1998). It describes the use of a TM-based DNA computer to solve the travelling salesperson problem described in Topic 1.5.

Questions

4 What is a Turing machine?

5 What is the principle of universality?

6 Explain what is meant by a universal Turing machine.

7 This question is about universality. Which one of the following does not belong: supercomputer, coffee maker, Java programming language, MS Excel, mobile phone, DNA computer?

8 Explain why programs can be treated as data.

9 Explain one consequence of the principle of universality for microprocessor systems which are used as microcontrollers or embedded computers.

10 What is meant by computability?

In this topic you have covered:

- why Turing machines are studied
- Turing machines with one or more tapes
- state transition diagrams for Turing machines
- unary representation
- how to use transition rules to represent a Turing machine
- how to track the execution of a Turing machine
- how programming language statements are represented in a Turing machine
- rigorous meaning of the term 'algorithm'
- why a task is computable if and only if it can be computed by a Turing machine
- meaning of the term 'computability'
- why all other types of computing machine are reducible to an equivalent Turing machine
- why no physical computing device can be more powerful than a Turing machine
- programs and data can be treated as the same thing.

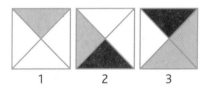

Computation has limits

Computer scientists know that there are algorithms that can't be written. For example, you cannot write an algorithm that can always tell whether some other algorithm will actually work. How about intelligence? Can we write an algorithm such that a computer following it would actually be thinking?

It is useful to classify problems into those that are algorithmic in nature, i.e. have the potential for their solution to be described by rules or steps, and those which are non-algorithmic. An example of a non-algorithmic problem is the problem of answering the question, What is the meaning of life? An example of an algorithmic problem is, How does one make an omelette?

Finite problems are solvable

Any algorithmic problem with a finite set of inputs is solvable. For example, a decision problem whose sole legal inputs are values 1, 2, ..., n and which outputs either yes or no can be solved by an algorithm containing a table mapping each of the n inputs to the appropriate output. In contrast, algorithmic problems that have infinite sets of legal inputs are less accommodating.

Non-computable problems

Here is a problem adapted from the third edition of *Algorithmics: The Spirit of Computing* by David Harel and Yishai Feldman (Addison Wesley 2004). You are given the task of covering large areas using coloured tiles. A tile is defined to be a 1×1 square divided into quarters by its diagonals; each quarter is coloured with some colour. The tiles are assumed to have fixed orientation and are not rotatable. An input is a finite number of tile descriptions. Tile types 1, 2 and 3 are shown in Fig. 1.5.1.

The problem asks whether any finite area of any size and with integer dimensions can be covered using only tiles given above and following the constraint that colours on the touching edges of any two adjacent tiles must be identical. An unlimited number of tiles of each of the three types is available. One solution to this problem is shown in Fig. 1.5.2 for a 3×3 tiling.

Fig. 1.5.1 *Tile types 1, 2 and 3*

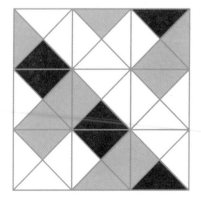

Fig. 1.5.2 *One solution for a 3×3 tiling*

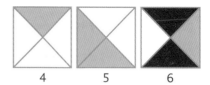

If the tile types are as shown in Fig. 1.5.3, it becomes impossible to use them to tile even very small room sizes (Fig. 1.5.4).

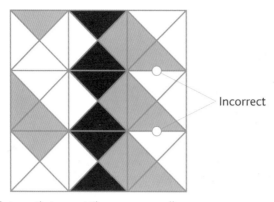

Fig. 1.5.3 *A different set of three tile types*

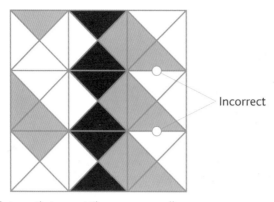

Incorrect

Fig. 1.5.4 *Tile types that cannot tile even very small rooms*

Now imagine that we try to construct an algorithm to be run on a computer, any computer, regardless of the amount of time and memory space required, that will have the ability to decide whether arbitrary finite sets of tile types can tile areas of any size. We do not want the algorithm to output the tiling pattern when it finds a solution; we just want it to output yes or no. Unfortunately, there is no way to construct such an algorithm. An algorithmic problem that admits no algorithm is **non-computable** and the algorithmic problem is non-solvable.

Decision problems

A **decision problem** is a yes/no algorithmic problem. For example, we require an algorithm to decide if a given positive integer n is prime. The algorithm is to output yes if n is prime and no if it isn't. Here is an algorithm for this problem expressed in the programming language Pascal:

```
Program FindPrimes;
Var
  i, n : LongWord;
  Prime : Boolean;
Begin
  Write('Input n: ');
  ReadLn(n);
  Prime := False;
  For i := 2 To Round(Sqrt(n))
    Do
      If (n Mod i) = 0
        Then
          Begin
            Prime := True;
            Break;
          End;
  If Prime
    Then WriteLn('Yes')
    Else WriteLn('No');
  ReadLn;
End.
```

If the decision problem has an algorithmic solution then it is **decidable**.

Key terms

Non-computable: describes an algorithmic problem that admits no algorithm.

Decision problem: a yes/no algorithmic problem.

Decidable: describes a decision problem that has a yes/no answer.

Undecidable algorithmic problems

Decision problems are problems that require a yes/no answer. If the algorithmic problem is non-computable and it is a decision problem, then the algorithmic problem is said to be **undecidable**. The tiling problem is an example of an undecidable problem.

Worked example

Look at the following statement and say whether it is true or false:

This statement is false.

Solution

If the statement is true, then the statement is telling us that it is false. On the other hand, if the statement is false, then the statement is telling us that it is true. Both interpretations are contradictory. The conclusion is therefore that the answer is undecidable.

Tractable and intractable problems

Even if the problem is an algorithmic problem and it is computable, whether a solution can be produced may still depend on the size of the input. If the problem scenario in Fig. 1.5.5 were to include 100 interconnected cities, the time taken to find a solution would be so great that the problem could not be solved by searching all possible routes. Problems that have reasonable (polynomial) time solutions are called **tractable**. Problems that have no reasonable (polynomial) time solutions are called **intractable** and are considered unsolvable by a standard that requires an algorithm to terminate with the right answer within polynomial time.

Worked example

An intractable problem

If there are N cities in the travelling salesperson problem, what is the maximum number of routes that we might need to compute to find the cheapest round-trip route that takes the salesperson through every city and back to the starting city? There is no way except to compute all possible routes. Assume there is a flight available between every pair of cities. Fig. 1.5.5 shows an example with four cities.

Pick a starting city
Pick the next city, then $N - 1$ choices remain } How to build a route
Pick the next city, then $N - 2$ choices remain
Maximum number of routes is $(N - 1) * (N - 2) * (N - 3) * ... * 2 * 1$

If $N = 12$ then the maximum number of routes is 39 916 800. On a medium-speed computer, it will take approximately 39 seconds to evaluate all routes. If $N = 23$ then a medium-speed computer will take approximately 51 years. This is an example of an intractable problem, because the time taken to solve the problem increases dramatically as the number of cities increases.

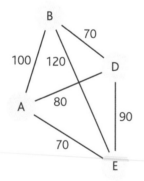

Fig. 1.5.5 *Cities and flight paths with the cost of each in pounds (£)*

For some intractable problems, a solution can be verified in reasonable time; if you guess a solution, it can be checked relatively quickly. These problems are called NP-type problems. Tractable problems are called P-type problems. Computer scientists want to know whether it is worth continuing to search for P-type solutions to NP-type problems. The challenge is to prove, one way or another, if the class of problems known as NP problems can be reduced to the class of P-type problems. This is known as the P = NP challenge.

Approximate solutions

Many intractable problems are concerned with scheduling or matching. Class scheduling in schools and colleges is one example – the timetabling problem. It is not too difficult to come up with an exponential time algorithm for solving the timetabling problem. An exponential time algorithm will take too long to run for anything except very small inputs. However, timetables get produced in time for the start of an academic year. So how is this possible? The answer is that the algorithms that get used ignore some of the constraints to produce solutions that are compromises.

None of these algorithms are guaranteed to work in reasonable (polynomial) time and to produce the right answer for each possible input situation. For example, the solution may require some additional classroom to be used and some particular teacher to teach an extra period, even though neither is actually necessary. The solutions that are found are sub-optimal but they are often usable. Guessing a solution is one way that polynomial time solutions can be found for intractable problems. Knowing how to guess is a matter of experience and know-how. This is known as **heuristic** knowledge.

Many intractable problems also lend themselves to solutions in polynomial time in specific cases but they remain intractable for more general cases.

Did you know?

There is a $1 million prize offered by the Clay Mathematics Institute for the first person to prove P = NP or P ≠ NP (www.claymath.org/millennium/P_vs_NP).

PC activity

List four problems that are classified as NP problems. You may find them using a search engine such as Google. The hardest NP problems are called NP-complete problems.

PC activity

Research approximate solutions to intractable problems.

Key terms

Heuristic: describes an approach that uses know-how and experience to make informed guesses that assist in finding a polynomial time solution to an intractable algorithmic problem.

Questions

1. A person who shaves another person is called a barber. A certain village has just one barber who is male. This barber shaves everyone who does not shave himself and no one else. (a) Who shaves the barber? (b) How would you classify this problem?

2. Use an exponent calculator (**www.webwinder.com/wwhtmbin/jexpont.html**) to calculate (i) 2^{10}, (i) 2^{20}, (iii) 2^{30}, (iv) 2^{40}, (v) 2^{50}, (vi) 2^{60}, (vii) 2^{120}.

3. A courtier presented the Persian king with a beautiful, hand-made chessboard. When the king asked what he would like in return, the courtier surprised the king by asking for two grains of rice on the first square, four grains on the second, eight grains on the third, and so on. The king readily agreed and asked for the rice to be brought. How many grains of rice were placed on (i) the 4th square, (ii) the 10th square and (iii) the 64th square?

4. Find out roughly how many atoms there are in the world. How would you classify the problem in question 3?

5. In the context of computation, define tractability and intractability. A young person is offered two choices for increasing her weekly allowance. The first option begins at £0.01 and doubles each week, whereas the second option begins at £1 and increases by £1 each week. What is the young person's weekly allowance in each case after (i) 10 weeks, (ii) 20 weeks, (iii) 52 weeks?

6 Imagine having a pond with water lily leaves floating on the surface. The lily doubles in size every day and if left unchecked will smother the pond in 30 days, killing all the other living things in the water. Day after day the plant seems small, so it is decided to leave it to grow until it half-covers the pond, before cutting it back. On what day will this occur?

7 Suppose that you are organising 300 students into groups of 30. You have been given a list of pairs of incompatible students. Members of a pair must not be together in any group. The number of ways that 30 students can be chosen from 300 students is about 6×10^{68}. It is not possible to build a computer capable of solving this problem by brute force. However, it is relatively easy to check if a given choice of 30 students is satisfactory, i.e. no pair within the 30 also appears on the forbidden list. How would you classify this problem?

Key terms

Halting problem: is it possible in general to write a program that can tell, given any program and its inputs and without executing this program, whether the given program with its given inputs will halt?

PC activity

Go to **http://planetmath.org/ encyclopedia/HaltingProblem. html** and **www.bbc.co.uk/dna/ h2g2/A1304939** for proofs of the halting problem's conclusion.

Activity

Does the algorithm on the left terminate for $x = 15$?
Does it terminate for $x = 105$?
Does it terminate for any positive x?

 PC activity

Code the algorithm in the programming language that you are most familiar with.

Halting problem

The **halting problem** asks 'Is it possible in general to write a program that can tell, given any program and its inputs and without executing this program, whether the given program with its given inputs will halt?' It sheds light on why it is not possible to predict in advance when a computer will crash, i.e. get stuck in some loop, therefore enabling such a situation to be avoided. Predicting in advance would require a method that could decide, just by inspecting another program and its inputs, whether or not the program would go into an infinite loop on the given input; an infinite loop often signifies a bug. A general method to do this for any program and its inputs does not exist and can be proven to not exist; see the PC activity.

Here is an example of an algorithm that may or may not go into an infinite loop.

1 Input x.

2 While x is not equal to 1, do the following:
   If x is even, divide x by 2.
   Otherwise, set x to $3x + 1$.

How long should one wait?

Often it is difficult to tell whether a program has entered an infinite loop, because it may be that the program just needs a little longer to do its calculations. Here is an example.

In mathematics, a perfect number is defined as a positive integer that is the sum of its positive divisors excluding the number itself. For example, 6 is a perfect number because its divisors are 1, 2 and 3 and $1 + 2 + 3 = 6$. The next two perfect numbers are 28 and 496. Table 1 shows that we can express these perfect numbers as $1 + kx$, where k and x are integers such that $k, x > 0$.

Given x, is there a perfect number n of the form $1 + kx$ for some $k > 0$ and $k < s$? The following program outputs 6, 28, 496, 8128 when x = 1 and s = 27, 29, 497, respectively. The program takes a long time to find the perfect number 8128. When x = 2 the program does not halt; it searches for odd perfect numbers. Finding an odd perfect number has defeated the best mathematicians to date.

```pascal
Function FindPerfectNumber(x, s : Integer) : Integer;
  Var
    Sum, i, n : Integer;
    Found : Boolean;
  Begin
    FindPerfectNumber := -1;
    Found := False;
    n := 1;
    While Not Found
      Do
        Begin
          Sum := 0;
          i := 1;
          While i < n
            Do
              Begin
                If (n Mod i) = 0 {Find next factor}
                  Then Sum := Sum + i; {Add factor to Sum}
                i := i + 1;
              End;
          If (Sum = n) And (n >= s)
            {If true then found first perfect number after s}
            Then
              Begin
                FindPerfectNumber := n;
                Found := True;
                Break;
              End;
          If Not Found
            Then n := n + x; // Try next n
        End;
  End;
Var
  x, s : Integer;
Begin
  Repeat
    Write('Input x: ');
    ReadLn(x);
    Write('Input s: ');
    ReadLn(s);
    If x > 0
      Then Writeln(FindPerfect(x, s));
  Until x = 0;
  ReadLn;
End.
```

Here is a program that calls a procedure Test. Procedure Test takes as input a function, F, and a single parameter, x, and executes F on input x.

```pascal
Program Project1;
{$APPTYPE CONSOLE}
Uses
  SysUtils;
Type
  TFunction = Function (y : Integer) : Integer;
    {Declare a type which is a function with a single integer
    parameter y and which returns an integer result}
```

Table 1 $1 + kx$ for the first three perfect numbers

x	k	$1 + kx$
1	5	6
5	1	6
1	27	28
3	9	28
9	3	28
27	1	28
3	165	496
5	99	496
9	55	496
11	45	496
15	33	496

🖥 PC activity

Write a program based on the code to find a perfect number and try with x = 1 and s = 7, 29, 497. Next try x = 2 and s = 2.

```
Function A (Value : Integer) : Integer;
  Begin
    A := 2 * Value; {Function returns 2 times Value}
  End;
Procedure Test (F : TFunction;  x : Integer);
  { Takes as input a function F and executes function F on
    input Parameter}
  Begin
    WriteLn(F(x));
  End;
Begin
  Test(A,6); {Executes function F on input 6}
  ReadLn;
End.
```

How useful is a procedure that is designed to accept as input another subprogram, e.g. a function, plus the input to be run by this subprogram? It is very useful, because subprograms such as the function FindPerfectNumber which halt for values of x = 1 and s = 7, 29 and 497 but not for values of x = 2 could be submitted to a differently constructed procedure Test that would be used to determine without executing FindPerfectNumber if FindPerfectNumber halts for the given input values of x and s. This would be extremely useful, because it would solve the problem of having to wait an indeterminate amount of time for the subprogram to terminate.

Is it possible to construct such a procedure Test whose purpose is to accept as input a subprogram or program and its input, and to determine whether the subprogram will halt on this input? Unfortunately, the answer is no. This has serious implications for algorithms in general. To discover if an algorithm will halt, it needs to be run on its range of specified inputs. There is no other way, in general. But when running the algorithm, if we find ourselves waiting for a long time, then do we conclude that the algorithm is stuck in a loop or do we conclude that we have not allowed enough time for the algorithm to calculate its output?

In this topic you have covered:

- there are algorithmic problems that are non-computable

- non-computable decision problems are called undecidable problems

- some computable problems are tractable and some are intractable

- it is possible to guess a solution for some intractable problems and the guessed solution can be checked in polynomial time

- some algorithms that involve too many steps to be solvable in a reasonable time by computer in the general case can be solved for specific cases in a reasonable time

- it is impossible to write a program to determine, in general, if another program will halt.

Question

8 Is it possible to write a program that reads in another program and its inputs and decides whether or not it goes into an infinite loop? An infinite loop often signifies a bug.

1.6 Regular expressions, BNF and RPN

🖥 PC activity

Go to Google's natural language translation service at **http://translate.google.com** and experiment with translating from one language to another.

■ Did you know?

Language translation was one of the first applications that computer pioneers envisaged in the mid-20th century. In 1954 IBM scientists and Georgetown University linguists demonstrated a machine that produced Russian-to-English translations and began a long tradition in this field of overpromising and underdelivering on the quality of the results.

■ Natural language

English, French, Chinese, Gujarati, Hindi, whichever language you learned as a child, all are examples of natural languages. Natural languages have features in common:

■ A natural language comprises a set of words.

■ A natural language is governed by rules that define the order in which words may be put together to create speech. These rules define the grammar or syntax of the language.

Here are two valid constructs using the grammar of the English language:

Clever young students work hard.

The peanut ate the monkey.

And here is an invalid construct:

Work students young hard clever.

The constructs that the rules of syntax allow are called sentences of the language. A natural language is also governed by rules that define a relationship between a sentence and concepts in the real world. These are the rules of semantics. The rules of semantics are used to define the meaning of a sentence.

For example, 'The peanut ate the monkey' has no possible relationship with any concept in the real world, i.e. it has no meaning. Writing rules for a natural language is a very demanding task. It is partly because of this difficulty that formal languages are used to specify the required behaviour of computing systems.

Basing translation on sophisticated grammars produced by linguists has proved to be inferior to the Google approach based on statistical translation pioneered by IBM in the 1990s. This translation model is not rules-based but is produced by software that looks for patterns, comparing words and phrases, in millions of paired documents, one in the original language and one in the target language. The model now outperforms the best rules-based language translation service on offer from Systran.

■ Formal language

A formal language is defined using two components: its alphabet and its rules of syntax.

The alphabet of a formal language is equivalent to the words of a natural language, except that the alphabet is precisely defined as a finite set. Elements of the set are called symbols of the language.

The rules of syntax of a formal language define how to construct *strings* of the language out of symbols. The strings of a formal language are the equivalent of the sentences of a natural language. For example, a formal language is used for describing the hardness of the lead in pencils.

Its alphabet is {H, B, 2, 3, 4} and the strings in the language are {"4B", "3B", "2B", "B", "HB", "H", "4H", "3H", "2H"}. Note that "4B", "4B", "3B", "2B", etc., are strings in the language, not symbols of its alphabet. To distinguish a string from a symbol, strings are put in double quotes.

In the formal language for pencil hardness there are nine strings. This language is unusual in having a finite number of valid strings. Generally this is not the case, so it is not feasible to list all the valid strings of the language. Instead, a notation is needed to express the rules governing the construction of these strings out of symbols. We call these notations metalanguages. Two metalanguages are regular expressions and Backus–Naur Form (BNF).

Worked examples _____

1   A formal language is used for car number plates.

(a)   Write down some strings in this language.

(b)   Define the alphabet of this language.

2   Write down some DNA strings.

Solutions

1(a)   Here are some strings in the car number plate language: "KD02 NGN", "OY08 BYO", "V2 GRC", "S278 EFC", "LS56 OHT".

1(b)   The alphabet for the car number plate language is {A–Y, 0–9}.

2   The alphabet for DNA is {A, C, G, T}.

Regular language

A **regular language** is any language that a finite state machine (FSM) will accept, e.g. a language composed of the strings generated by a(a|b)*, e.g. {a, aa, ab, aab, abb, ... }, where | means OR and * means zero or more instances. A regular expression, a deterministic finite state automaton and a non-deterministic finite state machine are equivalent ways of defining a regular language. To find a language that is not regular, we must construct a language that requires an infinite number of states.

Regular expressions

One of the most basic and important computing tasks is the manipulation of text, e.g. word-processing documents, DNA sequences, Pascal or Delphi programs. Another important text-processing problem is pattern matching. This often involves searching for one occurrence or all occurrences of some specific string in a large document. For example, we might want to search for the word "haystack" in a large word-processing document, or we might want to search for all occurrences of the string "GATCGGAATAG" in the human genome.

Often there is a need to check whether or not an e-mail address is syntactically valid. For example, fred@www.educational-computing. co.uk looks like an e-mail address, but er!@;#£M does not. A simple test for a valid e-mail address might be a sequence of one or more lower case letters, followed by the @ symbol, followed by another sequence of lower case letters followed by . followed by another sequence of lower case letters followed by co. then uk.

Regular expressions offer a way to specify such patterns and also to solve the corresponding pattern-matching problem.

Regular expression notation

The notation a(a|b)* is called a regular expression, regex or pattern. A **regular expression** describes a set of strings, e.g. the set of all valid e-mail addresses or the set of all binary strings with an even number of 1s. As the set might contain an infinite number of members, it is not possible simply to enumerate them all. The regular expression a(a|b)* describes the infinite set {a, aa, ab, aab, abb, ... }. Therefore, regular expressions are usually used to give a concise description of a set, without having to list all elements. For example, the set containing the three strings Michel, Michael and Michell can be described by the pattern Mich(e|ae|el) or, to put it another way, the pattern Mich(e|ae|el) matches each of the three strings.

A regular expression defines the valid strings of a formal language as patterns of symbols drawn from the alphabet of the language. If the alphabet of some formal language is {a, b} then here are some things we can say:

- a is a regular expression that matches a string consisting of just the symbol a.
- b is a regular expression that matches a string consisting of just the symbol b.
- ab is a regular expression that matches a string consisting of the symbol a followed by the symbol b. This regular expression is a concatenation of a and b.
- a* is a regular expression that matches a string consisting of zero or more a's.
- a+ is a regular expression that matches a string consisting of one or more a's.
- abb? is a regular expression that matches the string ab or the string abb. The symbol ? indicates there is zero or one of the preceding element.
- a|b is a regular expression that matches a string consisting of the symbol a or the symbol b.

To express the syntax of a language, these components of the notation are used in combination.

Key terms

Regular expression: a notation for defining all the valid strings of a formal language or a special text string for describing a search pattern.

Worked example _____

Define the syntax of a formal language with alphabet {a, b, c} in which valid strings consist of at least one a or at least one b, followed by two c's.

Solution

The language is L = (a+|b+)cc.

To interpret a regular expression requires knowledge of the order in which to apply the metasymbols. In arithmetic, we need to know whether $5 + 2 \times 6$ should be interpreted as $5 + (2 \times 6)$ or $(5 + 2) \times 6$ and we use brackets to define the order of evaluation. We use brackets with regular expressions and the following precedence rules:

- * and + are always done first
- concatenation is done next
- | comes last.

Here are some regular expressions that define languages over the alphabet {a, b, c}:

- abc defines the language with one string: "abc".
- abc|bac defines the language with two strings: "abc" and "bac".
- (a|c)b(a|c) defines the language with four strings: "aba", "abc", "cba", "cbc".
- a+ defines the language that contains the strings "a", "aa", "aaa", "aaaa", …
- ab* defines the language that contains the strings "a", "ab", "abb", "abbb", …
- (ac)* defines the language that contains the strings "", "ac", "acac", "acacac", …
- a*ca*ca* defines the language that contains the strings with any number of a's but exactly two c's
- (a|c)* defines the language that contains all possible strings of a and c, including the empty string.

Questions

1 A language L is defined by the alphabet {a, b, c} together with the regular expression (a|c)+bb. (a) Explain in English what constitutes a valid string in L. (b) Give two examples of valid strings in L.

2 The symbol + is not strictly necessary. Show that + is not necessary by rewriting the regular expression for L.

3 Here are some informal descriptions of languages. Write down a regular expression to define each language formally. The alphabet for the languages is {0, 1}. Note any ambiguity in the informal descriptions.

a all possible binary strings

b strings in the language consist entirely of 1s and do not include the empty string

c strings in the language start with a single 1 which may be followed by zero or more 0s

d strings in the language always start with either 110 or 011. The first three symbols may be followed by zero or more 0s or 1s in any order

e any non-empty string in the language as long as it ends with a 0

f any non-empty string that starts and ends with two 1s is a valid string in the language.

4 Write a regular expression to describe strings over the alphabet {x, y, z} that are in sorted order.

Metacharacters

There are 12 characters with special meanings:

- the vertical bar or pipe symbol |
- the question mark ?
- the asterisk or star *
- the plus sign +
- the opening round bracket (and the closing round bracket)
- the opening square bracket [and the closing square bracket]
- the backslash \

- the caret ^
- the dollar sign $
- the period or dot .
- the hyphen – when it appears inside square brackets.

These special characters are often called metacharacters.

Alternation

A vertical bar separates alternatives. For example, a|b can match a or b, bed|ban matches strings bed and ban.

Character class

An alternative way of expressing alternation uses square brackets [and], e.g. [ab] means either a or b. The regular expression b[ae]d matches bad and bed because [] encloses a list of alternative characters, one of which is selected for matching purposes. The contents of the square brackets define a character class.

This form is particularly useful when a range of characters are matched. For example, [a-z] matches all 26 lower case letters from a to z. The character class [a-zA-Z] matches upper case and lower case letters of the alphabet. The – is a metacharacter when it appears inside square brackets. Note that the only special characters or metacharacters inside a character class are the backslash \, the caret ^ and the hyphen -. The usual metacharacters are normal characters inside a character class and do not need to be escaped by a backslash.

Typing a caret after the opening square bracket will negate the character class. The result is that the character class will match any character that is *not* in the character class. Remember that a negated character class still has to match a character. n[^t] does *not* mean 'an n not followed by a t'. It means 'an n followed by a character that is not a t'. It will not match the n in string ben. It will match the n and the space after the n in ben played cricket.

Grouping

Parentheses, or round brackets, are used to define the scope and precedence of the operators, among other uses. For example, gray|grey and gr(a|e)y are equivalent patterns that describe the set containing gray and grey.

Quantification

A quantifier after a token (such as a character) or group specifies how often that preceding element is allowed to occur. The most common quantifiers are ?, *, and +.

Table 1 *Quantifiers for regular expressions*

Quantifier	Meaning
?	Indicates there is zero or one of the preceding element. For example, colou?r matches color and colour
*	Indicates there is zero or more of the preceding element. For example, ab*c matches ac, abc, abbc, abbbc, and so on
+	Indicates that there is one or more of the preceding element. For example, ab+c matches abc, abbc, abbbc, and so on, but not ac

These quantifiers can be combined to form arbitrarily complex expressions, similar to the construction of arithmetical expressions from numbers and the operations $+$, $-$, $\times$, $\div$. For example, `Mich(a?e|el)1` and `Mich(e|ae|el)1` are valid patterns that match the same strings.

Worked example

Write down the strings defined by the regular expression `b[ea]d?`. The strings are `be`, `ba`, `bed`, `bad`, because `b` means b, `[ea]` means either an e or an a, and `d?` means no d or one d.

Worked example

Write down the strings defined by the regular expression `10*1`. The strings are `11`, `101`, `1001`, `10001`, patterns with a sequence of 0's sandwiched between two 1's. This is because `1` means 1, `0*` means zero or more 0's, and `1` means 1.

Worked example

Write down the strings defined by the regular expression `10+1`. The strings are

`101`, `1001`, `10001`, patterns with a sequence of 0's sandwiched between two 1's. This is because `1` means 1, `0+` means one or more 0's, and `1` means 1.

Searching using regular expressions

A regular expression is also a special text string for describing a search pattern. Regular expressions define patterns of characters that, applied to a block of text, enable specific strings of characters to be located within the text. The most basic regular expression consists of a single literal character, e.g. `e`. It will match the first occurrence of that character in the string. If the string is `Bob ate his dinner`, it will match the e after the t. This regex can match the second e too. It will only do so when you tell the regex engine to start searching through the string after the first match. In a text editor, you can do this by using the Find Next or Search Forward function.

For example, the pattern `b(a|e)d` will find instances of `bad` and `bed` in this text:

`I slept badly in my bed at bedtime when I was bedded down for the night.`

The pattern will match `bad` in `badly`, `bed` in `bed`, `bed` in `bedtime` and `bed` in `bedded`. If this regular expression is part of a program used to search text, e.g. a web page, then the program will return substrings `bad` and `bed` if the text contains these substrings.

Regular expressions are composed of characters that directly match the text and metacharacters such as `|` to control how to achieve the matching.

Simple matching

Any single character matches itself, unless it is a metacharacter with a special meaning described below. A sequence of characters matches the corresponding sequence of characters in the target string, so the pattern `bed` matches substring `bed` in the target string `bedded`.

Characters that normally function as metacharacters are preceded by a backslash `\` when they need to be interpreted literally. This is called escaping the character. For example, to use the metacharacter * as a character to be matched requires that * be preceded by \.

The dot matches almost any character

The dot matches a single character, without caring what that character is, unless it is the newline character. So .an matches strings ban, can, dan, fan, ian, lan, man, nan, pan, ran, tan, van, wan because . matches any single character.

Predefined shorthand classes

With predefined classes the metacharacter \ functions to escape the normal meaning of the following character, e.g. \d means treat d as a metacharacter not as the literal character d. The following predefined classes have meaning:

- x\d matches "x0", "x1", "x2", "x3", "x4", "x5", "x6", "x7", "x8", "x9" because \d matches a single numeric character.

- be\w matches "bed", "bee", "beg", "ben", "bet", "beD", "beE", "beG", "beN", "beT","be0", "be1", ..., "be8", "be9" because \w matches a single alphanumeric character (a..z, A..Z, 0..9) and the underscore character _ .

- be\W matches "be!", "be"", "be£", "be$", "be%", "be^", etc., because \W matches a single non-alphanumeric character. \W is short for [^\w].

- \D matches a single non-numeric character and is equivalent to [^\d].

- \s matches a single space.

- \S matches any single non-space character and is the equivalent of [^\s].

Worked example _____

The regular expression for any integer is [+\-]?\d+.

This is because [+\-] matches a single character which is + or -. The \ is used because – is a metacharacter; – is used in [a-z], for example. [+\-]? matches zero or one character which is + or -. \d matches any digit. \d+ matches one or more digits.

Examples: [+\-]?\d+ matches 351, -7851, +3567.

Worked example _____

The regular expression for a real number is [+\-]?\d+(\.\d+)?

This is because [+\-] matches a single character which is + or -. The \ is used because – is a metacharacter; – is used in [a-z], for example. [+\-]? matches zero or one character which is + or -. \d matches any digit. \d+ matches one or more digits. \. matches the decimal point (\ is used to escape the metacharacter meaning of ., which is match any character). (\.\d+) means match a decimal point followed by one or more digits. (\.\d+)? means no instance or a single instance of a decimal point followed by one or more digits.

Examples: [+\-]?\d+(\.\d+) matches 351, -7851.4, +3567.456.

Worked example _____

The regular expression for an e-mail address is [_a-zA-Z\d\-.]+@ ([_a-zA-Z\d\-]+(\.[_a-zA-Z\d\-]+)+)

This is because [_a-zA-Z\d\-.] matches a single character which is the underscore character or a single character from the range a–z or A–Z or a digit or a hyphen or a full stop. [_a-zA-Z\d\-\.]+ matches one or more characters as described. @ matches the @ character. [_a-zA-Z\d\-]+ is as above but omitting the full stop character. (\.[_a-zA-Z\d\-]+) means match a full stop followed by one or more characters from a–z, A–Z, digits and a hyphen. (\.[_a-zA-Z\d\-]+)+ means match one or more times what is matched by the round brackets.

Example:
[_a-zA-Z\d\-.]+@([_a-zA-Z\d\-]+(\.[_a-zA-Z\d\-]+)+)
matches fred@flintstone.com, mary@contrary.co.uk

Applications of regular expressions

Regular expressions are used extensively in operating systems for pattern matching in commands and when performing a search for files or folders. Often when editing text, you need to search for a word in a block of text. You can use a regular expression to find a word, even if it is misspelled. For example, if searching for the word separate (correct spelling) the regex sep[ae]r[ae]te would find separate, seearate, seperete and separete. The regex [A-Za-z_][A-Za-z_0-9]* could be used to search for an identifier in a programming language.

Other applications are scanning for virus signatures, search and replace in word processors, searching for information using Google, filtering text (spam, Net Nanny, Carnivore, malware, firewall traffic), validating data-entry fields (e-mail, dates, URLs, debit and credit card numbers).

■ Questions

5 Say which of the following strings match the regular expression be[ea]n: (a) ben, (b) been, (c) bean, (d) beean.

6 Say which of the following strings match the regular expression be?ad: (a) bed, (b) bad, (c) bead, (d) be?ad.

7 Say which of the following strings match the regular expression 10(1)*01: (a) 1001, (b) 100101, (c) 10101, (d) 1011101.

8 Say which of the following strings match the regular expression \d+(-|\s)\d+: (a) 01296-433006, (b) 01296--433006, (c) 01793   234589, (d) 01793 234589, (e) 01793234589.

9 Create a regular expression to validate website addresses which always begin with www., such as www.educational-computing.co.uk.

10 The word 'licence' has been spelled in the following ways in a piece of text: licence, license, lisence, license. Write a regular expression that will find all instances of the word 'licence' spelt in these different ways.

■ Backus–Naur form

Defining the syntax of a formal language by means of a regular expression can get very tedious for languages with large alphabets, because the notation of a regular expression does not allow the symbols of a language to be grouped into classes. For example, it would be exceptionally tedious but not impossible to define the syntax of an identifier in a programming language such as Pascal by means of a regular expression. However, there are some types of language whose syntax simply cannot be defined by a regular expression.

A very common language construct in computing involves brackets (...). For most purposes, it is required that the brackets are matched, i.e. every opening bracket has a corresponding closing bracket that comes after it and no closing bracket is allowed before it has a corresponding opening bracket. The nesting of brackets within other brackets also occurs quite often. The problem arises when it is necessary to allow any depth of nesting of brackets. It is not possible to define such a language using regular expressions. Instead we must express the rules of the language in a notation known as **Backus–Naur form** (BNF).

BNF notation

A program in any language can be viewed as a string of characters chosen from some set or alphabet of characters.

How do we prescribe which strings of characters represent valid programs? The syntax of a programming language defines the rules that tell us whether a string is a valid program. Consider this simpler example which lists the valid strings that describe pencil lead hardness: {"4B", "3B", "2B", "B", "HB", "H", "4H", "3H", "2H"}. The alphabet used is {H, B, 2, 3, 4}.

Now consider how, using BNF, the rules for constructing these valid strings can be specified:

```
<lead hardness> ::= HB | <scale of hardness> | <simple
hardness>
```

The lead hardness is defined as either the symbol H followed by the symbol B, or it is a scale of hardness or it is a simple hardness. The symbol ::= means 'consists of' or 'is defined as'.

- The phrases enclosed in angle brackets < and > are called non-terminal symbols of the grammar.
- The non-terminal lead hardness on the left-hand side of the rule is the equivalent in the formal language of a category such as noun or verb in the grammar of a natural language.
- H and B on the right-hand side of the rule are two terminal symbols of the grammar. Terminal symbols of grammar are symbols from the alphabet of the formal language.
- The vertical bar character | separates alternatives on the right-hand side of the rule.

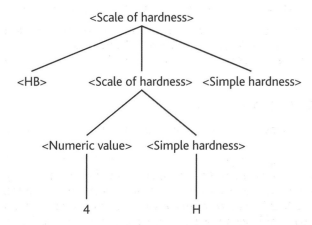

Fig. 1.6.1 *Parse tree for pencil hardness 4H*

Here is the completed grammar (syntax definition):

```
<scale of hardness> ::= <numeric value><simple hardness>
<numeric value> ::= 2 | 3 | 4
<simple hardness> ::= H | B
```

`<lead hardness>` is known as the starting symbol of the grammar; it defines the structure of a complete string in the language.

Worked example _____

Is the pencil hardness 4H valid? Fig. 1.6.1 shows that it is.

Recursive definitions

Simple definitions such as those for pencil hardness are adequate for many rule-based systems but some rule definitions need to use recursion. Consider, for example, the definition of an unsigned integer, i.e. a string of digits containing neither a sign nor a decimal point. Without using recursion, here is the only possible BNF definition:

```
<unsigned integer> ::= <digit>|<digit><digit>|<digit><digit>
<digit>|<digit><digit><digit><digit>|
|etc
<digit> ::= 0|1|2|3|4|5|6|7|8|9
```

Clearly, the definition of an unsigned integer is inadequate because it depends on the number of terms included as alternatives. A definition catering for every possible unsigned integer would have to contain an infinite number of terms. The solution is a **recursive definition**, in which the term being defined is also used in the definition:

```
<unsigned integer> ::= <digit>|<digit><unsigned integer>
<digit> ::= 0|1|2|3|4|5|6|7|8|9
```

Using this definition, it is possible to verify the validity of a string of digits such as 435 in the following way:

- 435 is not a digit
- 435 is an unsigned integer if 4 is a digit and 35 is an unsigned integer
    - 4 is a digit
    - 35 is not a digit
    - 35 is an unsigned integer if 3 is a digit and 5 is an unsigned integer
        - 3 is a digit
        - 5 is a digit and hence an unsigned integer
    - 35 is an unsigned integer
- 435 is an unsigned integer.

Syntax of a programming language

The syntax of a programming language is more complex than the case of pencil hardness. Nevertheless, BNF can be used to specify the rules for valid statements as follows:

```
<statement> ::= <assign_statement>|<for statement>|<if
statement>|etc.
<assign_statement> ::= <identifier><assign_op><expression>.
<expression> ::= <term><arithmetic_operator><term>.
<term> ::= <identifier>|<constant>|<expression>
<arithmetic_operator> ::= <multi_op>|<add_op>|etc.
<add_op> ::= + | -
etc.
```

Key terms

Recursive definition: is one that is defined in terms of itself.

Activity

Express the steps that verify that 435 is an unsigned integer as a parse tree; see Fig. 1.6.1. Check that 4*5 is not an unsigned integer using the approach given above.

Activity

Use a search engine such as Google to search for the BNF definition of the programming language that you are most familiar with.

Natural language and BNF

Natural language has a very complicated set of rules for constructing grammatically correct sentences. Sentences are constructed from nouns, verbs, adjectives, prepositions, the definite article, the indefinite article and adverbs.

In BNF a subset of the English language can be specified as follows:

```
<sentence> ::= <noun phrase><verb phrase><noun phrase>.
<noun phrase> ::= <preposition> <article><noun>
<verb phrase> ::= <verb>|<adverb><verb>
<article> ::= The|the|a|an|A|An
<preposition> ::= in|on|at|of
<noun> ::= cat|mat|fire|front|mouse
<verb> ::= sat|lay|eat|caught|slept
<adverb> ::= slowly|quickly|languidly
```

The non-terminal symbol <sentence> is the starting symbol.

For example, the sentence

The cat sat on the mat.

can be analysed and broken down as shown in Fig. 1.6.2.

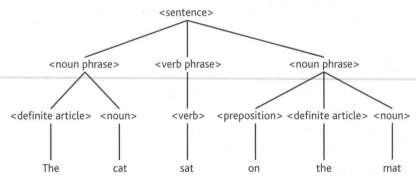

Fig. 1.6.2 *Parse tree for a simple sentence*

A parse tree is a pictorial representation showing how a valid sentence conforms to the rules for constructing grammatically correct sentences.

Syntax diagrams

Syntax diagrams are an alternative way of defining the syntax rules of a language. Suppose that we need to define a subset of the English language that includes the following sentence.

The cat caught the mouse.

We consider a sentence to be composed of a subject followed by a verb followed by an object followed by a full stop (Fig. 1.6.3). Each of the boxes except the last one, which needs no further expansion, can be defined diagrammatically (Fig. 1.6.4).

Sentence:

Fig. 1.6.3 *We consider a sentence to be composed of a subject followed by a verb followed by an object followed by a full stop*

Check whether these sentences are valid sentences according to the syntax defined by Fig. 1.6.4:

1 A mouse ate the cat.

2 A small bird caught the thin mouse.

3 The black cat saw the fly.

4 The fat bird ate fly.

5 A bird saw a fly and a mouse.

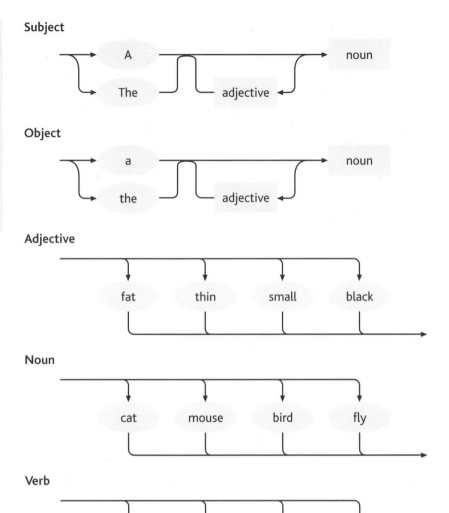

Fig. 1.6.4 *Syntax diagram for a subset of the English language*

Each part of a syntax diagram defines a non-terminal. Here are the non-terminals in Fig. 1.6.4:

Sentence, Subject, Object, Adjective, Noun, Verb

Each diagram has an entry point and an end point. The diagram describes possible paths between these two points by going through other non-terminals and terminals. Terminals are represented by oval boxes and non-terminals are represented by square boxes. Here are the terminals in Fig. 1.6.4:

caught, ate, saw, killed, a, the, A, The, cat, mouse, bird, fly, fat, thin, small, black

Questions

11 Draw a syntax diagram which defines the Roman numerals from 1 to 10: I, II, III, IV, V, VI, VII, VIII, IX, X. Your diagram should not consist merely of ten alternatives.

12 An identifier in a programming language consists of a letter followed by zero or more letters or digits. Draw a syntax diagram for valid identifiers in this language.

13 A user ID for logging into a computer system consists of two digits followed by one of the abbreviations H, L, D, R, Pa, Ph, followed by a surname consisting of upper case letters A..Z only followed by a single initial chosen from the set of upper case letters A..Z. Draw a syntax diagram for user IDs to this system.

Reverse Polish notation

The arithmetic expression 5 + 6 contains two operands and one operator. The operands are 5 and 6 and the operator is +. The expression 5 + 6 is an infix expression because the operator appears between the two operands. Other examples of infix expressions are

(a) 36 + 4 * 3

(b) (x − y)/(x + y)

(c) x ↑ 2.

In (a) the operands are 36, 4 and 3. The operators are the addition operator + and the multiplication operator *. In (b) the operands are x and y, the operators are the subtraction operator −, the addition operator + and the division operator /. In (c) the operands are x and 2. The operator is the exponentiation operator ↑. Case (c) means x raised to the power of 2 or x squared.

There is a potential problem with infix. In (a) do we evaluate 36 + 4, producing 40 and then multiply by 3, producing the answer 120, or do we evaluate 4 * 3, producing 12 and then add 36, producing 48? As humans, we have been drilled to evaluate multiplication before addition. However, for programming machines to follow such a rule is an unnecessary complication. If we need to add first, then we could make this clearer by putting round brackets (or parentheses) around 36 + 4 so the expression becomes (36 + 4) * 3.

The round brackets show that we evaluate 36 + 4 then multiply by 3. But a machine would need to be programmed with this rule. This seems an unnecessary complication. Is there a way of writing an expression without brackets that has only one order of evaluation and that would be easy for a machine to evaluate? Yes, it is called postfix or reverse Polish notation (RPN). In this representation the operator is placed after the operands it acts upon. For example, the reverse Polish or postfix expression 36 y + is 36 + y in infix notation.

Consider the following postfix expressions: (a) x y − x y + /, (b) x 2 ↑ and (c) x y 2 ↑ +. In infix, (a) is (x − y)/(x + y), (b) is x ↑ 2 and (c) is x + (y ↑ 2). Case (c) raises y to the power of 2 and then adds x. RPN expressions have an advantage over infix expressions because they do not need brackets to show the correct order of evaluation. They are simpler to evaluate by a machine.

Did you know?

Please excuse my dear Aunt Sally: parentheses, exponentiation (roots and powers), multiplication, division, addition, subtraction.

Did you know?

In the early days of electronic calculators, precedence rules proved difficult to implement in calculator hardware. In the 1920s Polish mathematician Jan Lukasiewicz showed that writing operators in front of their operands, instead of between them, made brackets unnecessary. In the 1950s Charles L. Hamblin proposed a scheme where the operators follow the operands (postfix operators); this led to RPN. RPN has the advantage that the operators appear in the order required for computation.

Questions

14 Convert these infix expressions using variables x and y into RPN expressions: (a) x + y, (b) (x + y)/2, (c) (x + y) * (x − 4), (d) x ↑ y, (e) x + y ↑ 2, (f) (x + y)/(x − y).

15 Convert these RPN expressions using variables x and y into infix expressions: (a) x y *, (b) x y + 6 *, (c) x y + x y − /, (d) 2 x * 3 y * + 8 /, (e) x y + 2 ↑ 6 x − *.

☑ *In this topic you have covered:*

- regular expressions define valid strings in a formal language
- a regular expression is equivalent to a finite state automaton
- regular expressions are used to check that a string is a valid postcode or valid e-mail address
- regular expressions are used when searching for particular strings in documents or operating system directories and folders
- there are some formal languages that regular expressions cannot define
- these languages can be defined using Backus–Naur form (BNF)
- BNF is used to define the syntax of a programming language
- syntax diagrams are another way to define the syntax of a programming language
- reverse Polish notation (RPN) eliminates the need for brackets in arithmetic expressions and makes it easier for a machine to evaluate expressions.

2 Programming concepts

2.1 Programming paradigms

The first high-level programming languages appeared in the 1950s. Hundreds more have been invented since. Some are still in common use today. Why are there so many? For each specific area where computers are used, the methods used to solve problems have different requirements. For example, Fortran was designed for numerical applications and is still used by mathematicians, scientists and engineers. Cobol was designed for business applications. Pascal was designed as a language to teach structured programming; see page 89 in the AS book.

A programming paradigm is a fundamental style, or methodology, of computer programming. There are several programming paradigms:

- imperative (procedural)
- functional
- logic
- event-driven
- object-oriented.

A programming language supports one or more paradigms; see Table 1.

Imperative programming

The first computers could only be programmed in machine code, then assembly code. Both machine and assembly code required detailed knowledge of the architecture of the particular processor. Registers were addressed directly. These languages were known as low-level languages; see pages 184–185 in the AS book.

Later, high-level languages were invented. There are many different high level languages, designed to solve different types of problem. Programs were written using sequences of instructions that were executed by the processor in the order the programmer designed. This is the imperative paradigm. Among the earliest languages were Fortran and Cobol, which are still in use today. An imperative program manipulates variables and data structures. For extensive examples of imperative programming, see Section 2 in the AS book.

Functional programming

In the functional programming paradigm, programs define mathematical functions. A solution to a problem consists of a series of function calls. There are no variables or assignment statements, but lists and functions that manipulate lists. An example of a functional programming language is Haskell. Here is the Haskell code for the classic recursive algorithm to calculate $n!$ (Topic 2.2):

```
factorial :: Integer -> Integer
  factorial 0 = 1
  factorial n | n > 0 = n * factorial (n-1)
```

And here is an iterative solution of *n*! in Lisp:

```
(defun factorial (n)
  (loop for i from 1 to n
        for fact = 1 then (* fact i)
        finally (return fact)))
```

■ Logic programming

A logic program consists of a set of facts and rules. A knowledge base is built up through writing facts and rules about a specific area of expertise. Then an inference engine, a program, with an ability to backtrack will use the knowledge base to answer queries presented in the form of a goal.

The best-known language is Prolog, extensively used for artificial intelligence and expert systems. Here is an example of a Prolog program for a small family tree:

```
parent(jackie, laura).
parent(jackie, tim).
parent(rachel, david).
parent(rachel, jonathan).
parent(joyce, jackie).
parent(joyce, rachel).
parent(janet, paul).

parent(paul, laura).
parent(paul, tim).
parent(andrew, david).
parent(andrew, jonathan).
parent(bill, jackie).
parent(bill, rachel).
parent(john, paul).

male(david).
male(jonathan).
male(paul).
male(tim).
male(john).
male(andrew).
male(bill).

female(jackie).
female(laura).
female(rachel).
female(janet).
female(joyce).

mother(Mother,Child) IF parent(Mother,Child) AND female(Mother).
father(Father,Child) IF parent(Father,Child) AND male(Father).
sibling(Sib1,Sib2) IF parent(P,Sib1) AND parent(P,Sib2) AND NOT Sib1=Sib2.
grandfather(GF,Child) IF father(GF,P) AND parent(P,Child).
grandmother(GM,Child) IF mother(GM,P) AND parent(P,Child).
  goal
grandmother(jackie, GrandChild).
```

A fact

Paul is a parent of Laura

A rule

GM is the grandmother of Child if GM is the mother of P and P is a parent of Child

A goal

Who are the grandchildren of Jackie?

Event-driven programming

An event is an action or occurrence detected by a program. Instead of all the program instructions being executed in the order the programmer designed, subroutines are executed in response to events. They could be actions the user performs, such as clicking on a button or choosing a menu option in a form (Window). Here is an example of an event-handling procedure in Delphi, executed when the user clicks on the button `btnGreeting` in the form `frmHello`:

```
Procedure TfrmHello.btnGreetingClick(Sender: TObject);
Begin
  lblMessage.Caption := 'Hello World';
End;
```

The run method of the application starts a system loop which continues until the application is closed. This system loop processes system messages. When an event occurs, a message is sent to the application. The application will execute the relevant event-handling code. If several events occur, their respective messages form a queue and the application will execute the relevant event handlers in turn.

Table 1. *Programming languages and their paradigms*

Language	Imperative	Functional	Logic	Object-oriented	Event-driven
Algol	✓				
Basic	✓				
C	✓				✓
C++	✓			✓	
Cobol	✓			✓ (current versions)	
Delphi (ObjectPascal)	✓			✓	✓
Fortran	✓			✓ (current versions)	
Haskell		✓			
Java	✓			✓	✓
Lisp		✓			
Pascal	✓			✓	
Prolog			✓		
Python	✓	✓		✓	✓
Simula				✓	
Smalltalk				✓	✓
Visual Basic.NET				✓	✓

Question

1 Find as many high-level programming languages as you can, then classify them as in Table 1.

Object: an instance of a class

Instantiation: an object is defined based on a class

Class definition: a pattern or template that can be used to create objects of that class.

Encapsulation: combining a record with the procedures and functions that manipulate it to form a new data type, a class.

Object-oriented programming

The structured programming approach involves breaking down a problem into smaller problems until routines can be written that execute single tasks. These routines operate on data passed to them through interfaces (parameters). Software engineering concerns itself with writing robust code. Reusing tried and tested code is a way to reduce development time and to improve the reliability of the code. Many routines are available in libraries.

Object-oriented programming takes this one step further by combining the routines and the data they operate on into a single unit called a class. The data items stored for a class are known as fields properties. The routines that operate on these fields are known as methods.

When a programmer wants to use a class, they declare instances of the class, known as **objects**. This is known as **instantiation**. The real benefit of working with classes is that a new class can be based on an existing class. The new class inherits all the fields and methods from the existing class, and the programmer declares other fields or methods that are specific to the new class.

The new class is known as a subclass or derived class of the existing class. The existing class is known as the superclass or parent class. If the superclass is the highest in the hierachy then it is also known as the base class. Two other key terms are **class definition** and **encapsulation**.

ClockExample1 is written using the imperative paradigm

The variables Hours and Minutes represent the clock settings

The main program body calls routines that access variables.

These variables can be altered from anywhere within the main program body without calling the procedure SetTime

```
Program ClockExample1;
{$APPTYPE CONSOLE}
Uses SysUtils;
Var Hours, Minutes : Integer;
Function GetHours : Integer;
  Begin
    GetHours := Hours;
  End;
Function GetMinutes : Integer;
  Begin
    GetMinutes := Minutes;
  End;
Procedure SetTime (h, m : Integer);
  Begin
    Hours := h;
    Minutes := m;
  End;
//********** main program body ***************
Begin
  SetTime(15,25);
  Hours := Hours + 1;
  WriteLn('The time is ',GetHours,':',GetMinutes);
  ReadLn;
end.
```

ClockExample2 is written using the imperative paradigm but the variables are grouped into a record with fields that represent the clock settings. This makes the code more transparent

```
Program ClockExample2;
{$APPTYPE CONSOLE}
Uses SysUtils;
Type TClock = Record
                  Hours: Integer;
                  Minutes: Integer;
              End;
Var Clock : TClock;
```

```
Function GetHours : Integer;
  Begin
    GetHours := Clock.Hours;
  End;
Function GetMinutes : Integer;
  Begin
    GetMinutes := Clock.Minutes;
  End;
Procedure SetTime (h, m : Integer);
  Begin
    Clock.Hours := h;
    Clock.Minutes := m;
  End;
//********** main program body ****************
Begin
  SetTime(15,25);
  Clock.Hours := Clock.Hours + 1;
  WriteLn('The time is ',GetHours,':',GetMinutes);
  Readln;
End.
```

> The clock settings can still be altered from anywhere in the main program body without calling the procedure SetTime

```
Unit Unit1;
Interface
Type TClock = Record
                Hours : Integer;
                Minutes : Integer;
              End;
Implementation
End.
```

> ClockExample2 is split into the main program, ClockExample3, and a unit that stores the type declaration, Unit1

```
Program ClockExample3;
{$APPTYPE CONSOLE}
Uses SysUtils, Unit1 In 'Unit1.pas';
Var Clock: TClock;
Function GetHours : Integer;
  Begin
    GetHours := Clock.Hours;
  End;
Function GetMinutes : Integer;
  Begin
    GetMinutes := Clock.Minutes;
  End;
  Procedure SetTime (h, m : Integer);
  Begin
    Clock.Hours := h;
    Clock.Minutes := m;
  End;
//********** main program body ****************
Begin
  SetTime(15,25);
  Clock.Hours := Clock.Hours + 1;
  WriteLn('The time is ',GetHours,':',GetMinutes);
  Readln;
End.
```

> Clock is a record of type TClock. Note that the record fields are still accessible anywhere in the program

ClockExample4 uses an object Clock of class TClock, declared in Unit2

Before an object can be used, it needs to be created

Note that the clock fields are still accessible from anywhere in the program

When an object is no longer required, the memory it occupies must be released

This is Unit2. The **Interface** part contains the class definition

The **Implementation** part contains the code for the class methods

```
Program ClockExample4;
{$APPTYPE CONSOLE}
Uses SysUtils, Unit2 In 'Unit2.pas';
Var Clock : TClock;
Begin
 Clock := TClock.Create;
 Clock.SetTime(15,25);
 Clock.Hours := Clock.Hours + 1;
 WriteLn('The time is ',
              Clock.GetHours,':',Clock.GetMinutes);
 Clock.Free;
 ReadLn;
End.
```

```
Unit Unit2;
Interface
Type TClock = Class
                  Hours : Integer;
                  Minutes : Integer;
                  Function GetHours : Integer;
                  Function GetMinutes : Integer;
                  Procedure SetTime(h, m : Integer);
              End;
Implementation
Function TClock.GetHours: Integer;
   Begin
     GetHours := Hours;
   End;
Function TClock.GetMinutes: Integer;
   Begin
     GetMinutes := Minutes;
   End;
Procedure TClock.SetTime (h, m : Integer);
   Begin
     Hours := h;
     Minutes := m;
   End;
End.
```

```
Unit Unit2;
Interface
Type TClock = Class
                  Private
                    Hours : Integer;
                    Minutes : Integer;
                  Public
                    Function GetHours : Integer;
                    Function GetMinutes : Integer;
                    Procedure SetTime(h, m : Integer);
                    Procedure Increment Time;
                  End;
Implementation
{methods code as above for ClockExample4}
Procedure TClock.IncrementTime;
   Begin
     Minutes := Minutes + 1;
     Sleep(60000); // wait one minute
```

To make the final program fully object-oriented, the clock's fields are made inaccessible from the program by declaring them as private. The only way to access the fields now is through TClock's public methods

When you try to run ClockExample4 with this amended Unit2, you will find that the program cannot access the private field Clock.Hours

To increment the time of the clock, a new method needs to be written to update this field

```
        If Minutes = 60
          Then
            Begin
              Hours := Hours + 1;
              Minutes := 0;
              If Hours = 24 Then Hours := 0;
            End;
      End;
```

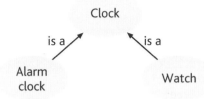

PC activity

1 Copy the program code for ClockExample1, ClockExample2, ClockExample3 and ClockExample4. Make sure the programs work correctly.

2 Edit ClockExample4 so that it is a fully object-oriented program as shown above.

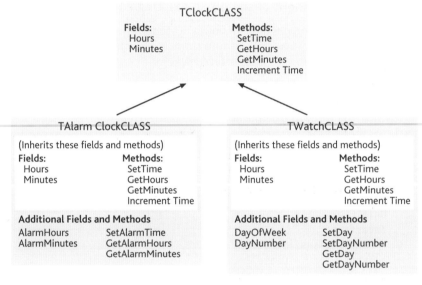

Fig. 2.1.1 *An inheritance diagram*

Fig. 2.1.2 *A class diagram*

Key terms

Inheritance: defining a class and then using it to build a hierarchy of descendant classes with each descendant inheriting access to all its ancestors' code and data.

Declaring subclasses of existing classes

Two further classes are required, TAlarmClock and TWatch. They can be based on the existing class, TClock. This uses the idea of **inheritance**.

```
Type TAlarmClock = Class (TClock)
                     Private
                       AlarmHours: Integer;
                       AlarmMinutes: Integer;
                     Public
                       Function GetAlarmHours: Integer;
                       Function GetAlarmMinutes: Integer;
                       Procedure SetAlarmTime(h, m : Integer);
                     End;
```

PC activity

1. Complete the program code for AlarmClockExample then test it.

2. Write the necessary code to implement class TWatch then write a program to test a TWatch object.

Here is a simple Pascal program that uses this class:

```
Program AlarmClockExample;
{$APPTYPE CONSOLE}
Uses SysUtils, Unit2 In 'Unit2.pas';
Var AlarmClock: TAlarmClock;
Begin
  AlarmClock := TAlarmClock.Create;
  AlarmClock.SetTime(15,10);
  AlarmClock.SetAlarmTime(15,15);
 Repeat
  AlarmClock.IncrementTime;
  WriteLn(AlarmClock.GetHours,':',AlarmClock.GetMinutes);
   Until (AlarmClock.GetAlarmHours = AlarmClock.GetHours)
     And (AlarmClock.GetAlarmMinutes = AlarmClock.GetMinutes);
   WriteLn('Wake up');
   AlarmClock.Free;
   ReadLn;
End;
```

Writing a component based on an existing component

In Delphi, every component is an object descended from TComponent, TControl or TGraphicControl, or from some other existing component such as TCustomPanel and TCustomGroupBox.

1. Define a subclass based on the class that is most what you want.
2. In the public area of the class definition you can redefine any methods which you want to redefine at runtime using Override.
3. You can add new methods.
4. In the implementation part, write the definitions of any methods you declared in the class definition.

Class definition using Pascal

```
Unit ClassDefs;
Interface
  Uses Classes, StdCtrls;
  Type TClock = Class (TLabel)
                       Private
                         Hours : Integer;
                         Minutes : Integer;
                         Function IntToStrF (i : Integer) : String;
                       Public
                         Constructor Create (AOwner : TComponent);
                         Override;
                         Procedure IncrementTime;
                         Procedure DisplayTime;
                     End;
Implementation
  Uses SysUtils, StrUtils;
  Constructor TClock.Create (AOwner : TComponent);
    Begin
      Inherited Create(AOwner);
      Top := 20;
      Left := 20;
      Hours := 0;
      Minutes := 0;
      Caption := '00:00';
    End;
  Procedure TClock.IncrementTime;
```

The **TClock** class is derived from the **TLabel** class

Any methods you want to redefine at runtime, you reference here with **Override**

Always call the inherited constructor. Then you can add any other code you want to run on creation of the control, such as sizing the object

```
      Begin
        Minutes := Minutes + 1;
        If Minutes = 60
          Then
            Begin
              Hours := Hours + 1;
              Minutes := 0;
              If Hours = 24
                Then Hours := 0;
            End;
      End;
  Function TClock.IntToStrF (i : Integer): String;
  Var StringI : String[2];
    Begin
      StringI := IntToStr(i);
      If Length(StringI)=1
        Then IntToStrF := '0' + StringI
        Else IntToStrF := StringI;
    End;
  Procedure TClock.DisplayTime;
    Var StrMinutes, StrHours : String[2];
    Begin
      StrMinutes := IntToStrF(Minutes);
      StrHours := IntToStrF(Hours);
      Caption := StrHours + ':' + StrMinutes;
    End;
End.
```

Using the example in a Pascal program

```
Unit ClockForm;
Interface
 Uses
    Windows, Messages, SysUtils, Variants, Classes, Graphics,
    Controls, Forms, Dialogs, ClassDefs, ExtCtrls;
 Type
    TForm1 = Class(TForm)
                tmrClockTick : TTimer;
                Procedure FormCreate(Sender : TObject);
                Procedure tmrClockTickTimer(Sender : TObject);
              Public
                Clock : TClock;
            End;
 Var
    Form1 : TForm1;
Implementation
{$R *.dfm}
 Procedure TForm1.FormCreate(Sender : TObject);
    Begin
      Clock := TClock.Create(Self);
      Clock.Parent := Self;
      tmrClockTick.Enabled := True;
      tmrClockTick.Interval := 60000; // tick every minute
    End;
 Procedure TForm1.tmrClockTickTimer(Sender : TObject);
    Begin
      Clock.IncrementTime;
      Clock.DisplayTime;
    End;
End.
```

The unit name of the component library

Declare the clock object

When you call the component's constructor, you must pass a parameter specifying the owner of the component. This is usually Self, i.e. the form

Set the parent property. You only do this for controls, not other components, before any other properties. This causes the control to display on the parent (Form 1)

PC activity

1 Use the code on page 77 to implement a clock that shows the current time and displays it on a form (Fig. 2.1.3).

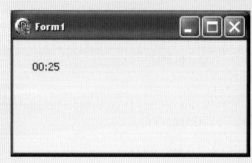

Fig. 2.1.3 *Form*

2 Extend the program from Question 6 to display seconds as well.

3 Write a program that implements an alarm clock as a component. This is a more challenging question.

Key terms

Polymorphism: giving an action one name that is shared up and down a class hierarchy. Each class in the hierarchy implements the action in a way appropriate to itself.

Making a method virtual means it can be redefined

*Methods to be redefined are referenced with **Override***

Polymorphism

In the following example, the method Display is used in the base class as well as in the derived classes, but each class implements this method differently. This is known as **polymorphism**.

```
Unit Unit1;
Interface
Uses
    Windows, Messages, SysUtils, Variants, Classes, Graphics,
    Controls, Forms, Dialogs, StdCtrls;
Type
    TForm1 = Class(TForm)
                btnRun : TButton;
                Procedure btnRunClick(Sender : TObject);
             End;
    TShape = Class
                Procedure Display; Virtual;
             End;
    TRectangle = Class (TShape)
                Procedure Display; Override;
                End;
    TEllipse = Class (TShape)
                Procedure Display; Override;
                End;
Var
    Form1 : TForm1;
Implementation
    Procedure TShape.Display;
      Begin
        Form1.Canvas.LineTo(100,200);
      End;
    Procedure TRectangle.Display;
      Begin
        Form1.Canvas.Rectangle(150,20,250,200);
      End;
```

```
Procedure TEllipse.Display;
  Begin
    Form1.Canvas.Ellipse(300,100,500,200);
  End;
Var Shape : TShape;
{$R *.dfm}
Procedure TForm1.btnRunClick(Sender: TObject);
  Begin
    Shape := TShape.Create;
    Shape.Display;
    Shape.Free;
    Shape := TRectangle.Create;
    Shape.Display;
    Shape.Free;
    Shape := TEllipse.Create;
    Shape.Display;
    Shape.Free;
  End;
End.
```

Question

2 Draw an inheritance diagram of the classes in the above program.

In this topic you have covered:

- the characteristics of imperative and functional programming
- an example of logic programming using Prolog
- the characteristics of event-driven programming
- object class, instantiation, encapsulation, inheritance and polymorphism
- a practical introduction to programming with objects.

2.2 Recursion

In this topic you will cover:

- recursive algorithm for *n*!

- how to represent recursive calls when dry running such a routine

- how to write a recursive routine

- the use of the stack when routines are called recursively

- the classic recursion example of the Towers of Hanoi puzzle.

Key terms

Recursive routine: a routine defined in terms of itself.

General case: the solution in terms of itself for a value *n*.

Base case: a value that has a solution which does not involve any reference to the general case solution.

Recursive call

What is recursion?

Recursion describes the ability of a routine to call itself. This means a **recursive routine** is defined in terms of itself.

Recursion is very powerful and often results in a very elegant solution to a problem. However, iterative solutions usually make more efficient use of computer time and memory space.

A classic example of a recursive routine is *n* factorial. The mathematical definition is:

$n! = n \times (n - 1)!$
Example: $3! = 3 \times 2! = 3 \times 2 \times 1$
because $1! = 1$

Recursive solutions to problems have a **general case** and a **base case**.

In the example of the factorial function, the general case is
$n! = n \times (n - 1)!$
and the base case is
$1! = 1$.

Programming the factorial definition using Pascal gives the following code:

```
Function Factorial (n : Integer) : Integer;
  Begin
    If n = 1
      Then Result := 1
      Else Result := n * Factorial(n-1)
  End;
```

To illustrate the recursive calls, dry run the function with an initial call to calculate 5! (Table 1).

Table 1 *Dry run to calculate 5!*

Call number	Function call	*n*	Result =	Result =	Return value
1	Factorial(5)	5	5 * Factorial(4)	5 * 24 =	120
2	Factorial(4)	4	4 * Factorial(3)	4 * 6 =	24
3	Factorial(3)	3	3 * Factorial(2)	3 * 2 =	6
4	Factorial(2)	2	2 * Factorial(1)	2 * 1 =	2
5	Factorial(1)	1	1		1

Explanation

Note that every time the routine executes the Else part of the code, it invokes another call to itself. However, each time the value of the parameter changes and eventually the parameter value is 1. This time the Then part of the function code is executed and the function returns normally, supplying the return value to the previous invocation of the routine.

In the above example, the function calls 1 to 4 don't run to completion until call number 5 of function returns the value 1 to function call 4. This call can then return normally, providing the value 2 to function call 3. This will then provide the return value 6 to function call 2, which in turn provides the return value of 24 to function call 1. Finally, function call 1 can return the answer, 120.

Here is another way of representing the recursive calls of Factorial(5):

```
Factorial(5)
   Factorial := 5 * Factorial(4)
   Factorial(4)
      Factorial := 4 * Factorial(3)
      Factorial(3)
         Factorial := 3 * Factorial(2)
         Factorial(2)
            Factorial := 2 * Factorial(1)
            Factorial(1)
               Factorial := 1
               Return 1
            Return 2
         Return 6
      Return 24
   Return 120
```

It shows how the call Factorial(1) does not make a recursive call but returns normally with a return value, causing the previous calls to unwind.

The mechanism of recursive routines

Recursion works only if the routine is called with the current value or values passed as parameters. It would not work with global variables.

Each time a routine is called, a special area of main memory, called the stack, is used. There the return address is stored as well as the contents of registers. Any local variables and the routine's parameters are also allocated space on the stack. The stack locations for one routine call are known as a **stack frame**. When a routine ends, control normally passes to the stored return address and its stack frame is removed from the stack.

If many recursive calls are made, the stack space could run out. This is known as stack overflow. For example, if the above function Factorial were called with a parameter of 0, recursive calls would not terminate normally as the base case of 1 would never be reached. Eventually stack overflow would occur. Because of the stack overheads, recursive algorithms may not be as efficient as iterative solutions.

AQA Examiner's tip

You may be asked to dry run a recursive algorithm.

Key terms

Stack frame: the locations in the stack area used to store the values referring to one invocation of a routine.

 PC activity

1 Test the recursive routine Factorial.

2 Write an iterative solution for Factorial. Test your solution.

 PC activity

1 Dry run the following algorithm with the procedure call
   PrintSequence(5). Clearly show the values of the parameter at each
   call and the printed output.

```
Procedure PrintSequence(n)
    n ← n - 1
    If n > 1
      Then
          PrintSequence(n)
    EndIf
    Output(n)
EndProcedure
```

2 Dry run the following algorithm with the procedure call
   PrintSequence(5). Clearly show the values of the parameter at each
   call and the printed output.

```
Procedure PrintSequence(n)
    n ← n - 1
    If n > 1
      Then
          Output(n)
          PrintSequence(n)
    EndIf
EndProcedure
```

■ How to write a recursive routine

Using the recursive factorial definition as an example, here are the steps
to follow when writing a recursive routine.

Code the general case:

```
Result := n * Factorial(n-1)
```

Determine the condition(s) for the base case:

```
If n = 1
```

Code the base case:

```
Result := 1
```

The base case must not contain a recursive call. Ensure that the base case
is reached after a finite number of recursive calls:

```
If n < 1 Then report an error
```

Note that the factorial function would cause an infinite number of
recursive calls if it was called with a parameter less than 1. This sort of
error needs to be trapped.

Putting these parts together gives the following code:

```
Function Factorial (n : Integer) : Integer;
  Begin
    If n < 1
      Then Error
      Else
        If n = 1
          Then Result := 1
          Else Result := n * Factorial(n-1)
  End;
```

The Tower of Hanoi

According to legend, an order of Buddhist monks in Hanoi has been engaged for many years in the following task. The monks have three vertical pegs and a set of 64 circular discs of different sizes; each disc has a hole in the centre which allows it to be slid onto any of the pegs. Initially the discs were all placed on a single peg, one on top of the other in order of decreasing size, so that they formed a single tower (Fig. 2.2.1). The tasks the monks have set themselves is to transfer this original tower to one of the other pegs, moving only one disc at a time and ensuring that no disc ever rests on top of a smaller one.

Assume the peg supporting the original tower is called A, the peg to which the tower is to be moved is called B, and the third peg is called C. Given the rules governing the movement of discs, it is clear that the only way in which the bottom disc of the original tower can be moved to form the base of the new tower, is to first get the 63 discs on top of it out of the way. The only place to put these 63 discs is on the third peg, so here is an algorithm for transferring the entire tower from peg A to peg B:

1 Transfer the top 63 discs from peg A to peg C.

2 Move the bottom disc from peg A to peg B.

3 Transfer the 63 discs from peg C to peg B.

We can generalise this for transferring n discs from a peg called Source to a peg called Destination (given a third peg called Workspace):

1 Transfer $n - 1$ discs from Source to Workspace.

2 Move 1 disc from Source to Destination.

3 Transfer $n - 1$ discs from Workspace to Destination.

This algorithm is clearly recursive, and the number of discs to be moved on each recursive call is successively reduced by 1. An escape route from successive calls is provided when only a single disc is to be transferred between pegs; in this case you just pick it up and move it. This is the base case.

Here is the complete algorithm for transferring n discs from Source to Destination:

```
Procedure MoveTower (N, Source, Destination, Workspace)
  If N=1
    Then MoveDisk (Source, Destination)
    Else
        MoveTower (N-1, Source, Workspace, Destination)
        MoveDisk (Source, Destination)
        MoveTower (N-1, Workspace, Destination, Source)
  EndIf
EndProcedure
```

The above algorithm is a very concise and elegant solution to a decidedly non-trivial problem. Iterative methods do exist, but their derivation requires considerable insight.

PC activity

1 Write a recursive function Fibonacci(n) which calculates the nth integer in the sequence of Fibonacci numbers. The general case is defined mathematically as
$f_n = f_{n-1} + f_{n-2}$
The base cases are
$f_0 = 0, f_1 = 1$.
Test your function.

2 Write a recursive function Power(A, n) which calculates the value of a^n. Test your function. Hint: the general case is $a^n = a \times a^{n-1}$ and the base case is $a^0 = 1$.

Fig. 2.2.1 *The Tower of Hanoi puzzle*

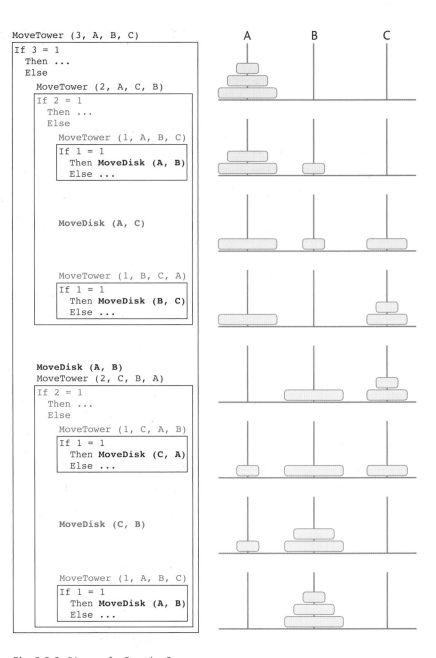

```
MoveTower (3, A, B, C)
If 3 = 1
  Then ...
  Else
    MoveTower (2, A, C, B)
    If 2 = 1
      Then ...
      Else
        MoveTower (1, A, B, C)
        If 1 = 1
          Then MoveDisk (A, B)
          Else ...


        MoveDisk (A, C)


        MoveTower (1, B, C, A)
        If 1 = 1
          Then MoveDisk (B, C)
          Else ...


    MoveDisk (A, B)
    MoveTower (2, C, B, A)
    If 2 = 1
      Then ...
      Else
        MoveTower (1, C, A, B)
        If 1 = 1
          Then MoveDisk (C, A)
          Else ...


        MoveDisk (C, B)


        MoveTower (1, A, B, C)
        If 1 = 1
          Then MoveDisk (A, B)
          Else ...
```

Fig. 2.2.2 *Diagram for Question 3*

For other recursive algorithms, look at Topic 2.5 on graphs and trees and Topic 2.6 on sorting and searching.

In this topic you have covered:

- how to dry run a recursive routine

- how to write a recursive routine

- how the stack is used by recursive routines.

Questions

1 How many moves must be made as a minimum (if no redundant moves are made) to move *n* discs?

2 Research on the Internet to find a non-recursive solution to the Tower of Hanoi problem.

3 Dry run the Tower of Hanoi algorithm with three discs.

2.3 Lists and pointers

In this topic you will cover:

- the concept of abstract data types

- the concept of linear lists and their representation using one-dimensional arrays

- the structure of linked lists and their representation as nodes linked by pointers

- the use of free memory, the heap and pointers.

Key terms

List: a collection of elements with an inherent order.

Abstract data type (ADT): a data type whose properties are specified independently of any particular programming language.

Abstract data types

Programming languages distinguish between different data types such as integer, real and string (see pages 37–40 in the AS book). High-level languages also provide the programmer with data structures such as records and arrays (see page 41 and pages 67–73 in the AS book). Object-oriented programming languages allow the declaration of classes, data structures combined with the methods that act on them (see Topic 2.1 in this book).

Real-life problems often refer to other structures, or containers, to store data items or objects, also called elements. Lists are examples of these structures. We will meet other examples in Topic 2.4 on stacks and queues and Topic 2.5 on graphs and trees. We write shopping lists and to-do lists and we can set up playlists on our media players. People use an endless number of lists.

Elements can be added and deleted from a list. Therefore a list can grow and shrink. This is known as a dynamic structure. A **list** is a collection of elements with an inherent order. How can lists be implemented in programmed solutions?

We are going to view the list as an **abstract data type (ADT)** – as a data type whose properties are specified independently of any particular programming language.

The operations that need to be performed on a list are:

- initialise list (i.e. start a new list)
- insert an element
- find an element
- delete an element
- get length of list
- output entire list.

Linear lists

A linear list stores its elements in adjacent locations. Elements in an array are stored physically in adjacent locations in main memory. When an array is declared, the compiler reserves the space for the array elements. This means that the array is a static structure.

A one-dimensional array can be used to store the elements of a list. However, the array needs to be declared with enough locations to store the maximum number of elements the list may contain at any one time.

How can the list operations be implemented?

- **Initialisation of list:** declaration of the array and initialising a variable NumberOfElements.

- **Insertion of an element:** store the element in the next available space; increment the variable NumberOfElements.

- **Search for an element:** see the section on linear search (*AQA Computing A2*, page 91).

- **Deleting an element**: find the element to be deleted and move subsequent elements up one space; decrement the variable NumberOfElements.
- **Get the length of the list**: this is the variable NumberOfElements
- **Output the entire list**: start at the beginning of the array and output each element in turn until the last element is reached.

Advantages

- It is easy to program.
- If elements are stored in key order, a binary search is possible.

Disadvantages

- Memory locations may be wasted due to arrays being static.
- Insertion of an element within an ordered list requires moving elements.
- Deletion of an element within a list requires moving elements.

PC activity

1. Write a program that uses a one-dimensional array to store names of friends to invite to a party. Allow a maximum of 30 names to be stored.

   Your program should ask you for the names of your friends to be added to the list until you type in the rogue value 'XXX'.

   Your program should then give you the following options: add another name, print the list of names, output the number of names in the list.

   Test your program to ensure it will not allow you to enter more names than there are spaces in the list.

2. This is a stretch and challenge question. Look at Topic 2.6 and add the following options to your program from Question 1: find a name, delete a name. Test that your program stores the remaining list of names accurately after the deletion of a name.

3. Adapt your program from Question 1 or Question 2. Declare the list array as an array of records. As well as recording your friends' names, you also want to store whether they have replied to your invitation or not. Add two further options to your program:

   - print list of names of all those definitely coming to the party

   - print list of names of all those who have not replied yet.

Key terms

Pointer: a variable that contains an address. The pointer points to the memory location with that address.

Null pointer: a pointer that does not point to anything, usually represented by Ø or −1.

Linked lists

Imagine list elements stored wherever there is space and linked to form a sequence. Each element of the list, known as a node, can be represented as a record of data fields, with an extra field used as a **pointer** that links a node to the next node in the list (Fig. 2.3.1). A special pointer, the start pointer, points to the first node of the list. The last node in the list has a **null pointer** in the pointer field.

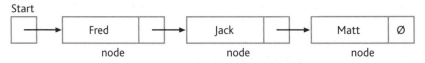

Start

| | Fred | | Jack | | Matt | Ø |

node   node   node

Fig. 2.3.1 *An extra field links a node to the next node in the list*

This concept of a linked list makes insertion and deletion of elements much less time-consuming. Just the pointer fields are changed. To insert a new node at the beginning of the list, the content of the start variable is copied into the new node's pointer field, then the start variable is set to point to the new node (Fig. 2.3.2).

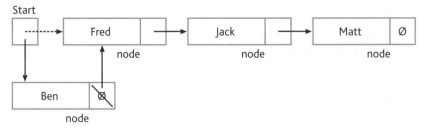

Fig. 2.3.2 *How to insert a new node at the beginning of the list*

To insert a new node between 'Fred' and 'Jack', the pointer field of the node for 'Fred' is copied to the pointer field of the new node. The pointer field of the node for 'Fred' is changed to point to the new node (Fig. 2.3.3).

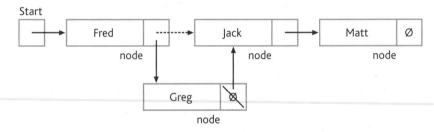

Fig. 2.3.3 *How to insert a new node between 'Fred' and 'Jack'*

What if the new node is to be added to the end of the list? The pointer field of the node for 'Matt' is changed to point to the new node (Fig. 2.3.4). Note that we can still use the step for the general case. The pointer field of the node for 'Matt' is copied to the pointer field of the new node. It just copies the null pointer.

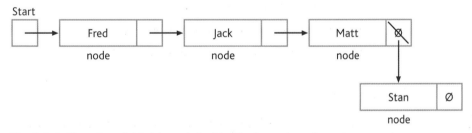

Fig. 2.3.4 *The pointer field of the node for 'Matt' is changed to point to the new node*

To delete the first node in the list, the pointer field of the node to be deleted is copied into the start variable (Fig. 2.3.5).

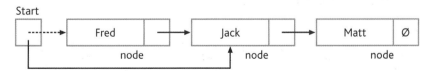

Fig. 2.3.5 *How to delete the first node in the list*

To delete the node for 'Jack', the pointer field of the node for 'Jack' is copied into the pointer field of the node for 'Fred' (Fig. 2.3.6).

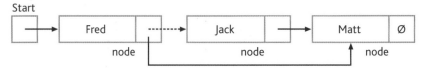

Fig. 2.3.6 *How to delete the node for 'Jack'*

What if the last node is to be deleted? Note that the step in the above example still holds. To delete the node for 'Matt', the pointer field of the node for 'Matt' is copied into the pointer field of the node for 'Jack' (Fig. 2.3.7).

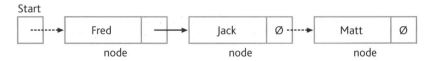

Fig. 2.3.7 *How to delete the last node in the list*

How can we program such a linked list?

These linked lists can be stored in an array, just as before. But instead of moving nodes to insert or delete elements, the nodes are connected via the pointers and the pointer values are the index of the array location of the node (Table 1). Tables 2 and 3 show two examples.

Table 1 *The nodes are connected via the pointers and the pointer values are the index of the array location of the node*

Index	Data fields	Pointer field
1	Fred	2
2	Jack	3
3	Matt	0
4		
5		
6		

Start: 1

Table 2 *To insert a new node for Greg, only the pointers are adjusted*

Index	Data fields	Pointer field
1	Fred	~~2~~ 4
2	Jack	3
3	Matt	0
4	Greg	2
5		
6		

Start: 1

Table 3 *To delete the node for Jack, only the pointers are adjusted*

	Index	Data fields	Pointer field
Start 1	1	Fred	4
	2	Jack	3
	3	Matt	0
	4	Greg	~~2~~ 3
	5		
	6		

But how can the now redundant node in array element 2 be reused? A second list can be produced by linking all the free nodes together (Fig. 2.3.8).

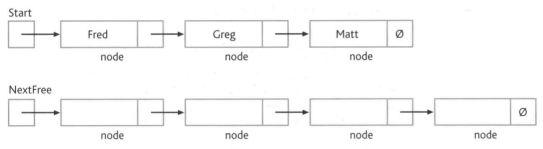

Fig. 2.3.8 *A second list can be produced by linking all the free nodes together*

Using an array, this would look like this (Table 4). Table 5 shows how to add a node at the beginning of the list.

Table 4 *A second list can be produced by linking all the free nodes together*

	Index	Data fields	Pointer field
Start 1	1	Fred	4
NextFree 2	2	Jack	5
	3	Matt	0
	4	Greg	3
	5		6
	6		0

Table 5 *How to add a node at the beginning of the list*

	Index	Data fields	Pointer field
Start ~~1~~ 2	1	Fred	4
NextFree ~~2~~ 5	2	Ben	~~5~~ 1
	3	Matt	0
	4	Greg	3
	5		6
	6		0

```
Node[NextFree].Data ← 'Ben'
Temp ← NextFree
NextFree ← Node[NextFree].Pointer
Node[Temp].Pointer ← Start
Start ← Temp
```

Table 6 shows how to add a node within the list shown in Table 1;
assume the new node is to be inserted after ThisNode,

Table 6 *How to add a node within the list*

	Index	Data fields	Pointer field
Start 1	1	Fred	~~2~~ 4
NextFree ~~4~~ 5	2	Jack	3
	3	Matt	0
	4	Greg	~~5~~ 2
	5		6
	6		0

```
Node[NextFree].Data ← 'Greg'
Temp ← NextFree
NextFree ← Node[NextFree].Pointer
Node[Temp].Pointer ← Node[ThisNode].Pointer
Node[ThisNode].Pointer ← Temp
```

Table 7 shows how to delete the first node of the list.

Table 7 *How to delete the first node of the list*

	Index	Data fields	Pointer field
Start ~~1~~ 2	1	Fred	~~2~~ 4
NextFree ~~4~~ 1	2	Jack	3
	3	Matt	0
	4		5
	5		6
	6		0

```
Temp ← Start
Start ← Node[Start].Pointer
Node[Temp].Pointer ← NextFree
NextFree ← Temp
```

Table 8 shows how to delete a node within the list; ThisNode is the node to be deleted. PreviousNode is the node before ThisNode.

Table 8 *How to delete a node within the list*

	Index	Data fields	Pointer field
Start [1]	1	Fred	2̶ 3
NextFree [1̶ 2]	2	Jack	3̶ 4
	3	Matt	0
	4		5
	5		6
	6		0

```
Temp ← NextFree
NextFree ← ThisNode
Node[PreviousNode].Pointer ← Node[ThisNode].Pointer
Node[ThisNode].Pointer ← Temp
```

Table 9 shows how to output the data elements of the list.

Table 9 *How to output the data elements of the list*

	Index	Data fields	Pointer field
Start [1]	1	Fred	4
	2	Jack	3
	3	Matt	0
	4	Greg	2
	5		
	6		

```
ThisNode ← Start
While Node[ThisNode].Pointer <> 0
  Do
    Output Node[ThisNode].Data
      ThisNode ← Node[ThisNode].Pointer
EndWhile
```

This has eliminated some of the disadvantages of linear lists, but not the fact that an array is a static structure whereas a list is really a dynamic structure.

 PC activity

Write a program based on the algorithms above that implements a linked list using an array of records.

Pointer type: a variable of pointer type stores an address of a data value.

Heap: the memory locations available to application programs for dynamic allocation.

Dynamic allocation: memory space is only allocated when required at run time.

Memory leakage: successive calls to allocate memory space are made, but memory locations that are no longer required are not released. Eventually no memory is left in the heap.

Use of free memory, the heap and pointers

Many high-level languages have a pointer type as a built-in data type. This **pointer type** is used to declare a variable to store an address, which is the location of a data value.

When a pointer variable is declared in a program, the compiler will reserve the space in memory for this pointer, but no space is reserved for the value or values it can point to. This memory space is allocated when required at run time from a pool of memory locations called the **heap**. This is known as **dynamic allocation**.

If the data value is an integer, the pointer type has to be declared as an integer pointer. For other data types the pointertype has to be declared accordingly.

Here is an example using Pascal syntax:

```
Var
    CounterPtr : ^Integer;
    AveragePtr : ^Real;
```

It is possible to declare pointer types. Here is an example using Pascal syntax:

```
Type
    TintegerPtr = ^Integer;
    TRealPtr = ^Real;
```

Pointer types can also be declared to point to user-defined types. Here is an example:

```
Type
    TNodePtr = ^TNode;
    TNode = Record
                Data : String;
                Ptr : TNodePtr;
            End;
```

When declaring a pointer, the pointer exists in memory but it is not pointing to anything. When it is required to point to a memory location, the memory location is allocated using the built-in procedure New. When the value is no longer required, the memory space must be released using the built-in procedure Dispose. The memory space is returned to the heap, the area of available memory. Failure to do so may result in **memory leakage**.

To store a value in the memory location pointed to by A:

```
A^ := 0;
```

Using dynamic storage allocation, there is no need to estimate maximum sizes and declare at compile time the amount of memory required for the list. Memory is allocated when required and disposed of when no longer required.

The following program was written in Pascal as an example of how pointer variables can be used. If you are using a different programming language, you need to explore whether it lets you access memory locations through the use of pointer variables.

```
Program LinkedList;
  {$APPTYPE CONSOLE}
Uses
  SysUtils;
```

```
Type
  TNodePtr = ^TNode;
  TNode = Record
             Data : String; // node consists of one data field
             Ptr : TNodePtr; // and a pointer to the next node
          End;
Var
  Start : TNodePtr;
Procedure InitList (Var List : TNodePtr);
  Begin
    List := Nil; // set up an empty list
  End;
Procedure AddItem (Var List : TNodePtr; NewItem : String);
  Var NewNode, ThisNode, NextNode : TNodePtr;
  Begin
    New (NewNode);              // allocate space for a new node
    NewNode^.Data := NewItem;
    NewNode^.Ptr := Nil;
    If List = Nil
      Then List := NewNode    // list points to the new node
      Else
        Begin
          NextNode := List;
          While NextNode <> Nil // find the end of the list
            Do
              Begin
                ThisNode := NextNode;
                NextNode := NextNode^.Ptr;
              End;
          ThisNode^.Ptr := NewNode;
                              // add new node to end of list
        End;
  End;
Procedure DeleteItem (Var List : TNodePtr; WantedData : String);
  Var ThisNode, PreviousNode : TNodePtr;
  Begin
    If List <> Nil
      Then
        Begin
          ThisNode := List;
          While ThisNode^.Data <> WantedData // find the node
            Do
              Begin
                PreviousNode := ThisNode;
                ThisNode := ThisNode^.Ptr
              End;
          PreviousNode^.Ptr := ThisNode^.Ptr;
        End;
      Dispose (ThisNode); // free the memory space
  End;
Procedure PrintList (List : TNodePtr);
  Var ThisNode : TNodePtr;
  Begin
    If List <> Nil
      Then
        Begin
          ThisNode := List; // start at the beginning
```

Pascal uses Nil for null pointer value

```
          Repeat
            WriteLn (ThisNode^.Data);
                              // output each node in turn
            ThisNode := ThisNode^.Ptr; // move to next node
          Until ThisNode = Nil;
                              // until end of list reached
        End;
      End;
    Begin
      InitList (Start);           // initialise the list
      AddItem (Start,'Fred');     // add Fred to the list
      AddItem (Start,'Jack');     // add Jack to the list
      AddItem (Start,'Matt');     // add Matt to the list
      PrintList(Start);           // print the names in the list
      WriteLn;
      DeleteItem(Start,'Jack');   // delete Jack from the list
      PrintList (Start);          // print the amended list
      ReadLn;
    End.
```

💻 PC activity

1. Write a user interface to test the functionality of the list operations in program LinkedList more thoroughly.

2. Add code to the program LinkedList so it gives a message if an attempt is made to delete a name that does not exist.

3. Extend the program above to find a name in the list. It should give a message if the name is not in the list.

4. Extend your program to give a message if an attempt is made to print an empty list.

5. Change the code for AddItem so the new node is added in the correct sequence to keep all nodes in ascending name order.

In this topic you have covered:

- the concept of abstract data types

- the concept of linear lists and their representation using one-dimensional arrays

- the structure of linked lists and their representation as nodes linked by pointers

- the use of free memory, the heap and pointers.

2.4 Stacks and queues

Key terms

Dynamic data structure: the memory taken up by the data structure varies at run time.

Static data structure: the memory required to store the data structure is declared before run time.

Stack: a last-in first-out (LIFO) abstract type data.

Stacks and queues are abstract data types (ADTs). Both are **dynamic data structures** rather than **static data structures**. Both can be seen as special cases of lists (Topic 2.3). They differ in the way elements are added and removed.

Stacks

A **stack** is also known as a last-in first-out abstract data type. Imagine a pile of plates in a restaurant on a spring-loaded rack (Fig. 2.4.1). Plates are added to the top and taken away from the top.

Fig. 2.4.1 *A stack of plates*

Two operations can be carried out on a stack (Fig. 2.4.2):

- add a new item to the top of the stack (known as pushing)
- remove an item from the top of the stack (known as popping).

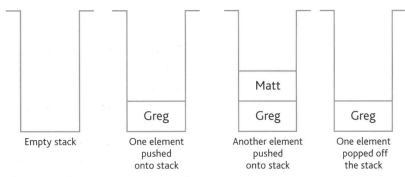

Fig. 2.4.2 *Diagram to represent a stack*

Here are two examples in a computing context:

- Stacks are used to store the return address, parameters and register contents when a procedure or function call is made. When the procedure or function completes execution, the return address and other data are retrieved from the stack; see Topic 2.2 on recursion.
- Stacks are used for compilers, when translating high-level language expressions in assignment statements; see Topic 1.6 on Reverse Polish Notation.

TopOfStackPointer

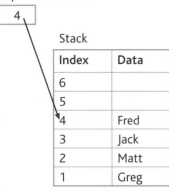

Fig. 2.4.3 *A pointer is required to point to the last item added to the stack*

Implementation

When implementing a dynamic structure using the linear list method, the structure becomes static.

Linear list method (using arrays)

A pointer is required to the last item added to the stack (Fig. 2.4.3). An empty stack has a `TopOfStackPointer` value of zero. To determine when the stack is full, the maximum index must be known.

Here is an algorithm to add an item to the stack (Fig. 2.4.4):

```
If Stack is full
  Then Error
  Else
    Increment TopOfStackPointer
    Stack[TopOfStackPointer] ← Datum
EndIf
```

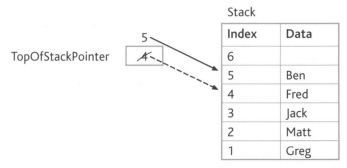

Fig. 2.4.4 *How to add an item to the stack*

Here is an algorithm to remove an item from the stack (Fig. 2.4.5):

```
If Stack is empty
  Then Error
  Else
    Return Stack[TopOfStackPointer]
    Decrement TopOfStackPointer
EndIf
```

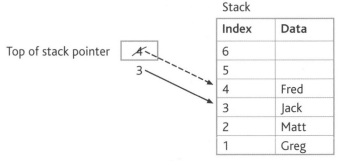

Fig. 2.4.5 *How to remove an item from the stack*

Linked list method

A stack can be seen as a linked list where elements are added and removed from the front of the list only. Fig. 2.4.6 shows how to add a new item to the top of the stack; the algorithm to add an element to the beginning of a linked list is described in Topic 2.3.

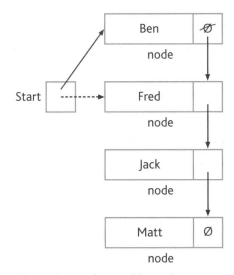

Fig. 2.4.6 *How to add a new item to the top of the stack*

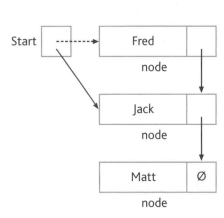

Fig. 2.4.7 *How to remove an item from the top of the stack*

Fig. 2.4.7 shows how to remove an item from the top of the stack; the algorithm to delete the first element of a linked list is described in Topic 2.3. The pointer type method can be used to implement a stack (Topic 2.3).

A stack can also be implemented by declaring a stack as a class:

```
Unit StackClass;
Interface
Type
  TStack = Class
              Type
                TNodePtr = ^TNode;
                TNode = Record
                              Data : String;
                              Ptr : TNodePtr;
                          End;
              Private
                TopOfStack: TNodePtr;
              Public
                Constructor Create;
                Procedure Push(NewItem: String);
                Function Pop: String;
                Function IsEmpty: Boolean;
                Procedure PrintStack;
            End;
Implementation
Constructor TStack.Create;
  Begin
    TopOfStack := Nil;
  End;
Procedure TStack.Push (NewItem: String);
  Var NewNode, ThisNode: TNodePtr;
  Begin
    New (NewNode); // create a new node
    NewNode^.Data := NewItem;
    ThisNode := TopOfStack; // remember the previous top of stack
    TopOfStack := NewNode; // Top of stack points to new node
    NewNode^.Ptr := ThisNode; // new node points to previous top
  End;
```

```
Function TStack.Pop: String;
  Var ThisNode: TNodePtr;
  Begin
    If IsEmpty
      Then WriteLn ('Stack Empty')
      Else
        Begin
          Pop := TopOfStack^.Data;
          ThisNode := TopOfStack;
          TopOfStack := TopOfStack^.Ptr;
          Dispose (ThisNode);
        End;
  End;
Function TStack.IsEmpty: Boolean;
Begin
  IsEmpty := (TopOfStack = Nil);
End;
Procedure TStack.PrintStack;
  Var ThisNode: TNodePtr;
  Begin
    Writeln('Contents of Stack:');
    If Not IsEmpty
      Then
        Begin
          ThisNode := TopOfStack;
          Repeat
            WriteLn (ThisNode^.Data);
            ThisNode := ThisNode^.Ptr;
          Until ThisNode = Nil;
        End
      Else WriteLn('Nil');
    WriteLn;
  End;
End.
```

Questions

1. (a) Draw a diagram of the state of a stack after Jones, Smith, Peters, Franklin and Taylor have been added to the stack, in the order given.
(b) Draw another diagram showing the state of the stack after two names have been popped off the stack.

2. Draw a diagram showing the array implementation of a stack after the words Plate, Saucer, Cup have been added to the stack, in the order given. You should also show the value of the variable TopOfStackPointer.

💻 PC activity

1. Write a program to implement a stack using the linear list method. Test that your program works correctly, including trying to add an element to a full stack and trying to remove an element from an empty stack.

2. Write a program to implement a stack using the linked list method with an array to store the nodes. Test that your program works correctly, including trying to add an element to a full stack and trying to remove an element from an empty stack.

3. Write a program to implement a stack using the linked list method with the pointer type and memory locations on the heap to store the nodes. Test that your program works correctly, including trying to remove an element from an empty stack.

4. Write a program that will test the stack class defined above.

Queues

A **queue** is also known as a first-in first-out abstract data type.

In everyday life, we encounter queues in lots of different situations: at bus stops, ticket counters and cafeterias, cars at traffic lights, aeroplanes waiting to take off.

Fig. 2.4.8 *A linear queue*

| Fred | Jack | Matt | Ben |

Front ↑   ↑ Rear

Fig. 2.4.9 *Diagram to represent a queue*

Two operations may be carried out on a queue:

- add a new item to the rear of the queue
- remove an item from the front of the queue.

Here are some examples of queues in computing context:

- print jobs waiting to be printed
- characters entered at the keyboard and held in a buffer
- jobs waiting to be executed under a batch operating system
- simulations (Topic 2.7).

A queue can be implemented in various ways. The simplest method is using an array. However, this makes the queue into a static data structure.

For dynamic implementations, memory locations are assigned from the heap and pointer type variables link the nodes.

Implementing queues using linear lists (arrays)

Fig. 2.4.10 on page 100 is an example of a queue after three people have joined it.

Queue

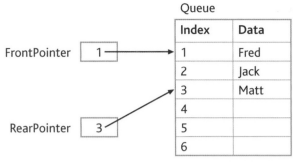

Index	Data
1	Fred
2	Jack
3	Matt
4	
5	
6	

Fig. 2.4.10 *A queue after three people have joined it*

Queue

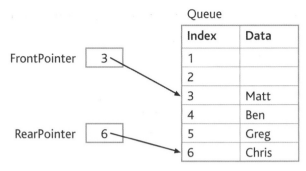

Index	Data
1	
2	
3	Matt
4	Ben
5	Greg
6	Chris

Fig. 2.4.11 *Three more people have joined the queue and two people have left the queue*

In Fig. 2.4.11 three more people have joined the queue and two people have left the queue.

What happens if another person wants to join the queue? The end of the array is reached. There are two possible solutions.

Solution 1: shuffle queue

Every time someone leaves the queue, everyone moves one position forward. This means the variable FrontPointer would not be required, because the front of the queue would always be in array element with index 1. However, this requires a lot of assignments, especially if the queue is long. This is not usually seen as a realistic solution, and circular queues are usually implemented instead.

Solution 2: circular queue

A **circular queue** allows the queue to wrap around to the beginning of the array and to reuse vacated locations.

Fig. 2.4.12 shows the situation after another person has left the queue and two more people have joined the queue.

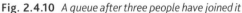

Key terms

Circular queue: when the array element with the largest possible index has been used, the next element to join the queue reuses the vacated location at the beginning of the array.

Queue

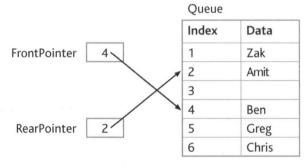

Index	Data
1	Zak
2	Amit
3	
4	Ben
5	Greg
6	Chris

Fig. 2.4.12 *Another person has left the queue and two more people have joined the queue*

The difficulty with this method is the representation of an empty queue and a full queue. It is easiest to keep a count of how many elements there are currently in the queue.

Here is an algorithm to add an item to a circular queue:

```
If Queue is full
    Then Error
    Else
        Increment RearPointer
        If RearPointer > MaxIndex
            Then RearPointer ← 1
        Queue[RearPointer] ← Datum
EndIf
```

Here is an algorithm to remove an item from a circular queue:

```
If Queue is empty
  Then
    Error
  Else
    Return Queue[FrontPointer]
    Increment FrontPointer
    If FrontPointer > MaxIndex
    Then FrontPointer ← 1
EndIf
```

Dynamic queue implementation using linked lists

Linear queue

In a **linear queue**, elements join the queue at one end and leave the queue at the other end. Two pointer type variables are required: one to point to the node at the front of the queue, and one to point to the node at the rear of the queue. Each node points to the node after it in the queue. The last node in the queue has a null pointer. Fig. 2.4.13 shows a queue with three people.

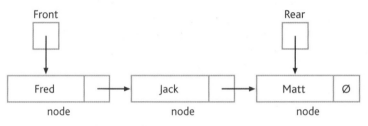

Fig. 2.4.13 *A queue with three nodes*

Ben is added to the back of the queue (Fig. 2.4.14).

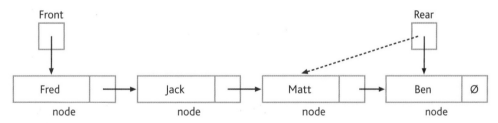

Fig. 2.4.14 *A new node is added to the rear of the queue*

Fred is removed from the front of the queue (Fig. 2.4.15).

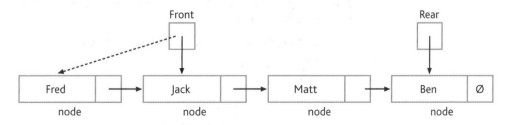

Fig. 2.4.15 *A node is removed from the front of the queue*

Here is the relevant code:

```
Unit QueueClass;
Interface
Type
  TQueue = Class
              Type
                TNodePtr = ^TNode;
                TNode = Record
                          Data : String;
                          Ptr : TNodePtr;
                        End;
            Private
              Front: TNodePtr;
              Rear: TNodePtr;
            Public
              Constructor Create;
              Procedure Add(NewItem: String);
              Function Remove: String;
              Function IsEmpty: Boolean;
              Procedure PrintQueue;
          End;
Implementation
Constructor TQueue.Create;
  Begin
    Front := Nil;
    Rear := Nil;
  End;
Procedure TQueue.Add (NewItem: String);
  Var NewNode: TNodePtr;
  Begin
    New (NewNode); // create a new node
    NewNode^.Data := NewItem;
    NewNode^.Ptr := Nil;
    If IsEmpty
      Then Front := NewNode
      Else Rear^.Ptr := NewNode;
    Rear := NewNode;
  End;
Function TQueue.Remove: String;
Var ThisNode: TNodePtr;
  Begin
    If IsEmpty
      Then WriteLn ('Queue Empty')
      Else
        Begin
          Remove := Front^.Data;
          ThisNode := Front;
          Front := Front^.Ptr;
          Dispose (ThisNode);
        End;
  End;
Function TQueue.IsEmpty: Boolean;
  Begin
    IsEmpty := (Front = Nil);
  End;
```

```
Procedure TQueue.PrintQueue;
Var ThisNode: TNodePtr;
Begin
  Writeln('Contents of Queue:');
  If Not IsEmpty
    Then
      Begin
        ThisNode := Front;
        Repeat
          WriteLn (ThisNode^.Data);
          ThisNode := ThisNode^.Ptr;
        Until ThisNode = Nil;
      End
    Else WriteLn('Nil');
    WriteLn;
End;
End.
```

Priority queues

Each element in a **priority queue** has an associated priority. When an element is taken from the queue, the element with the highest priority is chosen.

Priority queues are commonly used as event queues in simulations (Topic 2.7). Implementing a priority queue as a linear queue means that elements joining the queue will be added in such a way that the priority sequence is maintained. This means that, in effect, the implementation is the same as for a linked list; the order key is the priority.

Another way of implementing a priority queue is as a binary tree structure, also known as a binary heap.

🖥 PC activity

1 Write a program to implement the shuffle queue method. Test that your program works correctly, including trying to add an element to a full queue and trying to remove an element from an empty queue.

2 Write a program to implement the circular queue method using an array to store the elements. Test that your program works correctly, including trying to add an element to a full queue and trying to remove an element from an empty queue.

3 Write a program to implement a queue using the linked list method with the pointer type and memory locations on the heap to store the nodes. Test that your program works correctly, including trying to remove an element from an empty queue.

4 Write a program that will test the queue class defined above.

■ Question

3 (a) Draw a diagram showing the array implementation (maximum 6 elements) of a circular queue after Jones, Smith, Peters, Franklin and Taylor have joined the queue, in the order given. You should also show the Front and Rear pointers. (b) Draw another diagram showing the state of the queue after 2 people have left from the front of the queue. Also show the Front and Rear pointers. (c) Draw a third diagram showing the state of the queue after 3 more people have joined the queue from (b) above. Also show the Front and Rear pointers.

In this topic you have covered:

■ the concept of a stack as an abstract data type

■ the possible operations on a stack

■ the methods of implementing a stack in program code

■ the concept of a queue as an abstract data type

■ the possible operations on a queue

■ the methods of implementing a queue in program code.

2.5   Graphs and trees

Key terms

Graph: a diagram consisting of circles, called vertices, joined by lines, called edges or arcs; each edge joins exactly two vertices.

Graphs

Introduction

Problems such as how to travel from Marylebone to Russell Square by London Underground or what is the shortest route by road from Aylesbury to Evesham (Fig. 2.5.1) are ideal for representation by graphs.

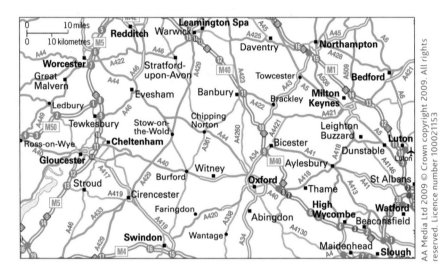

Fig. 2.5.1 *Road map*

In the first problem, we have tube stations interconnected by tube lines on which the underground trains run. In the second problem, we have villages, towns and cities interconnected by roads. We can use abstraction in each case to remove unnecessary details. The result is a diagram where the objects – tube stations, villages, towns and cities – are represented by circles and the interconnections between pairs of objects are represented by lines (not necessarily straight lines) joining the circles. Such a diagram is called a **graph**. The objects are called vertices or nodes and the lines representing the interconnections are called edges or arcs. Fig. 2.5.2 is an example of a simple graph. Fig. 2.5.3 is an abstraction of the road map of Fig. 2.5.1.

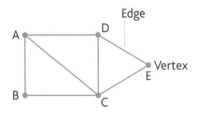

Fig. 2.5.2 *A simple graph*

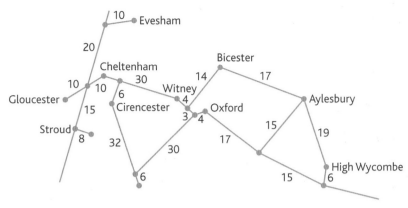

Fig. 2.5.3 *Road map showing distances in miles with unnecessary details removed*

Two vertices are **neighbours** if they are connected by an edge, and the **degree** of a vertex is its number of neighbours. In Fig. 2.5.2, vertex A and vertex B are neighbours. Vertex A has degree 3 because it has three neighbours: B, C and D.

A diverse range of systems may be represented by graphs (Table 1). Graph models can be used to solve problems in many different fields.

Table 1 *Some systems that can be represented by graphs*

Graph	Vertices	Edges
Internet	Web pages	Hyperlinks
Social networks	People, actors	Friendships, film casts
Circuits	Resistors, inductors, capacitors, power supplies, transistors, logic gates	Wires
Transportation	Airports	Air routes
Chemical compounds	Molecules	Chemical bonds

The Hollywood graph is an example of a social network system. It represents actors by vertices and connects two vertices when the actors represented by these vertices have worked together on a film. This graph is a simple graph. In January 2006 it contained 20 million edges and 637 099 vertices representing actors who had appeared in 339 896 films. Fig. 2.5.4 shows a very small part of this graph. Bruce Willis appeared with Sam Moses and Bradley Paterson in the film *16 Blocks* (2006) and with Robert Sedgwick and Samuel L. Jackson in the film *Die Hard: With a Vengeance* (1995).

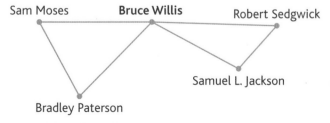

Fig. 2.5.4 *Part of the Hollywood graph*

Labelled or weighted graph: a graph in which the edges are labelled or given a value called a weight.

Automation: turning an abstraction into a form that can be processed by computer.

Directed graph or digraph: a diagram consisting of circles, called vertices, joined by directed lines, called edges.

Labelled graph

Fig. 2.5.3 shows part of the graph for the map in Fig. 2.5.1. The distances by road are shown as labels for each edge. A graph in which the edges are labelled is known as a **labelled graph** or **weighted graph**.

Fig. 2.5.3 illustrates abstraction, a key principle of computing or computer science. Unnecessary details of the problem have been removed so that the problem can be represented as a graph. This is known as problem abstraction and the graph is said to model the problem. Fig. 2.5.3 is an abstraction of Fig. 2.5.1. The next stage is to find a way of representing graphs that a computer program can process. This is known as **automation**, another key principle of computing or computer science.

Directed graph

A round-robin tournament is one in which every team plays every other team exactly once. Round-robin tournaments can be modelled using a kind of graph called a **directed graph** or **digraph** in which each team is represented by a vertex (Fig. 2.5.5). Note that each vertex has exactly five neighbours and that its degree is 5. This is to be expected as each team plays exactly five other teams in this round-robin tournament of six teams. Each edge has an arrowhead indicating which team won and which team lost when they played each other. Team A beat Team F because the edge is directed from Team A to Team F, the arrowhead points to Team F. This may be expressed algebraically as (Team A, Team F) for the edge connecting Team A to Team F. The graph tells us that Team C is undefeated and that Team F does not win a match.

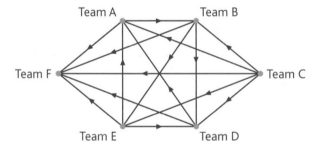

Fig. 2.5.5 *Round-robin tournament between six teams represented by a simple directed graph*

Fig. 2.5.6 shows how we can represent an undirected graph using the convention of a directed graph.

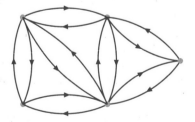

Fig. 2.5.6 *Undirected graph represented by multiple edges*

Fig. 2.5.6 is a multigraph because it has multiple edges connecting the same vertices. In fact, it is a directed multigraph. However, we may replace each of the links between vertices by a single undirected edge. The graph becomes a **simple graph** again, i.e. one without multiple edges and in which each edge connects two different vertices.

▉ Questions

1 What does the degree of a vertex in the Hollywood graph represent?

2 Draw a directed graph for a round-robin tournament involving three teams: A, B and C.

3 What is a graph?

4 Two utilities, water (W) and electricity (E), are to be supplied to houses A, B and C in the same road. Draw a graph for the connections that avoids the pipework and cables crossing each other in the same plane.

5 Different species of animal A, B, C, D, E need to be assigned holding cages so that the following rules are observed:

  A must not be in same cage as B and C.

  B must not be in same cage as D and E.

  C must not be in same cage as A and D.

  D must not be in the same cage as A, B and C.

  E must not be in the same cage as A, B and D.

  a Represent this problem as a graph.

  b What is the minimum number of cages that will be required?

Data representation of a graph

An adjacency matrix and an adjacency list are two ways to represent a graph without multiple edges so that the graph can be processed by a computer program.

Adjacency matrix

Undirected graph

Consider the simple graph shown in Fig. 2.5.7. We can represent this with a two-dimensional structure called a matrix (Table 2). If two vertices are connected then a 1 is placed in two positions in the matrix as follows:

▦ Find the row for the first vertex, move to the cell in this row which is in the column for the second vertex.

▦ Find the row for the second vertex, move to the cell in this row which is in the column for the first vertex.

For example, vertex 2 and vertex 4 in Fig. 2.5.7 are connected by an edge. To record this in Table 2, first move to row 2 and place a 1 in the fourth column. Next, move to row 4 and place a 1 in the second column. This process is repeated for all the other edges. Any cells without a 1 are now assigned a 0.

A special notation a_{ij} is used to refer to a particular cell of an adjacency matrix **A**, where i refers to the row number and j refers to the column number.

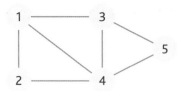

Fig. 2.5.7 *Undirected graph*

Table 2 *Adjacency matrix for the undirected graph in Fig. 2.5.7*

	1	2	3	4	5
1	0	1	1	1	0
2	1	0	0	1	0
3	1	0	0	1	1
4	1	1	1	0	1
5	0	0	1	1	0

PC activity

Obtain GraphDraw from **www. educational-computing.co.uk** and use it to explore adjacency matrices for undirected graphs.

Directed graph

The adjacency matrix **A** for an undirected graph is symmetric, $a_{ij} = a_{ji}$, because both of these entries are 1 when vertex i and vertex j are adjacent. We refer to vertex i algebraically as v_i and vertex j as v_j.

The adjacency matrix for a directed graph does not have to be symmetric, because there may not be an edge from v_j to v_i when there is an edge from v_i to v_j. Table 3 shows the adjacency matrix for the round-robin tournament of Fig. 2.5.5. The table is read row by row. A 1 in a row indicates that this row vertex beat the column vertex, e.g. for the first row Team A beat Team B and Team F.

Table 3 *Adjacency matrix for the round-robin tournament in Fig. 2.5.5*

	Team A	Team B	Team C	Team D	Team E	Team F
Team A	0	1	0	0	0	1
Team B	0	0	0	1	1	1
Team C	1	1	0	1	1	1
Team D	1	0	0	0	0	1
Team E	1	0	0	1	0	1
Team F	0	0	0	0	0	0

PC activity

Obtain GraphDraw from **www. educational-computing.co.uk** and use it to explore adjacency matrices for directed graphs.

PC activity

Obtain GraphDraw from **www. educational-computing.co.uk** and use it to explore adjacency lists for undirected graphs.

Adjacency list

Adjacency lists specify the vertices that are adjacent to each vertex of the graph.

Undirected graph

Table 4 is an adjacency list that represents the undirected graph in Fig. 2.5.8. It indicates that vertex 1 is connected to vertices 2, 3 and 4; vertex 2 is connected to vertices 1 and 4; vertex 3 is connected to vertices 1, 4 and 5; vertex 4 is connected to vertices 1, 2, 3, and 5; and vertex 5 is connected to vertices 3 and 4.

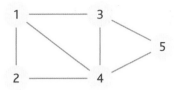

Fig. 2.5.8 *Undirected graph*

Table 4 *Adjacency list for the undirected graph in Fig. 2.5.8*

Vertex	Adjacent vertices
1	2, 3, 4
2	1, 4
3	1, 4, 5
4	1, 2, 3, 5
5	3, 4

Directed graph

With a directed graph, the adjacency list must reflect the direction of edges. Table 5 shows the adjacency list for the directed graph of Fig. 2.5.9. The adjacent vertices are called terminal vertices, and the vertex they are adjacent to is called the initial vertex. Table 5 shows that there are directed edges from vertex 1 to vertices 2 and 3, a directed edge from vertex 2 to vertex 4, directed edges from vertex 3 to vertices 4 and 5, directed edges from vertex 4 to vertices 1 and 5, and no directed edges from vertex 5.

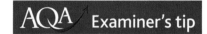

AQA Examiner's tip

The adjacency list in Table 4 is based on a list. An alternative uses a linked list as shown in the specimen paper for COMP3. Both approaches are valid.

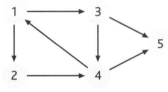

Fig. 2.5.9 *Directed graph*

Table 5 *Adjacency list for the directed graph in Fig. 2.5.9*

Vertex	Adjacent vertices
1	2, 3
2	4
3	4, 5
4	1, 5
5	

Labelled graph

If a graph is labelled as shown in Fig. 2.5.10, the value of each edge label is substituted for each 1 in the adjacency matrix, as shown in Table 6. Note that in some applications, 0 is a valid weight. In this case it can't be used as a no-edge value. Instead the infinity symbol (∞) may be used.

🖥 PC activity

Obtain GraphDraw from **www. educational-computing.co.uk** and use it to explore adjacency lists for directed graphs.

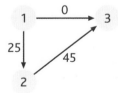

Fig. 2.5.10 *Weighted directed graph*

Table 6 *Adjacency matrix for a weighted directed graph*

	1	2	3
1	∞	25	0
2	∞	∞	45
3	∞	∞	∞

 PC activity

Obtain GraphDraw from **www. educational-computing.co.uk** and use it to explore adjacency matrices for labelled graphs.

In an adjacency list, we can add a new field in every node of every linked list, which holds the weight of that edge; they are shown in red in Table 7.

Table 7 *Adjacency list representation for a simple weighted directed graph*

Initial vertex	Terminal vertices
1	2, 25; 3, 0
2	3, 45
3	

Which is better, adjacency matrix or adjacency list?

If many vertex pairs are connected by edges, then the adjacency matrix doesn't waste much space and it indicates whether an edge exists with one access (rather than following a list). However, if the graph is sparse, so not many of its vertex pairs have edges between them, then an adjacency list becomes preferable. For example, if the graph has 1000 vertices and only about 2000 edges, its adjacency matrix representation will need 1 million (10^6) entries – 4 million bytes if each entry is a 4-byte word. Representing the same graph with an adjacency list might require, say, 1000 words to identify each node plus 2000 words for the list of neighbours, or 12 000 bytes. The difference may make one representation acceptable and the other not acceptable.

Questions

6 Represent the undirected graph in Fig. 2.5.11 as (a) an adjacency matrix and (b) an adjacency list.

7 Represent the directed graph in Fig. 2.5.12 as (a) an adjacency matrix and (b) an adjacency list.

8 Represent the weighted directed graph in Fig. 2.5.13 as (a) an adjacency matrix and (b) an adjacency list.

9 (a) When and why would it be appropriate to use an adjacency matrix?
(b) When and why would it be appropriate to use an adjacency list?

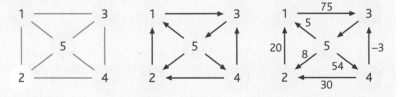

Fig. 2.5.11 *Undirected graph*

Fig. 2.5.12 *Directed graph*

Fig. 2.5.13 *Weighted directed graph*

Connectivity

Many applications of graphs involve getting from one vertex to another. For example, it may be required to find the shortest route between one place and another or a route out of a maze. Many problems like these can be modelled with paths formed by travelling along the edges of graphs. A graph is connected if there is a path between each pair of vertices and is disconnected otherwise.

Path

Informally, a path is a sequence of edges that begins at a vertex of a graph and travels from vertex to vertex along edges of a graph. In Fig. 2.5.4 two vertices, A and B, are linked when there is a chain of actors linking A to B. For example, Sam Moses is linked to Robert Sedgwick by the path Sam Moses–Bruce Willis–Robert Sedgwick. Sam Moses is adjacent to Bruce Willis because they acted together in the film *16 Blocks* and Bruce Willis is adjacent to Robert Sedgwick because they acted together in the film *Die Hard: With a Vengeance*. In the full Hollywood graph of 637 099 vertices, the Bacon number of an actor C is defined to be the length of the shortest path connecting C and the well-known actor Kevin Bacon. An actor who has acted with Kevin Bacon has a Bacon number of 1. Kevin Bacon has a Bacon number of 0. Table 8 was compiled from the Hollywood graph of early 2006.

Table 8 *Bacon number table*

Bacon number	Number of actors	Cumulative total number of actors
0	1	1
1	1902	1903
2	160 463	162 366
3	457 231	619 597
4	111 310	730 907
5	8168	739 075
6	810	739 885
7	81	739 966
8	14	739 980
9	1	739 981

Two very important path problems are the **explorer's problem** and the **traveller's problem**.

Explorer's problem

In the explorer's problem, an explorer wishes to find a route that traverses each road exactly once before returning to the starting point.

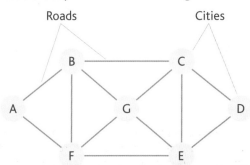

Fig. 2.5.14 *Road map for the explorer's problem and the traveller's problem*

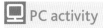 **PC activity**

Visit **http://oracleofbacon.org** and investigate the connections between Kevin Bacon and actors with whom you are familiar.

■ **Key terms**

Explorer's problem: the solution finds a route that traverses each road exactly once before returning to the starting point.

Traveller's problem: the solution finds a route that visits each city exactly once before returning to the starting point.

Fig. 2.5.14 shows a road map connecting cities A, B, C, D, E, F and G. For example, the explorer is required to find a route that starts at city A, travels along each road exactly once (in either direction) and finishes back at A. Two examples of such a route are ABCDEFBGCEGFA and AFGCDEGBCEFBA. In each case the explorer travels along each road once but may visit a particular city more than once.

Traveller's problem

In the traveller's problem, a traveller wishes to find a route that visits each city exactly once before returning to the starting point. Using Fig. 2.5.14 again, let's say that the starting point is city A then two possible routes are ABCDEGFA and AFEDCGBA.

Closed paths and cycles

Consider the graph in Fig. 2.5.15. A **closed path** or **circuit** is a sequence of edges of the form AB, BC, CF, FG, GC, CH, HA in Fig. 2.5.15 that starts and ends at the same vertex. A **cycle** is a closed path in which all the edges are different and all the intermediate vertices are different. For example, in Fig. 2.5.15 AB, BC, CD, DE, EF, FG, GH, HA is a cycle.

■ Trees

A **tree** is a type of graph that resembles a tree. In particular, a tree is a connected undirected graph with no cycles. Fig. 2.5.16 shows some examples of trees. There is just one path between each pair of vertices in a tree.

Fig. 2.5.16 *Graphs which are trees*

Rooted tree

A **rooted tree** is a tree in which one vertex has been designated as the root and every edge is directed away from the root (Fig. 2.5.17).

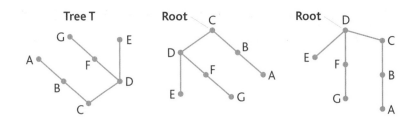

Fig. 2.5.17 *Graph T can be represented as a rooted tree with root C and as a rooted tree with root D*

■ **Key terms**

Closed path or circuit: a sequence of edges that starts and ends at the same vertex and such that any two successive edges in the sequence share a vertex.

Cycle: a closed path in which all the edges are different and all the intermediate vertices are different.

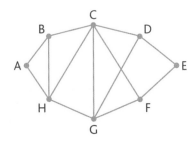

Fig. 2.5.15 *A connected graph*

■ **Key terms**

Tree: a connected undirected graph with no cycles.

Rooted tree: a tree in which one vertex has been designated as the root and every edge is directed away from the root.

■ **Key point**

There is just one path between each pair of vertices in a tree.

■ **Questions**

10 There are five unlabelled trees with four or fewer vertices. Draw them.

11 Explain why a tree with n vertices has $n - 1$ edges.

12 What is the difference between a tree and a rooted tree?

Standard algorithms

In a depth-first traversal, the first edge from the starting vertex, A, is followed to first neighbour B, then the first edge from this neighbour is followed to first neighbour D, and so on, until the traversal reaches the last vertex in the path. The algorithm then backtracks to the previous vertex and tries the next edge, to vertex E, applying the algorithm all over again. Once all the edges from B have been explored, B is marked as completely explored and the same is true of its neighbours, D and E (Fig. 2.5.18). The complete traversal is shown in Fig. 2.5.19. Note the use of a stack to enable backtracking.

PC activity

Obtain GraphDraw from **www. educational-computing.co.uk** and use it to explore traversing a graph.

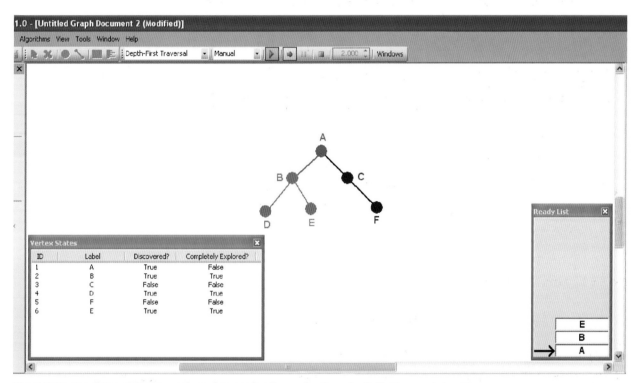

Fig. 2.5.18 *GraphDraw 1.0 part way through traversing the graph using a depth-first traversal algorithm*

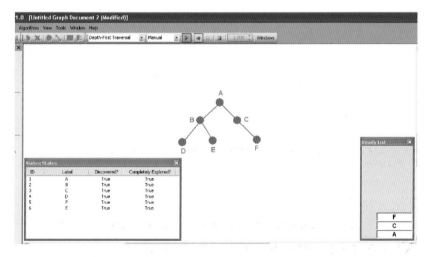

Fig. 2.5.19 *GraphDraw 1.0 having completed traversing the graph using a depth-first traversal algorithm*

What might the graphs in Figs 2.5.18 and 2.5.19 represent? Fig. 2.5.20 shows one possibility, a maze with entrance and exit from box A.

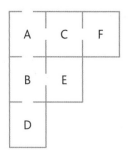

Fig. 2.5.20 *Maze with entrance and exit in the same place*

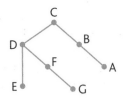

Fig. 2.5.21 *Undirected graph for Question 13*

Question

13 Show how the graph in Fig. 2.5.21 will be traversed using a depth-first traversal algorithm.

In this topic you have covered:

- representation of a problem as a graph consisting of vertices connected by edges
- 'use of a graph to represent complex relationships
- different types of graph: undirected, directed, and labelled or weighted
- representation of graphs using adjacency matrices and adjacency lists
- an adjacency matrix is better when the graph has a high ratio of edges to vertices
- an adjacency list is better when the graph has a low ratio of edges to vertices
- the meaning of graph connections and paths
- a tree is a connected undirected graph with no cycles
- a rooted tree is a tree in which one vertex is designated the root and every edge is directed away from the root
- traversal of a graph using a depth-first traversal algorithm which maintains two flags: discovered and completely explored.

2.6 Searching and sorting

Key terms

Linear search: this search method starts at the beginning of the list and compares each element in turn with the required value until a match is found or the end of the list is reached.

Bubble sort: during a pass through the list, neighbouring values are compared and swapped if they are not in the correct order. Several passes are made until one pass does not require any further swaps.

Before starting on this topic, make sure you can remember the standard algorithms of **linear search** and **bubble sort** in the AS book (pages 91–94).

Binary search

If we are working with an unordered list, then the linear search is the only methodical way of searching for a specific item. If we are working with an ordered list, there are faster methods than the linear search.

Consider a telephone directory with, say, 1000 names. If the names were not in any order, in the worst case all 1000 names would need to be checked to find a specific entry or to say that the required name does not exist in the directory.

Telephone directories are sorted by surname. If we use a linear search, the advantage is that, if the name does not exist, we can stop searching when we get past the position in the list where the name should be.

If we are looking for the telephone number of a person called Peters, we are unlikely to start at the beginning of the directory. We might make an educated guess and open the book nearer the middle. Assume the names on the open page start with the letter K, then we know to look in the second part of the directory. But if we open the directory where the names start with S, we know to look in the first part of the directory.

To summarise this method:

1 Look at the name in the middle of the list (the current item).

2 If the current name is the name sought, then the name is found.

3 If the current name is not the name sought, discard the half of the list that can't contain the name sought and repeat the same method with the other half of the list.

4 Keep repeating these steps until the name is found or the list contains no names.

Look at this example using the names in Fig. 2.6.1. Let's search for the name Peters.

▨ Find the middle name in the list of names, King

▨ King is not the name we are looking for.

▨ Peters is after King in the alphabet, so we can discard the first half of the list, including King, as we know this is not the name we are looking for.
  The discarded part of the list is shaded green in Fig. 2.6.1.

▨ Find the middle of the remaining list, Smith.

▨ Smith is not the name we are looking for.

▨ Peters is before Smith in the alphabet, so we can discard the second half of the current list, including Smith.

▨ Find the middle name of the remaining list, Nelson

▨ Nelson is not the name we are looking for.

▨ Peters is after Nelson in the alphabet, so we can discard the first part of the list, including Nelson

▨ The list now consists of a single name, Peters.

	List	
1	Adams	1
2	Bond	2
3	Clark	3
4	Farmer	4
5	Ford	5
6	Grant	6
7	Jones	7
8	King	8
9	Miller	9
10	Nelson	10
11	Peters	11
12	Smith	12
13	Thornes	13
14	Williams	14
15	Young	15

	List	
1	Adams	1
2	Bond	2
3	Clark	3
4	Farmer	4
5	Ford	5
6	Grant	6
7	Jones	7
8	King	8
9	Miller	9
10	Nelson	10
11	Peters	11
12	Smith	12
13	Thornes	13
14	Williams	14
15	Young	15

	List	
1	Adams	1
2	Bond	2
3	Clark	3
4	Farmer	4
5	Ford	5
6	Grant	6
7	Jones	7
8	King	8
9	Miller	9
10	Nelson	10
11	Peters	11
12	Smith	12
13	Thornes	13
14	Williams	14
15	Young	15

	List
	Adams
	Bond
	Clark
	Farmer
	Ford
	Grant
	Jones
	King
	Miller
	Nelson
	Peters
	Smith
	Thornes
	Williams
	Young

Fig. 2.6.1 *List of names*

How many names did we access before we found Peters? Four. If we had used the linear search method, we would have accessed eleven names. If we had searched for the name Philips, we would have known after accessing just four entries that the name was not in the list.

This new method does not look much of an improvement until we consider much larger lists. How many names would need to be checked at most to find a specific name in a list of 1000 names?

Remember that each time we check a name, we halve the size of the list we need to consider in the next step: 1000, 500, 250, 125, 62, 31, 15, 7, 3, 2, 1. In a list of 1000 names, at most 10 names would be checked before a specific name is found or it is definite that the name is not in the list.

In general, with N entries in the list, we make at most $(1 + \log_2 N)$ comparisons. This means the order of complexity for the binary search method is $O(\log_2 N)$; see Topic 1.2. This compares very favourably with the linear search, where the order of complexity is $O(N)$.

The method described above is known as the binary search or binary chop. It can be expressed more formally as an algorithm. First and Last are integer parameters storing the indices of the first and last list entries, respectively.

```
Procedure BinarySearch (List, First, Last, ItemSought)
   ItemFound ← False
   SearchFailed ← False
   Repeat
     Midpoint ← (First + Last) DIV 2 {DIV gives the integer
                                      part of division}
   If List[Midpoint] = ItemSought
     Then ItemFound ← True
     Else
       If First >= Last
         Then ItemSearchFailed ← True
         Else
           If List[Midpoint] > ItemSought
             Then Last ← Midpoint − 1
             Else First ← Midpoint + 1
           EndIf
```

```
            EndIf
          EndIf
        Until ItemFound OR SearchFailed
    EndProcedure
```

The binary search method is essentially a recursive method. After checking the middle entry of the list, either the first or second half of the list is searched using the binary search method. Here is the binary search method expressed as a recursive algorithm:

```
Procedure BinarySearch (List, First, Last, ItemSought)
  ItemFound ← False
  SearchFailed ← False
  Midpoint ← (First + Last) DIV 2 {DIV gives the integer
                                  part of division}
  If List[Midpoint] = ItemSought
    Then ItemFound ← True
    Else
      If First >= Last
        Then SearchFailed ← True
        Else
          If List[Midpoint] < ItemSought
            Then BinarySearch (List, Midpoint+1, Last, ItemSought)
            Else BinarySearch (List, First, Midpoint−1, ItemSought)
          EndIf
      EndIf
  EndIf
  If SearchFailed Then Output 'searchfailed'
  If ItemFound Then Output 'itemfound'
EndProcedure
```

Compare the iterative and recursive algorithms very carefully. Can you see the difference?

Both algorithms check the middle item and if this is not the wanted item, either the top or bottom boundary is adjusted, to discard the unwanted part of the list. The iterative algorithm repeats the process using a Repeat loop. The recursive algorithm calls itself with the new boundary parameters. Tables 1 and 2 show dry runs of the two algorithms.

Table 1 *Dry run of the iterative algorithm using Fig. 2.6.1 and searching for Miller*

ItemSought	First	Last	Midpoint	List[Midpoint]	ItemFound	SearchFailed
Miller	1	15	8	King	False	False
	9	15	12	Smith		
	9	11	10	Nelson		
	9	9	9	Miller	True	

Table 2 *Dry run of the recursive algorithm using Fig. 2.6.1 and searching for Miller*

Call	ItemSought	First	Last	Midpoint	List[Midpoint]	ItemFound	SearchFailed
1	Miller	1	15	8	King	False	False
2	Miller	9	15	12	Smith	False	False
3	Miller	9	11	10	Nelson	False	False
4	Miller	9	9	9	Miller	True	False

In Table 2 note that call 4 is the first instance of procedure BinarySearch that will return from the procedure call. Then execution will return to call 3, which will return to call 2, which will return to call 1. The stack is used to store return addresses and local variables when a procedure call is made. This means that recursive procedures have extra overheads (memory locations in use).

Questions

1 Dry run the iterative algorithm to search for Davidson in the list shown in Fig 2.6.1

2 Dry run the recursive algorithm to search for Davidson in the list shown in Fig 2.6.1. How many procedure calls are on the stack just before the search is abandoned?

PC activity

(a) Write programs in your chosen high-level language to implement the above algorithms. (b) Test your programs with a long list of several hundred entries. (c) Which program uses less main memory during execution? Why?

Insertion sort

It is much faster to search an ordered list using the binary search method than the linear search method. But to use the binary search method, a list may need to be sorted first, if it is not already sorted.

The bubble sort is a very simple algorithm, but it is very slow. For N elements to be sorted, in the worst-case scenario, $(N - 1) \times (N - 1)$ iterations are necessary. This means, its order of complexity is $O(N^2)$. There are other methods. Two of the best-known methods are the insertion sort and Quicksort.

We can divide a list into a sorted part and an unsorted part (Fig. 2.6.2). To start with, only the first element is sorted. Consider the next element as the current element. Is the current element smaller than the one above? If so, copy the larger element down a slot. Work up the list until the element above is smaller than the current element. Insert the current element at this position. Consider the next element of the unsorted part of the list. Continue this method until the unsorted part of the list is of length zero.

It can be expressed more formally as an algorithm. First and Last are integer parameters that store the indices of the first and last list entries, respectively. Fig. 2.6.3 shows a dry run of the algorithm.

	List	List	List	List	List	List	List	List
1	Williams	Smith	Jones	Jones	Jones	Jones	Adams	Adams
2	Smith	Williams	Smith	Nelson	Nelson	King	Jones	Bond
3	Jones	Jones	Williams	Smith	Peters	Nelson	King	Jones
4	Nelson	Nelson	Nelson	Williams	Smith	Peters	Nelson	King
5	Peters	Peters	Peters	Peters	Williams	Smith	Peters	Nelson
6	King	King	King	King	King	Williams	Smith	Peters
7	Adams	Adams	Adams	Adams	Adams	Adams	Williams	Smith
8	Bond	Bond	Bond	Bond	Bond	Bond	Bond	Williams

Fig. 2.6.2 *Insertion sort: the next element to be inserted into the correct place is shown in red, the sorted part of the list is shown in green*

```
Procedure Sort (List, First, Last)
  For CurrentPointer ← First + 1 To Last
    CurrentValue ← List[CurrentPointer]
    Pointer ← CurrentPointer - 1
    While List[Pointer] > CurrentValue AND Pointer > 0
      List[Pointer+1] ← List[Pointer]
      Pointer ← Pointer - 1
    EndWhile
    List[Pointer+1] ← CurrentValue
  EndFor
EndProcedure
```

First	Last	CurrentPointer	CurrentValue	Pointer	List						
					[1]	[2]	[3]	[4]	[5]	[6]	[7]
1	7	2	23	1	56	23	67	12	45	99	17
				1 0	56	56	67	12	45	99	17
					23	56	67	12	45	99	17
		3	67	2	23	56	67	12	45	99	17
					23	56	67	12	45	99	17
		4	12	3	23	56	67	12	45	99	17
				3	23	56	67	67	45	99	17
				2	23	56	56	67	45	99	17
				1 0	23	23	56	67	45	99	17
					12	23	56	67	45	99	17
		5	45	4	12	23	56	67	45	99	17
				4	12	23	56	67	67	99	17
				3 2	12	23	56	56	67	99	17
					12	23	45	56	67	99	17
		6	99	5	12	23	45	56	67	99	17
					12	23	45	56	67	99	17
		7	17	6	12	23	45	56	67	99	17
				6	12	23	45	56	67	99	99
				5	12	23	45	56	67	67	99
				4	12	23	45	56	56	67	99
				3	12	23	45	45	56	67	99
				2 1	12	23	23	45	56	67	99
					12	17	23	45	56	67	99

Fig. 2.6.3 *Dry run of an insertion sort: the ordered list is shown in green, the current value is shown in red*

Question

3 Dry run the insertion sort algorithm to sort the list 87, 72, 28, 45, 59, 36.

🖥 PC activity

1 (a) Using your preferred high-level language, write a program to implement the insertion sort algorithm. Your program should display the list after every iteration. (b) Test your program using the unsorted list from Fig. 2.6.2 as test data. Check that your program produces the same output as shown in the dry run (Fig. 2.6.3). (c) Try other sets of test data.

2 Write a program to perform a bubble sort. Compare the bubble sort and the insertion sort by running them with the same sets of test data. Keep a count of how many assignments have to be performed in each program to sort a set of data. How do the two methods compare for (i) a list that is almost in the correct order and (ii) a list that is in reverse order?

■ Quicksort

Quicksort is a sorting method developed by Tony Hoare in the 1960s. The idea behind it is to divide and conquer.

Split the list into two parts, one part containing values less than a pivot value, the other containing values greater than this pivot value. The pivot value can be arbitrarily chosen. In the worked example, the first item in the unordered list is used as the pivot.

The same process is now applied to each part list, repeatedly, until the parts contain just one value. Joining the part lists back together produces the ordered list.

Worked example ⎯⎯⎯⎯⎯⎯⎯⎯⎯⎯⎯⎯⎯⎯⎯⎯⎯⎯⎯⎯⎯⎯⎯⎯⎯⎯⎯⎯⎯⎯⎯⎯⎯⎯

The pivot value is shown in red; values in the correct position are shown in green. Consider the following list:

43	24	75	12	65	59	95	36	98	86

The leftmost number is the pivot value. Starting from the left-hand end of the list, find the first number that is greater than the pivot value. Starting from the right-hand end of the list, find the first number that is less than the pivot value.

43	24	75	12	65	59	95	36	98	86
↑		↑					↑		
Pivot value		Greater than pivot					Less than pivot		

Swap the two numbers. Continue to find pairs of numbers that need swapping (in this case there are none) so that two partitions are created: the left partition contains the pivot value and numbers smaller than the pivot value, and the right partition contains numbers larger than the pivot value.

43	24	36	12	65	59	95	75	48	86
Left partition				Right partition					

The pivot value is the largest value in its partition, so put it into its correct position by swapping it with the rightmost value in the left partition.

12	24	36	43	65	59	95	75	48	86
Left partition				Right partition					
			↑ This value is now in the correct position						

Now treat the values to the left of the pivot, and the values to the right of the pivot as two separate unordered sublists and repeat the process with each sublist unless the sublist is already in the correct order.

Left sublist			element in correct position	right sublist					
12	24	36	43	65	59	95	75	48	86
↑ Pivot value				↑ Pivot value		↑ Greater than pivot		↑ Less than pivot	
No value less than Pivot value can be found. Therefore Pivot value is in correct position already				Swap these values. This now gives a sublist with values less than the pivot values and a sublist with values greater than the pivot values.					
12	24	36	43	65	59	48	75	95	86
				Now swap the pivot value with the rightmost value in this partition					
12	24	36	43	48	59	65	75	95	86
						↑ This value is now in the correct position			

When there are only two values in a sublist, swap them, if necessary. The values in the first two sublists are already in the correct order.

12	24	36	43	48	59	65	75	95	86
							↑ Pivot value		

Repeating the process for the third sublist shows that the pivot value is the only element for the left partition; the right partition is now a set of two values that need to swap.

12	24	36	43	48	59	65	75	95	86

Here is the final ordered list:

12	24	36	43	48	59	65	75	86	95

The Quicksort method is another example of a recursive method. The outline algorithm is

split list,
Quicksort left partition,
Quicksort right partition.
Here it is in more detail:

```
Procedure Quicksort (List, First, Last)
  If First < Last        { if there are elements in the list}
    Then
      PivotValue ← List[First]
      LeftPointer ← First + 1
      RightPointer ← Last
      While LeftPointer <= RightPointer
        While List[LeftPointer] < PivotValue AND LeftPointer <= RightPointer
          LeftPointer ← LeftPointer + 1
        EndWhile
        While List[RightPointer] > PivotValue AND LeftPointer <= RightPointer
          RightPointer ← RightPointer - 1
        EndWhile
        If Left < Right
          Then Swap (List[LeftPointer], List[RightPointer])
        EndIf
      EndWhile
      Pivot ← RightPointer
      Swap (List[First], List[Pivot])
      Quicksort (List, First, Pivot - 1)
      Quicksort (List, Pivot + 1, Last)
    EndIf
EndProcedure
```

 Examiner's tip

You won't be expected to know the Quicksort algorithm for the COMP3 examination, but you may wish to use it in your COMP4 project.

Question

4 Dry run the Quicksort algorithm to sort the list 56, 23, 67, 12, 45, 99, 17.

🖥 PC activity

(a) Using your preferred high-level language, write a program to implement the Quicksort algorithm. (b) Test your program using the unsorted list from the worked example as test data. (c) Try other sets of test data.

In this topic you have covered:

- binary search
- insertion sort
- Quicksort.

2.7 Simulation

Key terms

Model: an abstraction of an entity in a real world or in the problem that enables an automated solution. The abstraction is a representation of the problem that leaves out unnecessary detail.

State history: consists of state descriptions at each of a chronological succession of instants.

Entities: the components that make up a system.

Attributes: a property of an object, eg. an object *car* has attributes *make, model, steering wheel, radio, engine, gearbox* etc. Some of these attributes are objects themselves.

What is simulation?

Simulation is the imitation of a process of a real system. Often the purpose of simulation is to find out what happens under different conditions or situations, real or imaginary. For example, a simulation of traffic flows could represent a road layout that does not exist, but the simulation might establish whether it is a feasible design. Experiments may be designed and the simulation can be run many times with different values. We may consider simulation because experimenting with the real system may cause unknown irremovable effects, or because we can experiment with a model more cheaply and at a time of our choosing.

Here we are concerned with digital computer simulation. This means setting up a computer **model** of a system and manipulating it to observe the results.

If the simulation results are to be at all meaningful, it is very important that the computer model reflects the key characteristics of the real system as accurately as possible. Too few characteristics and the model will not describe the behaviour of the system accurately, too many characteristics and the model will be unnecessarily complex.

Computer models for simulation can be produced to represent many types of system. Here are some examples: queuing systems, a machine or groups of machines, population growth, traffic flows, architectural designs, engineering, business, genetics, climate.

Digital computer simulation is the use of a digital computer to produce a chronological **state history** of a model which is regarded as the state history of the modelled system.

A system is made up of components, or **entities**. These entities have characteristics, or **attributes**.

Consider a simple queuing system. Customers arrive and queue, waiting to be served by a single human server. The entities of this system are Customer, Queue, Server. One attribute of a customer could be waiting.

The state of a system at any instant is determined by where the entities are, what they are doing and their attributes. A description of the state of a system at any specific instant will be called a state description. States of the modelled system are usually considered for a chronological succession of instants, and this leads to a state history.

We will consider systems that change discretely with time; i.e. systems that can change abruptly from one clearly identifiable state to some other clearly identifiable state. Any such change in state will take place at an instant in time.

An event has occurred when any change of state takes place; also whenever an event occurs, some change of state can take place. An activity is a time-consuming process. Here are the possible states of our simple queuing system:

- nobody in the queue, server waiting
- nobody in the queue, a customer being served
- customers in the queue, a customer being served.

Here are possible events in this system:

- a customer arrives
- end of serving.

Here are possible activities in this system:

- the serving of a customer
- the time between customers arriving.

The methodology of simulation

1 Problem formulation

- State the objectives: this is vitally important as a model can only answer the questions that it has been tailored to answer.
- State the criteria by which results will be measured: this helps us decide what accuracy is required and helps us make reasonable assumptions.

For example, we might wish to simulate the queuing system at a post office to decide whether there needs to be more than one counter. Should there be a single queue for several counters, or should there be a separate queue for each counter?

We might want to measure the results by calculating:

- average waiting time for customers
- average time of servers waiting with nothing to do
- maximum length of a queue or queues.

2 Observation of the real system

- Identify all the inputs and outputs.
- Decide what data is needed and how to gather it.
- Establish whether the system can be broken down into subsystems.
- List the parts of the system and their relationship.
- Identify the variables and parameters.

Example: consider the simple queuing example at the beginning of this section.

What is the probability of a customer arriving at any instance of time?

Data needs to be collected.

What time does it take for a customer to be served?

Data needs to be collected.

3 Formulation of the model

The principle of formulating the model is to make it as simple as possible initially and gradually make it more complex.

- From the list of parts, decide which are the important ones and find their properties and discrete states.
- Draw individual life cycle diagrams for each system part.

  Use a rectangle for an event and a circle for a queue.
- Link the individual diagrams to form a composite diagram.
- Recognise the assumptions and clearly state them.
- Think about the design of the experiment.

Consider the simple queuing example.

- The entities are customers and server.
- The events are customer arriving, customer being served.
- When customers wait, they join a queue.
- When a customer has been served they leave the system.
- When the server is idle, we can show this as the server **waiting in a queue**.

Fig. 2.7.1 shows the life cycle diagram for customers. Fig. 2.7.2 **shows the** life cycle diagram for the server. We can link Fig. 2.7.1 and Fig. 2.7.2 **to** create Fig. 2.7.3.

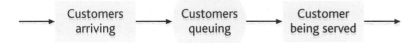

Fig. 2.7.1 *Life cycle diagram for customers*

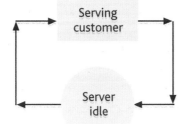

Fig. 2.7.2 *Life cycle diagram for the server*

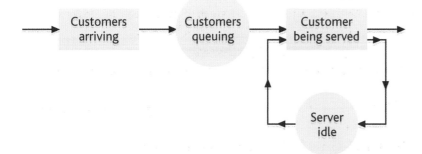

Fig. 2.7.3 *The result of combining Figs 2.7.1 and 2.7.2*

There are two main methods for running a discrete simulation:

- **Time-driven simulation**: the master clock is incremented in single time units and the program code checks what activity can start or finish in this time slot.
- **Activity-driven simulation**: a diary contains all the activities and when they are due to occur. The program checks which event is the next to occur and advances the master clock by the relevant amount of time.

4 Model validation

Before converting it into a program, ensure that the model is correct. It is useless to proceed with an invalid model.

■ Check thoroughly the logic of each life cycle diagram. This will almost certainly require the system to be reobserved.

■ Do a hand simulation on the composite diagram.

■ Check that your model can cope with exceptional conditions.

■ Is there a physical limit on some queue sizes?

Hand simulation for the simple queue example

Assume that a customer arrives at the end of every 3 minutes and serving takes 4 minutes. If we run the simulation for 20 minutes using time-driven simulation, we get Table 1.

Table 1 *Hand simulation for the simple queue example*

Master clock	Customer arriving	Customer being served	Customers in queue	Minutes in queue for all customers	Server status
1	–	–	0	–	Idle
2	–	–	0	–	Idle
3	Customer1	–	0	0	Idle
4		Customer1	0	0	Serving
5		Customer1	0	0	Serving
6	Customer2	Customer1	1	0	Serving
7		Customer1	0	1	Serving
8		Customer2	0	1	Serving
9	Customer3	Customer2	1	1	Serving
10		Customer2	1	3	Serving
11		Customer2	1	3	Serving
12	Customer4	Customer3	0	3	Serving
13		Customer3	1	4	Serving
14		Customer3	1	5	Serving
15	Customer5	Customer4	1	6	Serving
16		Customer4	1	7	Serving
17		Customer4	1	8	Serving
18	Customer6	Customer4	1	9	Serving
19		Customer4	2	11	Serving
20		Customer5	1	12	Serving
.	.	.	.	.	.
.	.	.	.	.	.
.	.	.	.	.	.

The average time a customer has to wait in the queue is given by this formula:

$$\text{Average customer wait} = \frac{\text{minutes in queue for all customers}}{\text{Number of customers}}$$

It is very unlikely that customers arrive at intervals of exactly 3 minutes and that every customer gets served in exactly 4 minutes. To make the simulation more realistic, we need to include a probability of such an event happening. Random number generators are used in computer models to give values based on probability as shown on next page.

5 Program formulation

There are specialist simulation programming languages such as Simula, SimPy and Simscript. They make it very straightforward to set up activities and queues. You can also write a program to simulate a system using your preferred high-level language.

■ Use object-oriented design for the parts that make up the model.

■ Include lots of diagnostics and comments.

■ Visualise the results of the simulation through tables, histograms, graphs or animation.

6 Program validation

If the system exists, then historical verification is possible. Known data from the past where the outcomes are known can be used. Run the simulation with that data and check that the results from the simulation match the historical outcome.

Verification by forecasting is also possible. Run the simulation to produce results for a future scenario. When this scenario occurs, check that the outcome matches the outcome the simulation predicted.

But how can we verify a program if the system does not exist? There is no way that we can prove that our model works. We can only cross-check that the assumptions we used for building the model were reasonable.

7 Design of experiment and analysis of results

Operational researchers use models and simulations to improve systems. Complex systems may involve many variables, so it can be very time-consuming to find an optimum combination of values. Then statistical methods are usually employed to analyse results. These methods are beyond the scope of this book.

The simulation needs to be run for long enough to find out what the effects of the variables really are. Look at the hand simulation above. After just 20 minutes it is not yet obvious that the queue is growing.

Even a simple queuing system can involve several variables:

■ The time it takes to serve a customer may be changed if more efficient methods are employed.

■ If the store becomes more popular, more customers may arrive in a given time span to join the queue.

■ More servers may be introduced when the queue grows above a certain size.

Analysing the effects of these variables can be quite complex. Finding an improvement is often all that can be hoped for, not the optimum.

The use of random number generators

Events rarely occur at set time intervals. When collecting data for a simple queue simulation, you may record the exact times of each customer as they arrive and how long it took to serve each one. This data may be useful to test your program for validity, but it is not sufficient to run simulation experiments.

Simulation techniques rely heavily on the element of randomness. You may collect averages such as how many customers arrive in a given period of time and then use the concept of probability to give you realistic arrival times for your simulation.

Probability is expressed as a number between 0.0 (never happens) and 1.0 (definitely happens). If you find that a customer arrives every 1 to 4 minutes, then the probability of a customer arriving in a particular minute is 0.25 (a 1 in 4 chance).

Computer systems have random number generators that produce random numbers when a function is called. These numbers are known as **pseudo-random numbers** as they are generated using an algorithm. If you start the random number generator with the same starting value (the seed), it will produce the same sequence of pseudo-random numbers.

In simulation we often want to repeat an experiment. If we have used truly random numbers, it is impossible to repeat the experiment under exactly the same conditions. To be able to generate the same set of random numbers is very useful.

For example, using Delphi, we can call the function random to return a value x such that $0 \leq x < 1$. A single call of the procedure randomize, near the beginning of the program, will get a different set of random numbers each time we run the program.

In the example above, to decide whether a customer has arrived in a given minute, we can use the following pseudo code:

```
ArrivalProbability ← 0.25
NextRandomNumber ← Random()
If NextRandomNumber <= ArrivalProbability
  Then CustomerArrived ← True
  Else CustomerArrived ← False
```

Key terms

Pseudo-random numbers: a series of numbers generated by computer with apparent randomness.

AQA Examiner's tip

You may wish to use a more complex queuing system as your COMP4 project topic.

Questions

1. Lorries arrive at a small warehouse with one loading bay. What are the entities and their attributes of this system? What are the possible states, events and activities of this system? Draw a life cycle diagram for the lorries and the loading bay. What are the possible variables in this system?

2. Use the system from Question 1. Assume between the hours of 0500 and 1500 a lorry arrives every 2 hours and it takes 3 hours to unload. Using a table with suitable headings, show the state of the system from 0500 hours until all lorries have been unloaded.

3. Adapt the system from Question 2 with the provision of two loading bays. Using a table with suitable headings, show the state of the system from 0500 hours until all lorries have been unloaded. Are there times when the second loading bay is underused?

🖥 PC activity

1 Use the system from Question 2. Write a program in your preferred programming language to simulate this system. This is a stretch and challenge question.

2 A small airline has a check-in desk for departures. The desk opens 2 hours before the flight is due to take off and closes half an hour before the flight is due to take off. Passengers arrive and wait to be checked in. What are the entities and attributes of this system? What are the possible states, events and activities of this system? Assume that 25 passengers have already arrived before the check-in desk opens. During the first and last half-hour of opening, one passenger arrives every 5 minutes. During the second half-hour, one passenger arrives every 3 minutes. The check-in process takes 2 minutes per passenger. Using a table with suitable headings, show the state of the system while the check-in desk is open. Have all passengers checked in half an hour before take-off? What would happen if the check-in process took longer? What would happen if more passengers arrived during the peak half-hour?

☑ *In this topic you have covered:*

- simulation through manipulating a computer model and observation of the results
- how a system is made up of components (entities) that have characteristics (attributes)
- how a state history shows the chronological succession of instants of the system
- the stages of simulation
- the use of random number generators to simulate the happening of an event.

3 Real numbers

3.1 Real numbers

Key terms

Real number: a number with a fractional part.

Scientific notation: a real number represented by a sign, some significant digits and a power of 10.

Significant digits: those digits that carry meaning contributing to the accuracy of a number. This includes all digits except leading and trailing zeros where they serve merely as placeholders to indicate the scale of the number.

Floating-point notation: a real number represented by a sign, some significant digits, and a power of 2.

Before starting on this topic, make sure you can remember how negative numbers are represented in two's complement format and how real numbers are stored as fixed-point binary numbers (Topic 5.1 in the AS book).

In the context of computing, **real numbers** are numbers with a fractional part, such as 17.84.

Real numbers can be stored in fixed-point representation (see pages 108–110 in the AS book) or in floating-point representation. Floating-point representation uses a similar format to scientific notation.

In **scientific notation**, denary real numbers are represented in the following way: a sign, some **significant digits** and a power of 10. Here are some examples of real numbers using scientific notation: 7.94×10^5, -3.123×10^9, 2.7×10^{-3}.

In **floating-point notation**, real numbers are represented in the following way: a sign, some significant digits expressed as a number with a fractional part, and an integer power of 2. Here are some examples of real numbers using floating-point notation: 4.6×2^6, -3.12×2^5, 6.2×2^{-3}.

The general format is $m \times 2^e$. The significant digits are called the mantissa (m) and the power of 2 is called the exponent (e). The exponent base, 2, is implicit and is not stored. The mantissa is stored as a fixed-point binary number. The exponent is stored as an integer. A real number can therefore be stored as a fraction m and an integer e.

Formats of floating-point numbers

Many formats have been used over the years. Different computer manufacturers designed different ways of representing floating-point numbers.

Two's complement format

Worked example

Calculate the value of the number in Fig. 3.1.1.

Fig. 3.1.1

The mantissa $m = 0.100100100_2$

The exponent $e = 000100_2 = 4_{10}$

Therefore the value is $0.1001001_2 \times 2^4 = 1001.001 = 9.125_{10}$

Worked example _____

Calculate the value of the number in Fig. 3.1.2.

Fig. 3.1.2

The mantissa is a negative value. Converting the two's complement gives $m = -0.011011100_2$

$e = 000100_2 = 4_{10}$

Therefore the value is $-0.011011100_2 \times 2^4 = -110.111_2 = -6.875_{10}$

Worked example _____

Calculate the value of the number in Fig. 3.1.3.

Fig. 3.1.3

The mantissa is $m = 0.101000000_2$

The exponent is a negative value. Converting the two's complement gives

$e = -000010_2 = -2_{10}$

Therefore the value is $0.101_2 \times 2^{-2} = 0.00101 = 0.15625_{10}$

IEEE standard for floating-point numbers

The most common representations for real numbers use the Institute of Electrical and Electronics Engineers (IEEE) standard. For single precision this uses 32 bits. The sign bit is 0 for a positive number and 1 for a negative number. The mantissa consists of an implicit leading bit and fractional bits. The exponent is stored in excess-127 mode. This means 127 is added to the exponent before it is stored.

Worked example _____

Calculate the value of the number in Fig. 3.1.4.

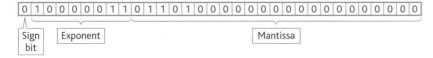

Fig. 3.1.4

The sign bit shows it is a positive number.

The exponent is $10000011_2 = 131_{10}$

It is stored in excess-127 mode, so $e = 131 - 127 = 4$

The mantissa has an implied 1-bit, so $m = 1.01101_2$

Therefore the value is $1.01101_2 \times 2^4 = 10110.1 = 22.5_{10}$

Worked example

Calculate the value of the number in Fig. 3.1.5.

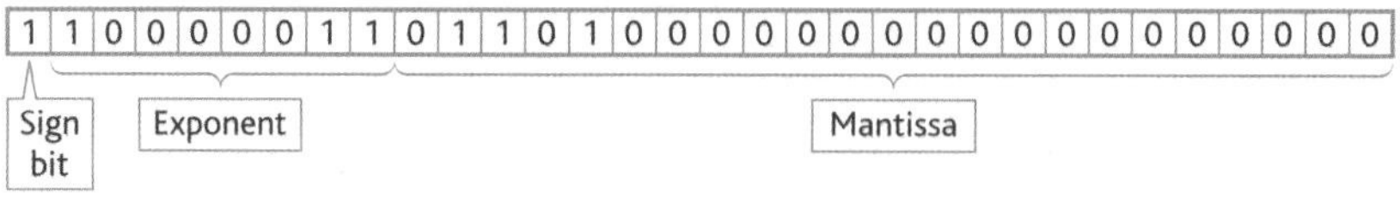

| 1 | 1 | 0 | 0 | 0 | 0 | 0 | 1 | 1 | 0 | 1 | 1 | 0 | 1 | 0 | 0 | 0 | 0 | 0 | 0 | 0 | 0 | 0 | 0 | 0 | 0 | 0 | 0 | 0 | 0 | 0 | 0 |

Sign bit Exponent Mantissa

Fig. 3.1.5

The sign bit shows it is a negative number.

The exponent is $10000011_2 = 131_{10}$

It is stored in excess-127 mode, so $e = 131 - 127 = 4$

The mantissa has an implied 1-bit, so $m = -1.011_2$

Therefore the value is $-1.01101_2 \times 2^4 = -10110.1 = -22.5_{10}$

Worked example

Calculate the value of the number in Fig. 3.1.6.

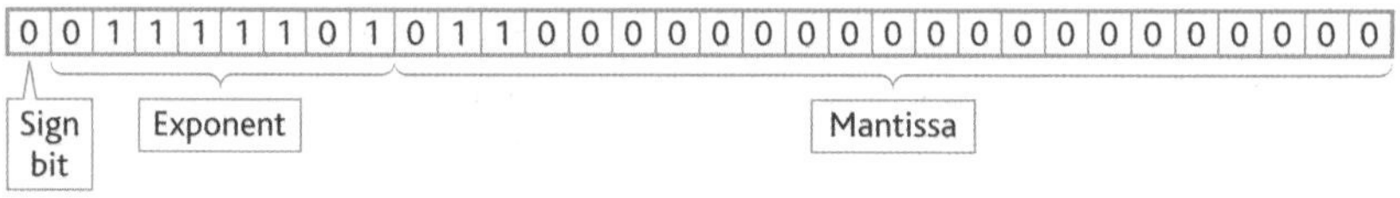

| 0 | 0 | 1 | 1 | 1 | 1 | 1 | 0 | 1 | 0 | 1 | 1 | 0 | 0 | 0 | 0 | 0 | 0 | 0 | 0 | 0 | 0 | 0 | 0 | 0 | 0 | 0 | 0 | 0 | 0 | 0 | 0 |

Sign bit Exponent Mantissa

Fig. 3.1.6

The sign bit shows it is a positive number.

The exponent is $01111101_2 = 125_{10}$

It is stored in excess-127 mode, so $e = 125 - 127 = -2$

The mantissa has an implied 1-bit, so $m = 1.011_2$

Therefore the value is $1.011_2 \times 2^{-2} = 0.01011 = 0.34375_{10}$

In the IEEE standard, an exponent of all 0s represents a special value and an exponent of all 1s represents a special value. If all bits of the exponent are zero and all bits of the mantissa are zero, the implied leading bit of the mantissa is then also implied to be zero. This bit pattern is taken to represent the value zero. Note that there is a representation for +0 and a representation for –0.

If all bits of the exponent are 1 and all bits of the mantissa are zero, the implied leading bit of the mantissa is then also implied to be zero. This bit pattern is taken to represent infinity. Note that there is a representation for $+\infty$ and a representation for $-\infty$. Operations with infinite values are defined in IEEE floating-point format. For example, dividing a real number by $+\infty$ will give the result zero.

Minifloat format

Minifloat format was invented by universities. It uses 1 sign bit, a 5-bit excess-15 exponent, 10 mantissa bits (with an implied 1-bit) and all the standard IEEE rules. It is ideal for understanding the IEEE standard without having to work with an unwieldy 32 bits.

Worked example

Calculate the value of the number in Fig. 3.1.7.

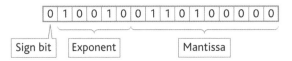

Fig. 3.1.7

The sign bit shows it is a positive number.

The exponent is $10010_2 = 18_{10}$

It is stored in excess-15 mode, so $e = 18 - 15 = 3$

The mantissa has an implied 1-bit, so $m = 1.01101_2$

Therefore the value is $1.01101_2 \times 2^3 = 1011.01 = 11.25_{10}$

Questions

1 Using the two's complement format (Fig. 3.1.8), convert the following binary floating-point numbers to denary: (a) 0101110010 000110, (b) 1010101000 000100, (c) 0110000000 111111, (d) 1010000000 111101.

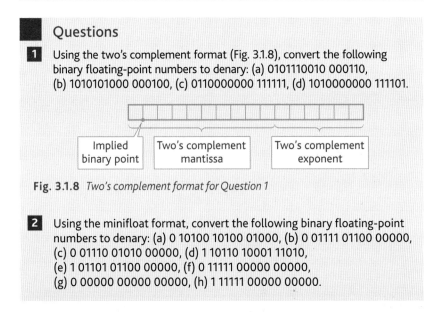

Fig. 3.1.8 *Two's complement format for Question 1*

2 Using the minifloat format, convert the following binary floating-point numbers to denary: (a) 0 10100 10100 01000, (b) 0 01111 01100 00000, (c) 0 01110 01010 00000, (d) 1 10110 10001 11010, (e) 1 01101 01100 00000, (f) 0 11111 00000 00000, (g) 0 00000 00000 00000, (h) 1 11111 00000 00000.

Normalisation

In scientific notation, denary real values can be represented in many different ways. The following numbers are all the same value: 0.004087325×10^6, 0.4087325×10^4, 4.087325×10^3, 4087.325×10^0, 40873.25×10^{-1}, 408732.5×10^{-2}, 4087325.0×10^{-3}. In normalised scientific notation there is just one digit before the decimal point and this must be non-zero. The exponent then ensures the correct magnitude of the number. So the example would be represented as 4.087325×10^3 in normalised scientific notation.

When representing real numbers in binary floating-point format, normalisation means the mantissa should have a significant first bit. This is important so that as few significant bits as possible are lost, because only a limited number of bits can be stored.

Normalised two's complement format

Look at this example. The denary value 14.65625 could be represented as a floating-point number: 0.111010101×2^4 or 0.0111010101×2^5 or 0.00111010101×2^6. If we have 10 bits available for the mantissa, the first representation will keep all significant bits, whereas the other two representations will lose the last significant 1.

> **Key point**
>
> Normalisation maximises precision for a given number of bits.

Look at another example. The denary value -45.375 could be represented as a floating-point number: $1.010010101_2 \times 2^6$ or $1.1010010101_2 \times 2^7$ or $1.11010010101_2 \times 2^8$. If we have 10 bits available for the mantissa, the first representation will keep all significant bits, whereas the other two representations will lose the last significant 1.

The first bit of the mantissa dictates whether the number is positive or negative. So the first fractional bit must be a significant bit in order to keep as many significant bits as possible. Note that this is a 1 if the number is positive, but a 0 if the number is negative.

Some interesting numbers

Table 1 contains some interesting numbers.

Table 1 *Some interesting numbers*

Mantissa	Exponent	$m \times 2^e$	Value	Explanation
0.111111111	011111	$0.111111111_2 \times 2^{31}$		Largest positive normalised value
0.1000 00000	000001	0.5×2^1	1	
0.1000 00000	000000	0.5×2^0	0.5	
0.1000 00000	100000	$0.5 \times 2^{-32} = 2^{-33}$		Smallest positive normalised value
1.0111 11111	100000			Smallest negative normalised value
1.0000 00000	011111			Largest negative normalised value

IEEE standard for floating-point numbers and normalisation

In IEEE standard format, the sign bit is separate from the mantissa. The first bit of the mantissa is implied to be 1 and not stored. This is a significant bit and therefore these numbers are normalised. IEEE floating-point numbers are normalised by definition. The IEEE standard also allows for denormalised numbers: the special case when all bits in the exponent are zero but not all bits in the mantissa are zero. The implied bit of the mantissa in this case is assumed to be 0. This is useful for representing very small values.

Worked example

Calculate the value of the number in Fig. 3.1.9.

Fig. 3.1.9

The sign bit shows it is a positive number.

The exponent is stored in excess-15 mode, so $e = -15$

The implied first bit of the mantissa is 0, so $m = 0.01101_2$

Therefore the value is $0.01101_2 \times 2^{-15} = 1101_2 \times 2^{-20} = 13 \times 2^{-20}$

Other interesting numbers

Table 2 contains other interesting numbers. Note that the negative values are symmetrical with the positive values.

Table 2 *Other interesting numbers*

Sign	Exponent	Mantissa	$m \times 2^e$	Value	Explanation
0	11111	00 0000 0000	Special case	∞	Infinity
0	11110	11 1111 1111	$1.1111111111_2 \times 2^{15}$ $= 1111111111100000_2$	65 504	Largest normalised value
0	01111	00 0000 0000	1.0×2^0	1	
0	01110	00 0000 0000	1.0×2^{-1}	0.5	
0	00001	00 0000 0000	1.0×2^{-14}		Smallest normalised value
0	00000	11 1111 1111	$0.1111111111_2 \times 2^{-15} =$ $1111111111_2 \times 2^{-25}$		Largest denormalised value
0	00000	00 0000 0001	$0.0000000001_2 \times$ $2^{-15} = 2^{-25}$		Smallest denormalised value
0	00000	00 0000 0000	Special case	0	

To convert a real number into floating-point format

Write the number in binary with a binary point in the appropriate place. Now normalise the binary number by shifting the binary point right or left as appropriate. Adjust the exponent accordingly to preserve the original magnitude of the number. Table 3 shows conversion examples for two's complement format and Table 4 shows conversion examples for minifloat format.

Table 3 *Two's complement format: conversion examples*

Real number	Binary	Two's complement	Normalised binary	Mantissa	Exponent
3.25	0011.0100	0011.0100	$0.1101000_2 \times 2^2$	0.1101 00000	000010
0.25	0000.0100	0000.0100	$0.1000000_2 \times 2^{-1}$	0.1000 00000	111111
−4.5	−0100.1000	1011.1000	$1.0111000_2 \times 2^3$	1.0111 00000	000011
−0.25	−0000.0100	1111.1100	$1.0000000_2 \times 2^{-2}$	1.0000 00000	111110

Table 4 *Minifloat format: conversion examples*

Real number	Binary	Normalised binary	Sign	Exponent (excess-15)	Mantissa (first bit implied)
3.25	11.01	$1.101_2 \times 2^2$	0	10001	10 1000 0000
0.25	0.01	$1.0_2 \times 2^{-2}$	0	01101	00 0000 0000
−4.5	−100.1	$-1.001_2 \times 2^2$	1	10001	00 1000 0000
−0.25	−0.01	$-1.0_2 \times 2^{-2}$	1	01101	00 0000 0000

Question

3 Take the following real numbers (i) 5.5, (ii) 0.375, (iii) −9.75 and (iv) −0.1875 then express them as (a) normalised two's complement format floating-point numbers and (b) minifloat format floating-point numbers.

Precision and errors

There are an infinite number of real numbers, but only a finite number of possible bit patterns to represent them. Inevitably, we will not be able to represent each one exactly. There will be loss of **precision** as significant bits can't be stored as part of the mantissa. Even double-precision and larger word formats will have this problem. The example in Fig. 3.1.10 uses the minifloat format.

Fig. 3.1.10

To represent the real number 208.1875, we say

$$208.1875_{10} = 11010000.0011_2 = 1.10100000011_2 \times 2^7$$

Note that the last significant bit did not fit into the space available for the mantissa. So the actual value stored is 208.125, a loss of precision of 0.0625.

Rounding errors

The precision of the result of an arithmetic operation is greater than the precision of the floating-point number format. The usual method to represent the approximated value is by rounding to the nearest representable value.

The following example assumes a maximum of 11 bits to store the mantissa (minifloat format). To convert the real number 72.1 into floating-point format:

$1.0010000001_2 \times 2^6$ is exactly 72.0625

$1.0010000010_2 \times 2^6$ is exactly 72.109375

To represent 72.1 using the minifloat format, we can either round down and store 72.0625 or round up and store 72.109375. The usual method is to round to the nearest value (72.109375 in this case). However, this introduces an error of 0.009375. This is known as the **absolute error**. Sometimes the precision is measured using relative error. The **relative error** is the difference of the real number and its representation divided by the real number.

In our example the real number 72.1 is rounded to the nearest representable value, 72.109375. The difference is 0.009375 (the absolute error). The relative error is 0.009375/72.1 = 0.00013.

Cancellation errors

Cancellation errors cause loss of accuracy during addition or subtraction of numbers of widely differing sizes, due to limits of precision. This example assumes a maximum of 11 bits to store the mantissa:

$$1.0110000000_2 \times 2^8 = 101100000.0000_2$$

$$1.1000000000_2 \times 2^{-5} = 000000000.000011_2$$

$$1.0110000000_2 \times 2^8 + 1.1000000000_2 \times 2^{-5} = 101100000.0000_2 +$$
$$000000000.000011_2$$

$$= 101100000.000011_2$$

$$= 1.0110000000_2 \times 2^8$$

Note that the effect of adding a very small number to a large number does not change the result.

Underflow

Underflow is where the result of a calculation is too small to be represented. The result will be stored as zero. For example, dividing a very small number might make it too small to be represented as a value above zero.

Overflow

Overflow is where the result of a calculation is too large to be represented. For example, when multiplying two large numbers together, the size of the exponent may be too big to fit the number of bits available. In IEEE standard floating-point format such a result will be stored as infinity.

Key terms

Underflow: the value is too small to be represented using the available number of bits.

Overflow: the value is too large to be represented using the available number of bits.

Questions

4 What is meant by the term 'precision' and why is precision important in the context of floating-point numbers?

5 Assuming a maximum of 11 bits to store the mantissa (minifloat format), convert the real number 36.1 into floating-point format. What error is introduced with this format?

6 Using minifloat format to represent the numbers, multiply $1.01100\,00000_2 \times 2^{12}$ by 2^7. What can you say about the result?

7 Using minifloat format to represent the numbers, divide $1.01100\,00000_2 \times 2^{-9}$ by 2^7. Comment on your result.

8 Represent the following numbers in minifloat format. Add them and comment on your result: $1.10100\,00000_2 \times 2^{12}, + 1.01000\,00000_2 \times 2^{-7}$.

Did you know?

The reason for the Ariane 5 rocket explosion (Fig. 3.1.11) was a floating-point number conversion that resulted in overflow.

PC activity

Find out more detail about the fate of the Ariane 5 rocket. Why did the floating-point number conversion cause overflow? Why were there no problems with Ariane 4?

AQA Examiner's tip

The IEEE standard is very unwieldy. You are more likely to be asked to work with the minifloat standard.

Fig. 3.1.11 *Ariane 5 rocket disaster*

In this topic you have covered:

- the method of storing real numbers as floating-point numbers
- how to convert decimal real numbers into floating-point representation
- how to convert floating-point representation into decimal real numbers
- the IEEE standard and the minifloat standard for representing floating-point numbers
- normalised and denormalised floating-point numbers
- how zero and infinity are represented
- the precision of floating-point representations
- rounding errors, cancellation errors, underflow and overflow.

4 Operating systems

4.1 Role of an operating system

Key terms

System program: a program that manages the operation of a computer.

Operating system: the most fundamental of all system programs.

Role of an operating system

Without its software, a computer is basically a useless collection of metal, silicon and plastic. With its software, a computer becomes a powerful information-processing tool.

Computer software can be divided into **system programs**, which manage the operation of the computer, and application programs, which solve problems for their users. The most fundamental of all the system programs is the **operating system**.

An operating system has these roles:

- Hide the complexities of the hardware from the user.
- Manage the hardware resources to give orderly and controlled allocation of the processors, memories and input/output (I/O) devices among the various programs competing for them, and manage data storage.

Operating system implementation

An operating system is the programs which make the hardware usable. The hardware is a collection of resources. Stored data are also a resource.

Managing resources

In a general-purpose computer, e.g. a desktop computer, one purpose of an operating system is to manage the hardware so that a satisfactory performance is achieved as judged by criteria such as the number of jobs completed per unit time or the response time to interactive users.

The operating system programs may be classified according to the resources they manage. Table 1 shows the key resources managed by an operating system and the corresponding operating system programs.

Table 1 *Key resources managed by an operating system and the corresponding OS programs*

Key resource	OS program
Processors	Processor scheduling
Storage	Memory management
Input/output devices	I/O management
Data	File management

One of the challenges facing operating system developers is keeping their operating systems flexible enough to run hardware produced by many different manufacturers. Today's operating systems can accommodate many different printers, disk drives and special peripherals in any possible combination.

General-purpose computers are not the only kind of computing device. In fact, the majority of computer systems in use today are embedded in other machinery, such as cars, telephones, appliances, and peripherals for computer systems. They are called embedded systems. Some embedded systems require no operating system because they function as very simple controllers. Others, such as mobile phones, do require an operating system. However, a mobile phone operating system has to manage a different set of resources. The resources include the keypad, the screen, the address book, the phone dialler, the battery and the network connection.

Virtual machine

Another purpose of an operating system is to hide from the user all the details of how the hardware works so that the user is presented with a machine which is much easier to use, a so-called **virtual machine**. These details are progressively hidden by placing layers of software on top of the hardware (Fig. 4.1.1). The final layers of the operating system are the user interface and a way for application programs to call on the services of the operating system, such as file creation. This is achieved with an application programming interface.

Key terms

Virtual machine: the apparent machine that the operating system presents to the user, achieved by hiding the complexities of the hardware behind layers of operating system software.

Application programming interface: a layer of software that allows application programs to call on the services of the operating system.

User interface	Application programming interface
I/O management	
File management	
Memory management	
Processor management	
Device drivers	
Kernel	
Hardware	

Fig. 4.1.1 *Layers of an operating system*

AQA Examiner's tip

Kernel: contains first level interrupt handler and dispatcher. For the exam, you do not need to know about interrupts or how processes/threads are dispatched.

Application programming interface

A standard **application programming interface** (API) allows a software developer to write an application on one computer and have a high degree of confidence that it will run on another computer of the same type, even if the other computer has a different specification. An operating system must ensure that applications continue to run when hardware upgrades and updates occur. This is the reason that the operating system, not the application, must manage the hardware and the distribution of its resources.

Application programs call subprograms provided by the programming language designer. The subprograms hook into the operating system so that the resources managed by the operating system can be accessed.

Here is a Delphi console mode program which uses the API function `FileOpen` to open a connection to a named disk file, the API function `FileSetDate` to update the date associated with the selected disk file and the API procedure `FileClose` to close the connection to the file. When executed, the program changes the date associated with file Example.Txt on the root of the C: drive.

```
Program APIExample;
{$APPTYPE CONSOLE}
Uses
  SysUtils;
Function SetFileDate(Const FileName : String;
                     Const FileDate : TDateTime): Boolean;
  Var
    FileHandle : THandle;
    FileSetDateResult : Integer;
  Begin
    Try
      Try
        FileHandle := FileOpen(FileName, fmOpenWrite OR fmShareDenyNone);
        If FileHandle > 0
        Then
          Begin
            FileSetDateResult := FileSetDate(FileHandle, DateTimeToFileDate(FileDate));
            SetFileDate := (FileSetDateResult = 0) ;
          End;
        Except SetFileDate := False;
      End;
      Finally FileClose (FileHandle) ;
    End;
  End;

Begin
  If SetFileDate('c:\Example.Txt', Now)
    Then WriteLn('Date of file successfully changed')
    Else WriteLn('Attempt to change date of file failed');
  ReadLn;
End.
```

User interface

User interfaces of interactive operating systems are classified as command line interfaces and graphical user interfaces.

Command line interface

In a command line interface (CLI), a user responds to a prompt to enter commands by typing a single command word, followed by zero or more parameters on a single line, before pressing the return key. The action of pressing the return key submits the command for processing. Fig. 4.1.2 shows an example. The command is dir. The operating system's command line interpreter responds by listing the files in the current directory, Test.

> ### ■ Key point
>
> Computer scientists are always working with two layers of abstraction: the layer above that calls on a service in the layer below, and the layer below that supplies the required service. Mathematicians and physical scientists work with just one level of abstraction; for example, entropy, S, represents the amount of disorder in a system as $S = k \ln W$ where W is the number of ways of arranging things.

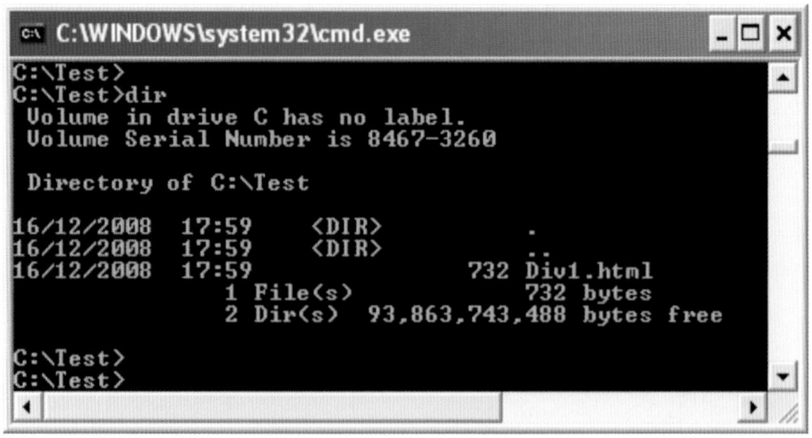

Fig. **4.1.2** *Command line interface*

Graphical user interface

A graphical user interface (GUI) is made up of windows. One window has the focus at any moment. GUIs are event-driven. Events are mouse button clicks, key presses or mouse movements. The operating system detects an event and correlates it with the current mouse position and the window currently in focus, in order to select an action to carry out.

Fig. **4.1.3** *Graphical user interface*

Questions

1 Computer software is divided into two categories. Name them.

2 What is the role of an operating system?

3 What are the four key resources managed by an operating system?

4 Name the operating system programs that manage the four key resources in Question 3.

5 What is a virtual machine?

6 What is an API?

7 Why is it important that an operating system provides a standard API?

8 Name two types of user interface.

9 How do operating systems for embedded computer systems differ from operating systems for general-purpose computers?

In this topic you have covered:

- an operating system is a type of system program

- an operating system is the most fundamental of all the system programs

- an operating system hides the complexities of the hardware from the user and this creates a virtual machine

- an operating system manages the hardware resources to provide orderly and controlled allocation of the processors, memories and I/O devices among the various programs competing for them.

4.2 Operating system classification

Key terms

Interactive operating system: an operating system in which the user and the computer are in direct two-way communication.

Real-time operating system: inputs are processed in a timely manner so that the output can affect the source of the inputs.

PC activity

Use the World Wide Web to research real-time operating systems.

Interactive operating system

Interactive processing is where the user interacts directly with the system to supply commands and data as the application program undergoes execution and the user receives the results of processing immediately. An operating system which allows such interaction supports interactive processing. An **interactive operating system** allows the user and the computer to be in direct two-way communication.

Real-time operating system

In a **real-time operating system** inputs are processed in a timely manner so that the output can affect the source of the inputs. The meaning of timely manner can be demonstrated by balancing a chair by supporting one leg in the palm of your hand. You will find yourself constantly making corrections to keep the chair balanced. Do take care if you try this; give yourself plenty of room.

Real-time operating systems are characterised by four requirements:

1. They have to support application programs which are non-sequential in nature, i.e. programs which do not have a START–PROCESS–END structure.

2. They have to deal with a number of events which happen in parallel and at unpredictable moments.

3. They have to carry out processing and produce a response within a specified time interval.

4. Some systems are safety-critical, so they must be fail-safe and guarantee a response within a specified time interval.

Here are some examples of real-time operating systems:

- **Airline reservation system**: up to 1000 messages per second can arrive from any one of 11 000 to 12 000 terminals situated all over the world. The response time must be less than 3 seconds.

- **Process control system**: up to 1000 signals per second can arrive from sensors attached to the system being controlled. The response time must be less than 0.001 second.

Real-time operating systems (RTOS) that are used to control machinery, scientific instruments and industrial systems typically have limited user-interface capability, and no end-user utilities, since the system will be a sealed box when delivered for use. Aircraft can now be landed automatically by a control system that operates in real time. Some RTOS manage the resources of the computer so that a particular operation executes in precisely the same amount of time every time it occurs. In a complex machine, having a part move more quickly just because system resources are available may be just as catastrophic as having it not move at all because the system is busy.

The airline reservation system is a different kind of real-time system. Here the time constraint is of the order of seconds. This is different from the time constraints imposed by flying or landing an aircraft automatically. That is why airline reservation systems are often called pseudo-real-time systems.

Network operating system

In a **network operating system**, a layer of software is added to the operating system of a computer connected to the network. This layer intercepts commands that reference resources elsewhere on the network, e.g. a file server. The network layer then redirects the request to the remote resource in a manner completely transparent to the user. In this way, files resident on a server are available to the client computer, exactly as if they were resident on that client computer's system. The client computer may have one or two local magnetic disk drives labelled C: and D: and one or more remote magnetic disk drives, perhaps labelled N: and P:, connected to a file server machine. All four drives appear as icons on the client computer's visual display unit. The remote drives are usually available to all client computers connected to the network.

A network operating system may also support interaction, so it can also be called an interactive network operating system. The computer on which a network operating system is installed may also have a real-time processing requirement and therefore the operating system may be called a real-time network operating system.

Key terms

Network operating system: a layer of software is added to the operating system of a computer connected to the network. This layer intercepts commands that reference resources elsewhere on the network, e.g. a file server, then redirects the request to the remote resource in a manner completely transparent to the user.

Questions

1. What is (a) an interactive operating system, (b) a real-time operating system and (c) a network operating system?

2. Explain why an airline reservation system and a system to land an aircraft automatically are considered to require a real-time operating system.

3. A user at a computer sees that she has access to four logical drives: C:, D:, E: and N:. (a) Suggest what each logical drive might represent. (b) What kind of operating system might be installed on this computer?

Device

In any computer-operated device that has an operating system (OS), there is usually a way to make changes to how the device works by changing the code of the operating system. This means that the device does not have to be scrapped when a different functionality is required. The change is effected not by rewiring physical circuits but by updating the operating system code. An important feature of modern operating systems is that the OS code is layered or modular and has clear interfaces between the layers or modules. The user interface may be changed simply by replacing the user interface layer with a different one.

Not all computers have operating systems. The computer that controls a washing machine, for example, doesn't need an operating system. It has one set of tasks to perform, very straightforward input to expect (a numbered keypad and a few preset buttons) and simple, unchanging hardware to control. For a computer-operated device like this, an operating system would be overkill and would drive up the development and manufacturing costs significantly, adding complexity where none is required. Instead, the computer in a washing machine runs a single firmware program all the time.

Computer-operated devices that carry out more than one major task benefit from having an operating system. Here are some things that an operating system allows:

- The device can multi-task.

- The device can operate in real time with critical timing constraints observed, if required.

- The hardware can be changed or upgraded without the need to change application code that runs on the hardware.

- New applications can be added fairly easily.

- Changes to basic functionality can be achieved by upgrading operating system code rather than by scrapping hardware and starting again.

- Applications can be developed in situ on the device or can be easily installed if developed on a more powerful machine.

- The entire OS can be replaced by a different OS, e.g. Windows Mobile can be replaced by Linux, where the new OS allows a much greater range of software changes to be made, e.g. changing a TiVo digital video recorder set up to record NTSC TV broadcasts so it can record PAL TV broadcasts.

- Open Source operating systems can be used. The source code is available for Open Source operating systems, which means that application developers can easily develop applications that will work on a device.

The growing interest in mobile devices (PDAs, mobile phones, car information systems, etc.) has led to the emergence of operating systems to support them. The computer in a typical modern mobile phone is now more powerful than a desktop computer from 20 years ago.

Operating systems for these devices need to consider the kind of resources available to these devices, in particular the energy, the physical context and the mobility of the user, and the limited amount of some resources such as memory or the central processor unit (CPU). An operating system for a mobile phone needs to manage a network connection, a keyboard that supports predictive text, a physically small display, an address book, a phone dialler and a battery of limited power.

These systems could be considered as embedded systems as they have to ensure some minimal running facilities in a strictly autonomous way, continually sending a message packet to base stations so the mobile phone location can be identified. There are real-time constraints on running multimedia applications, for example. The operating system needs to consider the instability of mobile phone networks (bandwidth, connection, etc.).

Smartphones

Smartphones differ from ordinary mobile phones in how they are built and what they can do. A smartphone is a mobile phone that offers advanced capabilities beyond a typical mobile phone, often with PC-like functionality. In order to achieve this, a smartphone must run complete operating system software, providing a standardised interface and platform for application developers. The operating system must support advanced features like e-mail and Internet capabilities and/or a full keyboard.

Most devices considered smartphones today use an identifiable and open operating system, often with the ability to add applications; this contrasts with regular mobile phones, which only support sandboxed applications (like Java games). A **sandbox** typically provides a tightly controlled set of resources for guest programs to run in, such as scratch space on disk and memory. Network access and the ability to inspect the host system or read from input devices are usually disallowed or heavily restricted in sandboxed systems.

PC activity

Use the World Wide Web to research operating systems for mobile devices.

Key terms

Sandbox: a tightly controlled set of resources for guest programs to run in.

Applications for smartphones may be developed by the manufacturer of the device, by the network operator or by any other third-party software developer, since the operating system is open. In terms of features, most smartphones support full e-mail capabilities with the functionality of a complete personal organiser.

Some operating systems that can be found on mobile devices are Symbian OS, RIM's Blackberry, Windows Mobile, Familiar's Linux distribution, Palm OS, Ångström's Linux distribution, and Darwin (iPhone OS). Android is a recent smartphone from the Open Handset Alliance (OHA). Google and T-Mobile launched the G1 phone with Android on 22 October 2008.

Personal digital assistants

Also known as a palmtop computer, a personal digital assistant (PDA) is a hand-held portable computer that can accomplish quite specific tasks and can take on the role of a personal assistant. Newer PDAs have colour screens and audio capabilities, so they can be used as mobile phones (smartphones), web browsers or portable media players. Many PDAs can access the Internet and intranets via Wi-Fi and many PDAs employ touch screen technology. Recently, PDA functionality has been integrated into smartphones, so sales of PDAs have declined and sales of smartphones have risen.

Operating systems for mobile devices such as PDAs and smartphones have to meet different requirements from operating systems for PCs. The operating system takes on the tasks of the basic input/output system (BIOS) in a PC and has to be designed to run on processors with low clock frequency and a main memory of limited capacity. The operating system must use various techniques to save energy and must cater for short reaction times. PDAs usually consist of a ROM for the operating system and RAM from 2 to 64 MB and above, plus a docking station to provide power and data synchronisation with a host PC. The synchronisation also backs up data from the PDA to the PC. Character input is achieved using a stylus and touch-sensitive screen; miniature PDA displays support high-resolution colour rendition with resolutions of approximately 640 pixels × 480 pixels.

Embedded computer systems

The majority of computer systems in use today are embedded in other machinery, such as cars, telephones, appliances and peripherals for computer systems. They are called embedded systems.

Today's motor cars may have 12 or more **embedded computer systems**. These types of embedded systems have a dedicated purpose, have a limited or non-existent user interface, and are designed to operate completely or largely autonomously within other machinery (e.g. an engine management system). They also have a limited memory capacity.

As each generation of hardware for embedded systems becomes more complex, and as more features are added, the applications they run increasingly require an operating system to keep the development time reasonable and to manage multiple tasks that need to meet specific time constraints. In the simplest system, a low-level piece of code switches between tasks or threads based on a timer (connected to an interrupt). This is the level at which the system is generally considered to have an operating system kernel.

As any code can potentially damage the data of another task in embedded systems, programs must be carefully designed and tested, and access

Key terms

Embedded computer system: a dedicated computer system with a limited or non-existent user interface and designed to operate completely or largely autonomously from within other machinery.

PC activity

Use the World Wide Web to research embedded computer systems for (a) motor cars driven by the general public and (b) Formula One cars. What operating systems are used for these embedded computer systems and why?

to shared data must be controlled by some synchronisation strategy. Operating systems for embedded systems are designed to work with the constraints of limited memory size and limited processor performance. In portable embedded systems, the operating system must also take account of limited battery life.

In addition to the core operating system, many embedded systems have additional upper-layer software components. These components consist of networking protocol stacks such as TCP/IP, FTP, HTTP and HTTPS, and also include storage capabilities such as flash memory management systems. If the embedded device has audio and video capabilities, then the appropriate drivers and codecs will be present in the system.

Desktop operating systems

All desktop computers have operating systems. The most common operating systems are the Windows family of operating systems developed by Microsoft, the Macintosh operating systems developed by Apple and the UNIX/Linux family of operating systems, developed over the years by many people, corporations and collaborators. **Desktop operating systems** must support a broad range of general-purpose tasks.

Desktop operating systems are very sophisticated because they have to manage many types of hardware and software resources. Modern PCs have large main memory capacities, multiple processors, huge disk storage capacities, various types of optical disks (read-only and read-write), and flash memory drives. They have real-time requirements for multimedia applications. Their operating systems must support a wide range of network protocols.

Operating systems for desktop computers are written in a layered or modular fashion so they can be updated easily. If the operating system is found vulnerable to a security threat, then a security update can be applied to counter the threat. Desktop operating systems support sophisticated GUIs. However, the memory footprint of desktop operating systems is very large and load times can be significant.

Desktop operating systems provide a virtual machine, which makes it easier for users to perform tasks than if they had to interact directly with the hardware. Desktop operating systems often act as the client operating system in a **client–server system**.

Server

A **server operating system** is an operating system optimised to provide one or more specialised services to networked clients, services such as file storage, domain control and running applications. They are optimised for the service they carry out. This leads to almost optimum performance, which would not be achieved if a server had to do a large amount of general-purpose processing.

PC activity

Use the World Wide Web to research the Linux operating system.

Key terms

Desktop operating system: an operating system that allows a user to carry out a broad range of general-purpose tasks.

Client–server system: a system in which some computers, the clients, request services provided by other computers, the servers.

Server operating system: an operating system optimised to provide one or more specialised services to networked clients.

PC activity

Use the World Wide Web to research server operating systems.

Questions

4 Give three computer-operated devices found in a home that do not require an operating system.

5 Give three computer-operated devices in the home that do require an operating system.

6 Explain why the operating system for a mobile phone will be very different from the operating system for a desktop computer.

7 Explain why the operating system for a smartphone will need to be more powerful than the operating system for a mobile phone.

8 State the requirements that an operating system for a PDA has to meet.

9 Explain the meaning of an embedded computer system for a car.

10 What are the constraints on an operating system for an embedded computer?

11 Why have operating systems for embedded computers had to become more sophisticated?

In this topic you have covered:

- the definitions of interactive, real-time and network operating systems

- the operational characteristics of these operating systems

- operating systems for devices such as smartphones and PDAs

- embedded operating systems, desktop operating systems and server operating systems.

Databases

Many computer systems are data-processing systems. They manipulate vast amounts of data. Traditionally this data was stored in computer files and programs accessed these files for reading or writing. During the AS course you learnt about saving data using files (Topic 2.7 in *AQA Computing AS*).

Remind yourself how you can write records of data to a file (pages 78–82 of *AQA Computing AS*). The record structure is defined as part of the program that manipulates the data. If you want to change the record structure of an existing file, you have to read the file of records using the old file structure and save the records to a new file using the new record structure. This is very inflexible and is an example of unproductive maintenance.

A modern approach is to pool all the data of an organisation into a single **database**, a structured collection of data. The software system used to define, create and maintain a database is called a **database management system** (DBMS). A DBMS also provides controlled access to the database.

Various database management systems are available. Whichever one you choose, it is important that the database is structured so as to minimise duplication of data.

For example, if storing details about customers, it is a waste of storage space to keep a customer's address more than once. It could also lead to data inconsistency if a change of address is updated in one place only.

Before a database system can be built successfully, the database designer needs to analyse the data requirements carefully and build a **data model** (Topic 5.1). There are a variety of data models; the most popular model is the relational model (Topic 5.2).

Key terms

Database: a structured collection of data.

Database management system: a software system that enables the definition, creation and maintenance of a database and which provides controlled access to this database.

Data model: a method of describing the data, its structure, the way it is interrelated and the constraints that apply to it for a given system or organisation.

5.1 Conceptual data modelling

In this topic you will cover:

- how to produce a data model from the given data requirements for a simple scenario

- how to describe the type of relationship and the degree of relationship between two entities.

Key terms

Conceptual model: a representation of the data requirements of an organisation constructed in a way that is independent of any software used to construct the database.

Entity: an object, person, event or thing of interest to an organisation and about which data is recorded.

Relationship: an association or link between two entities.

Degree of relationship: between two entities refers to the number of entity occurrences of one entity which are associated with just one entity occurrence of the other, and vice versa.

The **conceptual model** is created from the data requirements by establishing the **entities** and **relationships** from the data requirements and data constraints.

Entity–relationship modelling

Relationships between entities can be represented using Entity–Relationship diagrams. An entity is represented by a rectangular box and named using a singular noun; Fig. 5.1.1 shows an example. A relationship is represented by a line between two entities. There are four possible **degrees of relationship** (Fig. 5.1.2). Each relationship should also be labelled with its name.

Item

Fig. 5.1.1 *An entity is represented by a rectangular box and named using a singular noun*

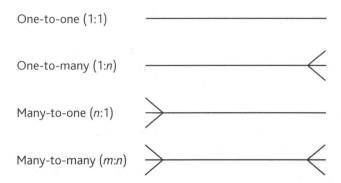

Fig. 5.1.2 *There are four possible degrees of relationship*

Worked example

A company provides some of its employees with a company car. The company keeps a record of the employee's name and unique employee number. The company records the registration number of the car and the model and make.

What are the entities about which data is stored? Employee, Car.

What is the relationship between Employee and Car? A car is allocated to a single employee. An employee is provided with a single car (Fig. 5.1.3).

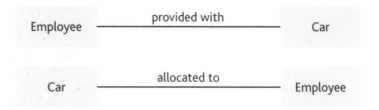

Fig. 5.1.3 *Entity–relationship diagram for one-to-one relationships*

Worked example _____

Consider the simple scenario of patients assigned to hospital wards. Each patient is assigned a unique patient ID. The following details are recorded about each patient: patient name and date of birth. Each ward has a unique name. The number of beds is recorded for each ward.

What are the entities about which data are stored? Ward, Patient.

What is the relationship between Ward and Patient? Each patient is allocated to a single ward. Each ward can accommodate one or more patients (Fig. 5.1.4).

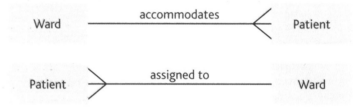

Fig 5.1.4 *Entity–relationship diagram for one-to-many and many-to-one relationships*

Worked example _____

Let's look at the scenario of an organisation that wants to set up online ordering facilities. Here are the data requirements for the underlying database:

- Each product item is assigned a unique item code and has an item description.
- The quantity in stock of each item is recorded.
- The unit price of each stock item is stored.
- Each order is assigned a unique order number.
- For each order, the customer name, delivery address and e-mail address are recorded.
- For each order, the order date is recorded.
- An order may consist of one or more different items.
- The quantity of an item ordered may be greater than one.
- Customers details will not be stored for future orders.

Two example orders are shown and part of the online catalogue.

Table 1. *Example of an order*

Order number	012367		
Deliver to		**Confirmation e-mail**	
Fred Bloggs 1, High Street Anytown		FredBloggs@NT.co.uk	
Order date		01/05/2009	
Order summary			
Item code	Description	Order quantity	Unit price
1234	Ring binder	3	1.50
3456	Stapler	1	2.99
8967	Divider	4	0.50

Table 2. *Part of online catalogue*

Catalogue			
Description	**Quantity in stock**	**Unit price**	**Item code**
Ring binder	342	1.50	1234
Hole punch	275	2.79	2189
Stapler	59	2.99	3456
.	.	.	.
.	.	.	.
,	,	,	,
Divider	187	0.50	8967
Scissors	47	1.99	9684

Table 3 *Example of an order*

Order number	034231		
Deliver to		**Confirmation e-mail**	
Joe Smith 7, The Lane Anytown		JoeSmith@NT.co.uk	
Order date		03/05/2009	
Order summary			
Item code	Description	Order quantity	Unit price
3456	Stapler	4	2.99
9684	Scissors	2	1.99

What are the entities about which data are stored? Item, Order.

What is the relationship between Item and Order? An order consists of one or more items. An item may appear in one, none or several orders.

When the degree of a relationship is not obvious, look at some of the **entity occurrences** in one list and link them with the members of the other list as in Tables 1 to 3. This shows that the relationship between Item and Order is many-to-many (Fig. 5.1.5).

■ Key terms

Entity occurrence: the details of one instance of the entity.

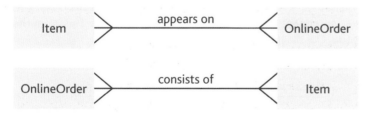

Fig. 5.1.5 *Entity–relationship diagram for many-to-many relationships*

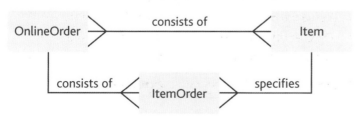

Fig. 5.1.6 *Entity–relationship diagram showing the link entity and one-to-many relationships to replace the many-to-many relationship*

■ **Key point**

ORDER is a reserved word in SQL. Do not use it as an entity name. Choose some other name when you build the database.

When we get many-to-many relationships, we need to analyse the scenario further. One order is typically made up of several single-item orders. So, in fact, we have another entity, ItemOrder. The diagram now looks like Fig. 5.1.6

Let's look at the scenario of a college that enrols students for AS and A2 courses. Here are the data requirements:

- ■ Each course is assigned a unique course code and has a course name.
- ■ Each student is assigned a unique student ID and has their name, address and date of birth recorded.
- ■ Each student enrols on one or more courses.
- ■ The students enrolled on a course will be assigned to one of several sets taught by different teachers.
- ■ Teachers are assigned unique initials.

The data constraint for this database is that teacher details will not be stored.

What are the entities about which data are stored? Course, Student, Set.

What is the relationship between Course and Student? A student may enrol on one or more courses. A course may be taken by one or more students.

What is the relationship between Course and Set? A course may consist of one or more sets. A set belongs to just one course.

What is the relationship between Student and Set? Students are assigned to one or more sets and each set will consist of one or more students (Fig. 5.1.7).

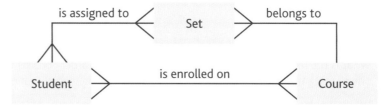

Fig. 5.1.7 *Students are assigned to one or more sets and each set will consist of one or more students*

When we analyse the many-to-many relationship, we find that there is an enrolment for each course the student chooses. This is another entity. Our diagram now looks like Fig. 5.1.8.

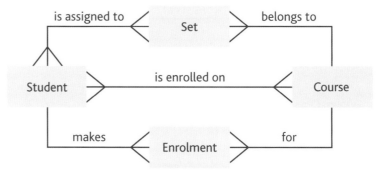

Fig. 5.1.8 *There is an enrolment for each course the student chooses*

Questions

1 A blind person may be given a guide dog. A guide dog will look after just one blind person and a blind person will only have one guide dog. Draw an entity–relationship diagram to represent this relationship.

2 Every car registered in the UK has a unique registration number and one registered keeper. The Driver and Vehicle Licensing Agency (DVLA) records the keeper's name and address. One person may keep several vehicles. Draw an entity–relationship diagram to represent this relationship.

3 A lending library lends out books to borrowers. Each borrower may borrow several books. There may be more than one copy of popular books. The library records names and addresses of borrowers and each borrower has a unique borrower ID. Each book title is identified by its ISBN. Each book copy is identified by a unique accession number. Draw an entity–relationship diagram to represent this system.

In this topic you have covered:

- how to produce a data model from given data requirements
- types and degrees of entity relationships.

5.2 Database design

Key terms

Relation: a set of attributes and tuples, modelling an entity (a table).

Attribute: a property or characteristic of an entity (a named column in a table).

Tuple: a set of attribute values (a row in a table).

Primary key: an attribute which uniquely identifies a tuple.

Relational database: a collection of tables.

Composite key: a combination of attributes that uniquely identify a tuple.

Foreign key: an attribute in one table that is a primary key in another table.

Relational databases

Did you know?

The relational database was invented by Dr Edgar (Ted) F. Codd in 1970. It is based on predicate logic, a branch of mathematics. The name comes from the mathematical concept of a relation, not the relationships that may exist between entities.

Fig. 5.2.1 *Dr Edgar F. Codd*

A **relation** consists of a heading and a body. A heading is a set of **attributes**. A body is a set of **tuples**. An attribute consists of an attribute name and a type name. A tuple is a set of attribute values. An attribute value is a valid value for the attribute type. A relation must have an identifier, an attribute that uniquely identifies a tuple.

A table can be seen as a representation of a relation. Data is stored in tables and each table must have a name and a **primary key**. The structure definition is the heading and the data in the table is the body. A tuple can be represented as a row in a table and an attribute can be represented as a named column of a table. Therefore, a **relational database** is simply a collection of tables.

When no single attribute is sufficient to identify a tuple, a combination of attributes may be used. This type of primary key is known as a **composite key**. Composite keys should always consist of the minimum number of attributes required to identify a tuple uniquely. Table 1 is the table for the entity Item.

When a database consists of more than one table and a relationship exists between these tables, the relationship is modelled by common attributes. An attribute in a table that is the primary key in another table is known as a **foreign key**.

Table 1 *Table form of a relation item*

	Description	Quantity in stock	Unit price	Item code	
Relation	Ring binder	342	1.50	1234	An attribute
	Hole punch	275	2.79	2189	A tuple
	Stapler	59	2.99	3456	
	.	.	.	.	
	.	.	.	.	
	.	.	.	.	

Look at the example of the online ordering system on page 187. When an item is ordered, the item code attribute from the Item table is stored as an attribute in the ItemOrder table. Since a customer should not be able to order an item that does not exist, a sensible method of validation is to check that the ItemCode entered into the ItemOrder table exists in the Item table. This is known as **referential integrity**.

Normalisation

The important thing about database design is that the correct attributes are grouped into the correct tables. The aim is to allow for all possible relationships between data and minimise the duplication of data, so that altering data does not lead to inconsistencies. A set of entities that satisfy these aims are called **normalised entities**.

Entity–Relationship modelling is one method of arriving at a set of normalised entities. Another method is the technique of **normalisation**.

Consider the online ordering example from page 187. Let's store all the data in a single table (Table 2). The primary key for this table would be OrderNumber, because it is unique for each order:

OnlineOrder(OrderNumber, CustomerID, DeliveryAddress, EmailAddress, OrderDate, ItemCode, Description, OrderQuantity, UnitPrice)

Table 2 *OnlineOrder*

Order Number	Customer ID	Delivery Address	Email Address	OrderDate	Item Code	Description	Order Quantity	Unit Price
012367	BLF1	Fred Bloggs 1, High Street Anytown	FredBloggs @NT.co.uk	01/05/09	1234	Ring binder	3	1.50
					8967	Divider	4	0.50
					3456	Stapler	1	2.99
034231	SMJ2	Joe Smith 7, The Lane Anytown	JoeSmith @NT.co.uk	03/05/09	9684	Scissors	2	1.99
					3456	Stapler	4	2.99

The problem with this table is that there are multiple entries for some of the attributes. How much space should be left for these entries? This could be wasteful of space or not allow for enough different items to be ordered. Such entries are known as **repeating groups** or **non-atomic** data.

The first stage of normalisation is to remove these attributes, with a copy of the primary key, to a separate table.

1NF: atomic data test

Given a table that has a primary key, it is in first normal form (1NF) if all of the data values are atomic values. That is, the table does not contain repeating groups of attributes.

Moving the repeating groups to a separate table gives us Table 3 and Table 4 in 1NF.

Table 3 *OnlineOrder*

OrderNumber	CustomerID	DeliveryAddress	EmailAddress	OrderDate
012367	BLF1	Fred Bloggs 1, High Street Anytown	FredBloggs @NT.co.uk	01/05/09
034231	SMJ2	Joe Smith 7, The Lane Anytown	JoeSmith @NT.co.uk	03/05/09

OnlineOrder(<u>OrderNumber</u>, CustomerID, DeliveryAddress, EmailAddress, OrderDate)

ItemOrder(<u>OrderNumber</u>, <u>ItemCode</u>, Description, OrderQuantity, UnitPrice)

Table 4 *ItemOrder*

OrderNumber	ItemCode	Description	OrderQuantity	UnitPrice
012367	1234	Ring binder	3	1.50
012367	8967	Divider	4	0.50
012367	3456	Stapler	1	2.99
034231	9684	Scissors	2	1.99
034231	3456	Stapler	4	2.99

Note that OrderNumber on its own is now not sufficient as a primary key. We need to use a composite key made up of OrderNumber and ItemCode.

There is another problem with these tables. We only store details in these tables about an item once we have sold one. In other words, the 'catalogue' of items is tied up with the orders. This problem is solved by finding all attributes that depend on only part of the primary key and removing them to a separate table. This means that we only need to consider tables with composite keys.

In our example, the order quantity depends on the item code and the order number. The description and the unit price do not depend on which order the item is in. Therefore unit price and description, together with a copy of the dependent part of the primary key, are moved to a separate table. This generates Tables 5 to 7.

2NF: partial key dependence test

A table is in second normal form (2NF) if it is in first normal form and contains no partial key dependencies.

Table 5 *OnlineOrder*

OrderNumber	CustomerID	DeliveryAddress	EmailAddress	OrderDate
012367	BLF1	Fred Bloggs 1, High Street Anytown	FredBloggs @NT.co.uk	01/05/09
034231	SMJ2	Joe Smith 7, The Lane Anytown	JoeSmith @NT.co.uk	03/05/09

Table 6 *ItemOrder*

OrderNumber	ItemCode	OrderQuantity
012367	1234	3
012367	8967	4
012367	3456	1
034231	9684	2
034231	3456	4

Table 7 *Item*

ItemCode	Description	UnitPrice
1234	Ring binder	1.50
8967	Divider	0.50
3456	Stapler	2.99
9684	Scissors	1.99

OnlineOrder(<u>OrderNumber</u>, CustomerID, DeliveryAddress, EmailAddress, OrderDate)

ItemOrder(<u>OrderNumber</u>, <u>ItemCode</u>, OrderQuantity)

Item(<u>ItemCode</u>, Description, UnitPrice)

If our customers return and order again, we store their details all over again. To avoid this problem, we move the attributes that depend on an attribute that is not the primary key to another table, with a copy of the attribute they depend on. DeliveryAddress and EmailAddress depend on CustomerID, not OrderNumber. This generates tables 8 to 10.

3NF: non-key dependence test

A table is in third normal form (3NF) if it is in second normal form and contains no non-key dependencies.

Table 8 *ItemOrder*

OrderNumber	ItemCode	OrderQuantity
012367	1234	3
012367	8967	4
012367	3456	1
034231	9684	2
034231	3456	4

Table 9 *Item*

ItemCode	Description	UnitPrice
1234	Ring binder	1.50
8967	Divider	0.50
3456	Stapler	2.99
9684	Scissors	1.99

Table 10 *OnlineOrder*

OrderNumber	CustomerID	OrderDate
012367	BLF1	01/05/09
034231	SMJ2	03/05/09

Table 11 *Customer*

Customer ID	DeliveryAddress	EmailAddress
BLF1	Fred Bloggs 1, High Street Anytown	FredBloggs @NT.co.uk
SMJ2	Joe Smith 7, The Lane Anytown	JoeSmith @NT.co.uk

OnlineOrder(<u>OrderNumber</u>, *CustomerID*, OrderDate)

Customer(<u>CustomerID</u>, DeliveryAddress, EmailAddress)

ItemOrder(*OrderNumber*, *ItemCode*, OrderQuantity)

Item(<u>ItemCode</u>, Description, UnitPrice)

We now have a set of tables with no unnecessary duplication; that is, no redundant data.

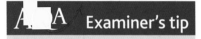

Examiner's tip

If you want to show which attributes are the foreign keys when you are handwriting a table definition, use a wavy underline. In typed text, a foreign key is shown in italics.

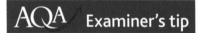

Examiner's tip

A table in 3NF is said to be fully normalised

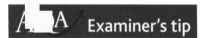

Examiner's tip

You may need to use a relational database as part of your Unit 4 project.

■ **Questions**

1 Use the worked example on page 154. Describe the fully normalised tables for this system.

2 A lending library lends out books to borrowers. Each borrower may borrow several books. There may be more than one copy of popular books. The library records names and addresses of borrowers and each borrower has a unique borrower ID. Each book title is identified by its ISBN. Each book copy is identified by a unique accession number. Describe the fully normalised tables for this system.

In this topic you have covered:

■ the concept of a relational database

■ database design and normalisation techniques.

5.3 Structured Query Language

In this topic you will cover:

- how to use SQL to define a database

- how to use SQL to retrieve, update, insert and delete data from several tables.

Did you know?

You can download and install MySQL server and the GUI tools for free. Online tutorials are also provided. Visit **www.mysql.com**. An ODBC interface called MyODBC allows additional programming languages that support the ODBC interface to communicate with a MySQL database.

AQA Examiner's tip

For your Unit 4 project, you may wish to create a database using SQL.

Structured Query Language (SQL) is a text-based querying system that has been adopted as standard by all major relational database management systems. The ANSI/ISO SQL standard has been evolving since 1986 and many versions exist. Here we will use generic SQL statements. SQL can be divided into two parts: Data Definition Language (DDL) is used to create a database and Data Manipulation Language (DML) is used to retrieve, update, insert and delete data in a database. SQL is a declarative language. This means we state **what** we want, rather than **how** what we want should be obtained.

The examples in this book were prepared using MySQL, the very popular Open Source database management system. The official way to pronounce MySQL is 'my ess que ell' not 'my sequel'. The MySQL GUI tools make this system very easy to use.

DDL

DDL is used to create the database structure; that is, to define which attributes belong in which tables. It also allows you to create users and grant access rights to users.

Table 1 *DDL commands*

Command	Effect
CREATE DATABASE	Creates a new database
CREATE TABLE	Creates a table with the attributes provided as parameters
CREATE USER	Creates new users (and sets a password)
GRANT	Sets access privileges for users
DROP	Deletes a database, table or user

To see how these commands are used, look at Fig. 5.3.1 and 5.3.2 This will create the database in the worked example on page 152 and in the normalisation example.

DML

Having created a database structure, we now want to add data to it and manipulate that data. Table 2 shows a selection of the most useful DML commands.

Table 2 *DML commands*

INSERT INTO	This will generate a new row in a table and store the supplied values in the columns as listed. (Fig. 5.3.3)
UPDATE	This will change values in a table, such as using a calculation (Fig. 5.3.4)
DELETE	This will delete a row in a table (Fig. 5.3.4)

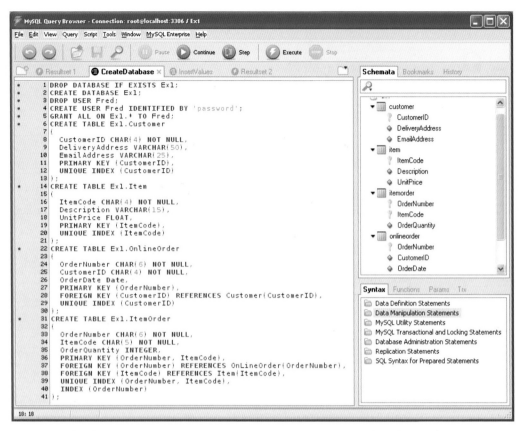

Fig. 5.3.1 *After this script was executed, it produced the schema (database) on the right*

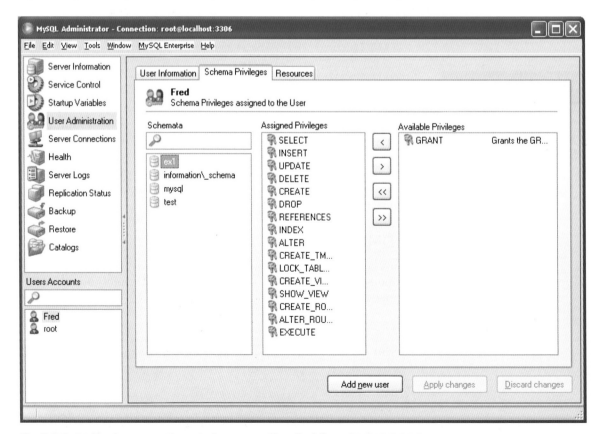

Fig. 5.3.2 *Fred has been correctly created as a user and has all privileges for the Ex1 database*

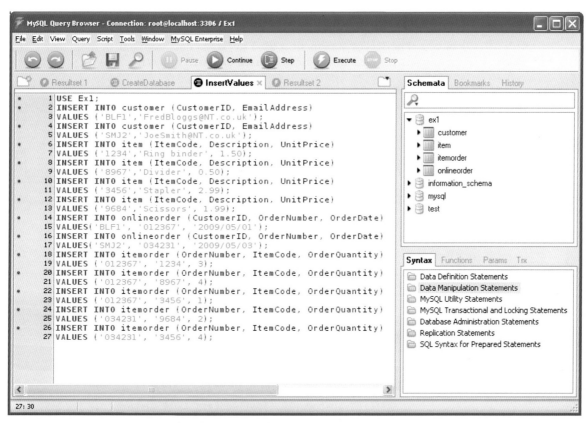

Fig. 5.3.3 *The script will store the values from page 160 into the tables*

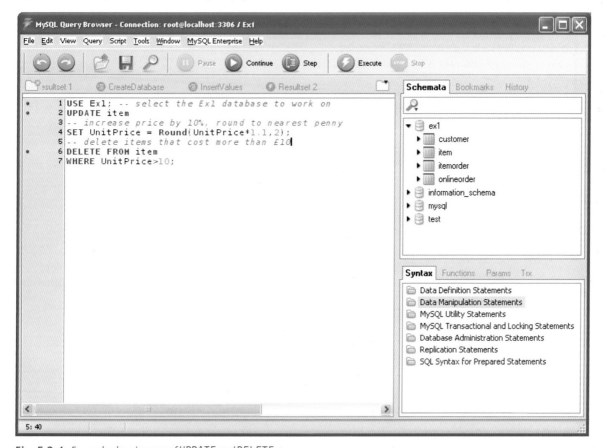

Fig. 5.3.4 *Example showing use of* UPDATE *and* DELETE

Querying a database

The SELECT statement is used to extract data from one or more tables. In its simplest form, it can be used to list all values in a table.

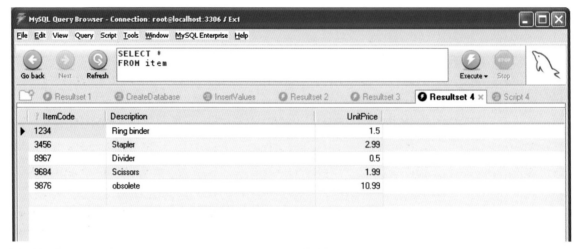

Fig. 5.3.5 *Answer table after running the query* SELECT * FROM item

The character * stands for 'all attributes'. Instead you can list the attributes whose values you want to see. Here is an example:

SELECT CustomerID, EmailAddress FROM customer

The WHERE clause is used to select which rows of a table are shown (Fig 5.3.6):

Fig. 5.3.6 *Finding the items ordered with order number 012367*

Table 3 explains the operators that can be used in WHERE clauses. Note that NULL means nothing has been entered in the field. This is different from zero or the empty string.

Table 3 *Operators that can be used in* WHERE *clauses.*

Operator	Meaning	Example
=	Equal to	OrderNumber = '012367'
>	Greater than	OrderDate > '2009/05/01'
<	Less than	OrderDate < '2009/05/02'

Table 3 continued

<>	Not equal to	`OrderDate <> '2009/05/03'`
>=	Greater than or equal to	`OrderDate >= '2009/05/01'`
<=	Less than or equal to	`OrderDate <= '2009/05/02'`
AND	Both parts of the expression must be true for the expression to be true	`ItemCode = '3456'` `AND OrderNumber = '012367'`
OR	At least one part of the expression must be true for the expression to be true	`ItemCode = '3456'` `OR ItemCode = '9684'`
NOT	Inverts the truth of an expression	`NOT ItemCode = '3456'`
IS NULL	To find a field that does not contain a value	`DeliveryAddress IS NULL`
BETWEEN ... AND ...	Within the given range (inclusive)	`OrderDate BETWEEN '2009/05/01'` `AND '2009/05/02'`
LIKE	Use _ to match any single character and % to match an arbitrary number of characters (including zero characters)	`CustomerID LIKE 'B%'` finds all customer IDs that start with B
IN	Equal to a value in a given set	`ItemCode IN ('3456', '1234')`

You can specify a sort order on one or more attributes using the ORDER BY clause. The answer table is presented in ascending order (ASC). For descending order use DESC. Here is an example:

```
SELECT * FROM item ORDER BY Description DESC
```

Using multiple tables

You can combine data from more than one table into a single answer table (Fig. 5.3.7). Note the contents of the WHERE clause in Fig. 5.3.7. This ensures that the foreign key–primary key link will list the rows in the table onlineorder with EmailAddress for the relevant CustomerID. Fig. 5.3.8 shows how to combine data from four tables.

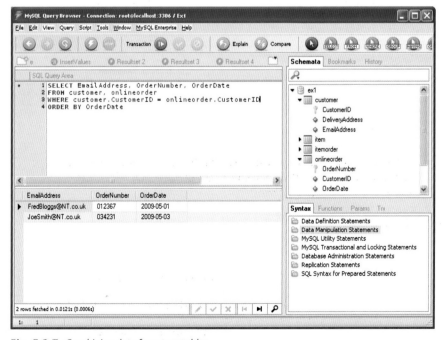

Fig. 5.3.7 *Combining data from two tables*

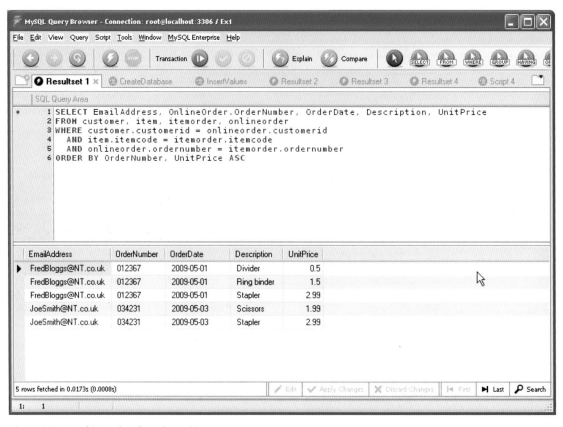

Fig. 5.3.8 *Combining data from four tables*

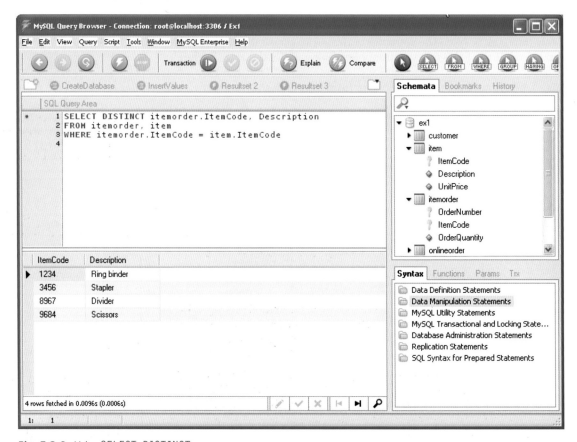

Fig. 5.3.9 *Using* SELECT DISTINCT

Carefully study the WHERE clause in Fig. 5.3.8. Notice that each foreign key reference is tested so that only the correct combinations of values are listed.

Notice too that sometimes the attribute is prefixed with the table name. This is only necessary when the attribute name on its own would cause ambiguity. That is, the same attribute name is present in more than one table.

Sometimes an answer table may contain duplicate rows. This can be avoided by using the keyword DISTINCT.

The GROUP BY clause

The GROUP BY clause allows us to use functions that operate on sets of values. They are known as aggregate functions. Examples are SUM, COUNT and AVG (Fig. 5.3.10).

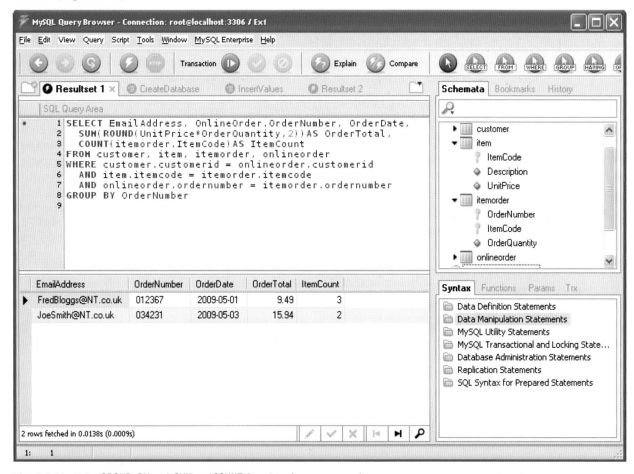

Fig. 5.3.10 *Using* GROUP BY *with* SUM *and* COUNT *functions for summary values*

Questions

1 (a) Using the data requirements from the worked example on page 154, write the DDL statements to create the database and all table structures. (b) Write a query using DML to list all courses. (c) Expand your query from (b) to include which students have enrolled on these courses.

2 (a) Using the library scenario from Question 2 on page 161, write the DDL statements to create the database and all table structures. (b) Write a query using DML statements to list all borrowers who have books on loan. (c) Expand your query from (b) to include the number of books each borrower has out on loan.

In this topic you have covered:

- how to create a database and tables using DDL

- how to manipulate data in a database using SQL.

6.1 Communication methods

Key terms

Data transmission: movement of data from one place to another.

Serial data transmission: single bits are sent one after another along a single wire.

Key point

In guided and unguided transmission media, the transmitted signal will decrease in strength with distance. If this is not corrected, the data encoded in the signal will not be recoverable accurately or at all.

Data transmission

Text, images, sound recordings, salaries, names, etc., can all be reduced to a numerical representation. The numbers may be in any number base but computers work best with binary digits. These binary digits represent data. The numbers need to be converted into a physical form that computers can manipulate and move from one place to another. This form is usually electrical, magnetic or electromagnetic. Moving data from one place to another is called **data transmission**.

Data transmission occurs between a transmitter and receiver over some transmission medium. The connection between transmitter and receiver is often called a communication channel. Transmission media may be classified as guided or unguided. In both cases, communication is in the form of electromagnetic waves. The data are encoded as electromagnetic signals. With guided media, the waves are guided along a physical path; examples of guided media are twisted pairs, coaxial cables and optic fibres. Unguided media provide a means for transmitting electromagnetic waves but do not guide them; examples are propagation through air, vacuum and sea water by radio waves ranging in frequency from very low to ultrahigh (microwaves). In guided and unguided transmission media, the transmitted signal will decrease in strength with distance. If this is not corrected, the data encoded in the signal will not be recoverable accurately or at all.

Serial data transmission

In **serial data transmission**, single bits (binary digits) are sent one after another along a single wire by varying the voltage on the wire. Fig. 6.1.1 shows a simple electrical circuit for sending single bits coded as 0 volts and 5 volts. When the switch is in position A the lamp bulb is connected to 5 volts. When the switch is in position B the lamp bulb is connected to 0 volts. We need to decide what the signal lamp on and the signal lamp off represent.

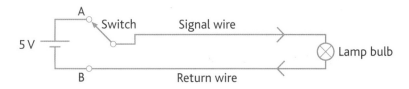

Fig. 6.1.1 *Simple circuit for sending binary digits serially*

If we are sending single bits along the wire, then we have one of two possible binary digit values to represent at any moment, 0 or 1. We may choose to let *lamp on* represent binary digit 1 and *lamp off* represent binary digit 0. The equivalent signals travelling along the signal wire represent binary digit 1 by 5 volts and binary digit 0 by 0 volts. The binary digits represent data and the voltages 0 volts and 5 volts their signal equivalent. Fig. 6.1.2 shows the transmission of a sequence of data bits using signals of 0 volts and 5 volts.

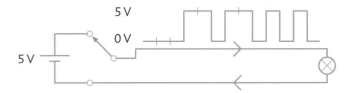

Fig. 6.1.2 *Serial data transmission of a sequence of data bits sent as electrical signals*

Serial data communication is used to network two computers using a crossover cable to join the network card in one computer with the network card in the other computer (Fig. 6.1.3). A crossover cable is a particular kind of two-way serial cable. Two-way communication requires two signal lines, as shown in Fig. 6.1.3. The Universal Serial Bus (USB) is another example of serial data communication. Fig. 6.1.4 shows serial data communication between a PC and a USB memory stick over a serial USB cable.

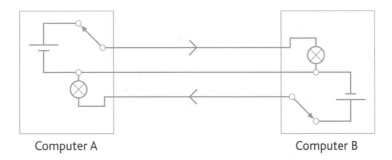

Computer A   Computer B

Fig. 6.1.3 *Simplified diagram to show two computers in communication using a network crossover cable*

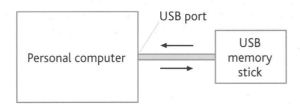

Fig. 6.1.4 *Example of serial data transmission*

Use of serial data transmission

Serial data transmission is used for long-distance communication. The main reason for using serial data transmission is that it needs only one signal pathway each way. This makes it easy to regenerate the signal. Signal strength can fall significantly over long distances. Serial data transmission makes it easier to route signals through telecommunication switches. It also saves on the cost of cabling.

Parallel data transmission

In **parallel data transmission**, bits are sent down several wires simultaneously. The connecting cable consists of many wires.

Fig. 6.1.5 shows a parallel connection that uses eight data wires, one return wire (the data wires can be individually shielded), one strobe wire and one ready/busy wire. The ready/busy wire is set to 5 volts or 0 volts. The strobe wire is set to 5 volts or 0 volts. The data wires are set to 5 volts or 0 volts.

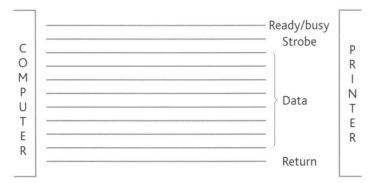

Fig. 6.1.5 *Parallel data transmission between a computer and a printer*

The transmission of data between computer and printer is controlled by the printer via the ready/busy wire. If the printer is ready to receive, the ready/busy wire is set by the printer at 5 volts, otherwise it is set to 0 volts. The computer reads the state of ready/busy wire. If it is set to busy, the computer does not send data. If it is set to ready, the computer places data signals onto the data wires. A short time later, the computer sets the voltage on the strobe wire to 5 volts. The printer detects this strobe signal voltage and starts to read the data on the data wires. At the same time it sets the ready/busy wire status to busy. When the printer is finished reading data, it sets the ready/busy wire back to ready.

Use of parallel communication

Parallel data transmission is used over short distances because it is difficult to keep the voltages on the eight wires in line with each other beyond a certain distance; the problem is called skew. This can lead to the voltage on each wire being read incorrectly. It is also expensive to run eight or more wires over long distances, especially if the signals on the wires need to be switched to a different path, e.g. in digital switching centres such as telephone exchanges. That is why parallel communication has been restricted to computer-to-printer connections and computer busses.

■ Baud rate

The **baud rate** sets the frequency at which signals may change. For example, if the computer's serial port is set to send at **1 baud**, the signal sent out by the computer can change only at the end of each elapsed second (Fig. 6.1.6). Table 1 shows the rates of signal change for some other baud rates.

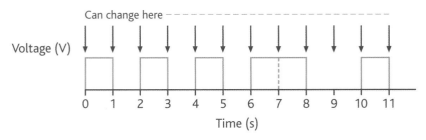

Fig. 6.1.6 *Timing of signal changes*

Table 1 *Baud rate and signal changes*

Baud rate	Time between signal changes (s)	Rate of signal change (changes per second)
2	0.5	2
4	0.25	4
1000	0.001	1000
10 000	0.0001	10 000

■ Bit rate

Bit rate is measured in bits per second. It is the number of bits transmitted per second. The **bit rate** is the same as the baud rate when one bit is sent between consecutive signal changes. However, it is possible to send more than one bit between signal changes if more than two voltage levels are used to encode bits. If the voltages 0 volts, 2.5 volts, 5 volts and 7.5 volts are used, then the decimal numbers in Table 2 can be encoded.

Table 2 *Linking voltage levels to number of bits encoded by these levels*

Signal level (volts)	Decimal number	Binary number
0	0	00
2.5	1	01
5	2	10
7.5	3	11

Fig. 6.1.7 shows how two bits of data are encoded per time slot on a 1 baud line, giving a bit rate of 2 bits per second.

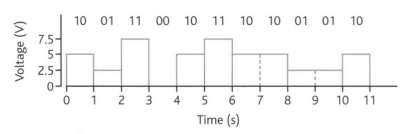

Fig. 6.1.7 *Sending data along a 1 baud line using four levels of voltage to encode bits*

■ Bandwidth

Bandwidth is a measure of how fast the data may be transmitted over the transmission medium. The greater the bandwidth, the greater the rate at which data can be sent.

The **bandwidth** of a transmission medium, e.g. copper wire, is the range of signal frequencies that it may transmit from one end of the wire to the other without significant reduction in strength. Bandwidth is measured in hertz (Hz), e.g. 500 Hz. The hertz is a unit of frequency equal to one cycle per second. Figs 6.1.8 and 6.1.9 show the effect of the transmission medium on two different frequencies.

Key terms

Bandwidth: for a transmission medium, e.g. copper wire, this is the range of signal frequencies that it may transmit.

Fig. 6.1.8 *Low-frequency signal injected onto wire at A arrives at B with its strength undiminished*

Fig. 6.1.9 *Higher-frequency signal injected onto wire at A arrives at B with its strength diminished significantly*

Although a given signal may contain frequencies over a very broad range, any medium used to transmit the signal will be able to accommodate only a limited band of frequencies. This limits the bit rate that can be carried on the transmission medium. Fig. 6.1.10 shows the effect of a 500 Hz bandwidth signal channel, e.g. a copper wire, on a transmission with bit rate of 2000 bits per second.

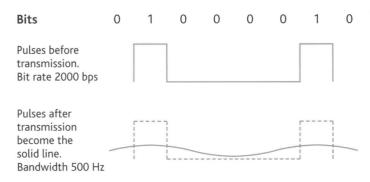

Fig. 6.1.10 *A 2000 bps transmission over a 500 Hz signal channel*

■ The relationship between bit rate and bandwidth

There is a direct relationship between bit rate and bandwidth. The greater the bandwidth of the transmission system, the higher the bit rate that can be transmitted over that system. If the data rate of the digital signal is W bits per second (bps) then a very good representation can be achieved with a bandwidth of $2W$ Hz.

■ Latency

Latency is the time delay that can occur between the moment something is initiated and the moment its first effect begins. In a wide area network involving satellites, significant time delay occurs because of the physical distance between the ground stations and the geostationary satellite. Requesting and receiving a web page can involve a considerable time delay, even though the bit rate of the uplink and downlink to the satellite is high, i.e. the bandwidth is large. The speed of microwaves is 3×10^8 m/s. With a round-trip distance of over 143 200 km, the propagation time delay is approximately 0.4 s.

> **■ Key point**
>
> The greater the bandwidth of the transmission system, the higher the bit rate that can be transmitted over that system.

Questions

5 Explain the difference between baud rate and bit rate.

6 What is the relationship between bandwidth and bit rate?

7 What is latency in the context of communications?

Key terms

Asynchronous serial data transmission: the arrival of data cannot be predicted by the receiver; so a start bit is used to signal the arrival of data and to synchronise the transmitter and receiver temporarily.

Asynchronous data transmission

In **asynchronous serial data transmission** the transmitter and receiver are not kept synchronised. Instead, the receiver is synchronised with the transmitter only at the time of transmission.

Start bit

The arrival of data at the receiver is signalled by a special bit called a start bit. As the arrival of data cannot be predicted by the receiver, the transmission is called asynchronous. The start bit is used to wake up the receiver. The receiver's clock is set ticking by the start bit.

The transmitter must operate a timing device, a clock, that is set at a rate determined by the baud rate. Signal changes take place at regular time intervals. The receiver must operate a timing device set at the same rate as the transmitter, so the received bits can be read at the same regular time intervals. It is important that the receiver reads each bit during the time that it is not changing, i.e. in the time interval between changes. This requires the receiver's timing device to be brought in step or synchronism with the transmission's timing. Bringing into step doesn't just mean setting the same rate. For example, two clocks could be ticking at the same rate but could be telling different times. It means that the timing of the transmitter's transmission of the bits should match the timing of the receiver's reading of the bits. This is achieved by a start bit that causes the receiver's clock to synchronise with the transmitter's clock.

Fig. 6.1.11 shows two computers with a serial connection between their serial ports. The connection is a special serial cable called a null modem cable. This cable's internal wiring between the end connectors ensures that each wire connects to the correct pin on each computer's serial port. For the link from computer A to computer B, the data wire is kept at the voltage level corresponding to a binary digit 1 when not sending – the idle state. A data transmission is started by changing the voltage level to the level for binary digit 0. This is the start bit. The transmitter then follows the start bit with 7 or 8 data bits depending on how the serial port has been configured. If parity is enabled, the last data bit is followed by a parity bit.

Stop bit

Finally, the transmitter attaches a stop bit. The voltage level chosen for the stop bit is the level for binary digit 1. The time interval for the stop bit allows the receiver to deal with the received bits, i.e. transfer them into the RAM of the computer.

AQA Examiner's tip

Typically the idle state is high (logic level 1) so that a broken cable can be deleted but be prepared to be asked questions where the idle state is low (logic level 0)

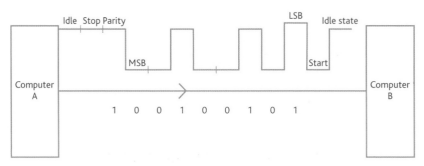

Fig. 6.1.11 *Asynchronous serial data transmission of 00100101 between computer A and computer B using even parity*

Asynchronous serial data transmission sends 7 or 8 data bits at a time. These 7 or 8 bits often represent character data from the ASCII character data set.

Odd and even parity

A check digit, called a parity bit, is used to check for changes to the data that can occur when the data is transmitted. The parity bit is an extra bit added to each 7 or 8 data bits that are transmitted. This parity bit is calculated from the 7 or 8 data bits and is either a 1 or a 0 depending on whether even parity or odd parity is chosen:

- **Even parity**: the parity bit is set to 1 or 0 so that the number of 1s across data bits and parity bit is an even number.
- **Odd parity**: the parity bit is set to 1 or 0 so that the number of 1s across data bits and parity bit is an odd number.

Fig. 6.1.12 *Even parity for 8 data bits*

Fig. 6.1.13 *Odd parity for 8 data bits*

The sending computer generates the correct parity bit and attaches it to the end of the data bits as they are transmitted. The receiving computer regenerates a parity bit from the received data bits and checks it against the received parity bit. If the two are different, an error occurred during transmission. Unfortunately, this checking method only detects an error when an odd number of data bit errors has occurred (e.g. 1, 3, 5, 7). Fig. 6.1.14 shows an asynchronous transmission of one character coded in 8 data bits. Notice the position of the parity bit in relation to the stop bit.

Fig. 6.1.14 *Sending a parity-protected character coded in 8 bits*

Handshaking protocols

Data transmission protocol

A **communication protocol** is a set of pre-agreed signals, codes and rules used to ensure successful communication between computers or a computer and a peripheral device such as a printer. Fig. 6.1.15 shows

Key terms

Communication protocol: a set of pre-agreed signals, codes and rules to be used for data and information exchange between computers, or a computer and a peripheral device such as a printer, that ensure that the communication is successful.

the pin configuration for a COM1 serial port found on older PCs. The port transmits on pin 2 and receives on pin 3. Pins 4, 7 and 8 are used to control a transmission. The signals on these pins play an important part in the handshaking protocol, a form of communication protocol.

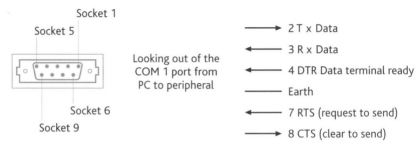

Fig. 6.1.15 *COM1 serial port on a PC, now largely replaced by USB ports*

Handshaking

A **handshaking protocol** is a data transmission protocol that involves an exchange of signals. In a handshaking protocol, the sending device checks first to see if the receiving device is present. If it is present, the sending device then enquires if the receiving device is ready to receive. The sending device waits for a response which indicates that the receiving device is ready to receive. On receipt of this signal, the sending device coordinates the sending of the data and informs the receiver that it is sending the data. The sender then waits for the receiver to become ready to receive more data. For example, in Fig. 6.1.16 a COM1 serial port of a computer is shown connected to the serial port of a printer.

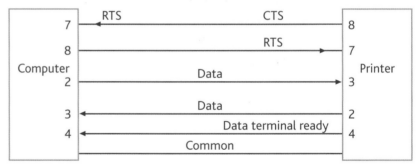

Fig. 6.1.16 *Serial port two-way communication using control signals RTS and CTS*

Assuming that the printer is present and switched on, Table 3 shows the handshaking protocol between the computer's serial port and the printer's serial port.

Table 3 *Handshaking protocol: C = computer, P = printer*

C	→	Are you ready?	→	P	Clear to send (P pin 8)
C	←	Yes I am	←	P	Request to send (C pin 7)
C	→	Here it is	→	P	Start bit
C	←	Busy	←	P	Clear to send (P pin 8)
C	→	That's it	→	P	Stop bit
C	←	I'm ready again	←	P	Clear to send (P pin 8)

When the computer wishes to send a byte of data to the printer, it checks the voltage on its request to send (RTS) pin. If this indicates that the printer is ready to receive, the computer starts sending. As soon as the printer receives the start bit, it sets its clear to send (CTS) pin to busy. When the stop bit arrives at the printer and the printer has transferred the received data bits into a buffer inside the printer, the printer sets its CTS pin to ready. This tells the computer that it can send the next byte of data. The start bit signals 'here it is' and the stop bit signals 'that's it'.

Questions

8 What is asynchronous serial data transmission?

9 In serial data transmission, what is the role of (a) the start bit and (b) the stop bit?

10 What is a communications protocol?

11 Describe the handshaking protocol used in serial data transmission.

12 Explain how odd and even parity bits are generated.

13 Describe how a receiver uses parity.

▧ Baseband

In a local area network (LAN) the transmission medium, the network cable, is often shared among several computers (Fig. 6.1.17). However, the set-up allows only one station to be sending at any moment. This

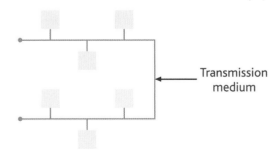

Transmission medium

Fig. 6.1.17 *In a LAN the network cable is often shared among several computers*

means that the whole bandwidth of the transmission medium is dedicated temporarily to one sending station and one receiving station, i.e. the whole bandwidth is dedicated temporarily to one data channel. Computers connected to this LAN must take turns to use the medium. The LAN is said to operate in baseband mode. **Baseband systems** tend to be used over short distances such as in LANs, where they offer high performance at low cost.

■ Broadband

A broadband system is a multichannel system. Several data channels are combined onto a carrier signal so that the bandwidth of the transmission medium can be shared by several data channels. **Broadband systems** are used for long-distance communication because long-distance communication media are expensive to install and maintain. It would be wasteful if each media path could support only a single data stream. Wide area networks (WANs) tend to use broadband media and operate in broadband mode. Broadband media allow two or more data streams to be carried at the same time.

■ Questions

14 What is baseband mode?

15 What is broadband mode?

16 Where would baseband mode be used and why?

17 Where would broadband mode be used and why?

In this topic you have covered:

- serial and parallel data transmission and where they are used
- the effect of distance on the transmission of data
- the meaning of baud rate, bit rate, bandwidth, latency
- the difference between baud rate and bit rate
- the relationship between bit rate and bandwidth
- asynchronous serial data transmission
- the purpose of start and stop bits
- odd and even parity and why parity is used
- the meaning of protocol in the context of computer communications
- a particular protocol called a handshaking protocol
- baseband and broadband operation and where they are used.

6.2 Networks

Key terms

Local area network: linked computers in close proximity.

Stand-alone computer: a computer that is not networked. It requires its own printer and other peripherals plus its own installation of application software.

Topology: in the context of networking, the shape, layout, configuration or structure of the connections that connect devices to the network.

Local area networks

Local area networks (LANs) emerged in the early 1970s as a substitute for large mainframe computers. People realised that for many companies it was more economical to have a number of small computers, each with the ability to run applications, rather than a single, large system. Each small computer needed access to peripherals, such as magnetic hard disks and printers, and needed to share data, so it became necessary to interconnect these small computers and the peripherals they shared. The interconnections became the **local area network**. A computer that is not interconnected is a **stand-alone computer**. A stand-alone computer needs its own printer, hard disk storage, and local installation of application software.

LANs cover a small geographic area such as a single building. The close proximity of computers to each other in a LAN enables communication links to be used that have higher speeds and lower error rates than in wide area networks (WANs). The links most commonly used in LANs are twisted pair, baseband coaxial cable, broadband coaxial cable and optical fibre.

Topology

Linking computers to form a network requires careful planning. Consider the problem of adding another computer to either of the layouts in Fig. 6.2.1. The way computers are cabled together or linked to form a network is very important. The term **topology** is used to describe the layout of a network.

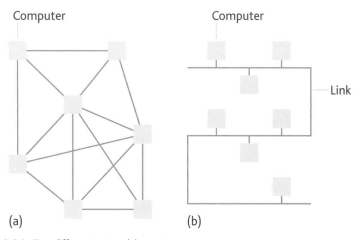

Fig. 6.2.1 *Two different network layouts*

Wide area network

Wide area networks (WANs) were invented to solve the problem of connecting a LAN to a distant workstation or another remote LAN. Fig. 6.2.2 shows a simple WAN. Often businesses have offices throughout a large region. For instance, the major banks have branch offices in every city and town throughout the country. LANs are perfect for sharing resources within a building or over a single site, but they cannot be used to connect distant sites. Wide area networks serve this need. Expressed simply, a wide area network is a set of connections between geographically remote local area networks. These connections may use one or more of the following:

- the public switched telephone network
- high-speed, high-bandwidth dedicated leased lines
- high-speed fibre-optic cable
- microwave transmission links
- satellite links
- radio waves
- the Internet.

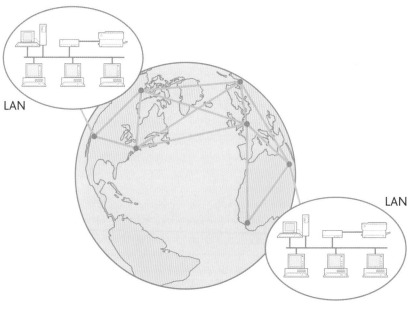

Fig. 6.2.2 *A WAN linking computers in different locations*

The mobile phone network is a WAN. It uses circuit switching for voice calls but packet switching for text messaging. Text messages are piggybacked onto the packets that mobile phones continually send so that base stations can locate them. These packets have 160 bytes of spare capacity. Circuit switching means that the network has to be able to find a complete pathway through the network before a call can be made. Packet switching means that a packet can be sent from the sender immediately, without setting up a path to the destination in advance.

Internetworking

When two LANs are interconnected by a WAN so that computers or nodes on one network are able to communicate with computers or nodes on the other network, and vice versa, the two LANs are said to be internetworked or to form an **internet**. The publicly accessible internet known as the Internet grew from wide area interconnections made between university campuses at the University of California, Stanford University, Massachusetts Institute of Technology, Carnegie Mellon University and other universities. In its early days it was known as ARPAnet. The Internet is a public internetwork or internet and, given its importance to the world, it is often given a capital I.

Questions

1 Define the following terms: (a) local area network, (b) stand-alone computer, (c) wide area network.

2 In the context of networking, what is a topology?

3 What is an internet?

LAN topologies

The most common network topologies are star and multi-access bus. They are shown in outline in Fig. 6.2.3.

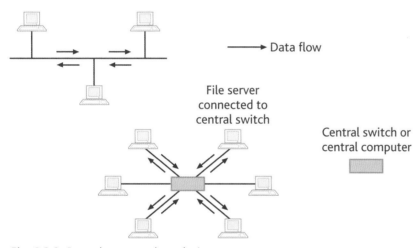

Fig. 6.2.3 *Bus and star network topologies*

Network adapter

A computer communicates on the network through a network interface card or network adapter. A network adapter plugs into the motherboard of a computer and into a network cable. Network adapters perform all the functions required to communicate on a network. They convert data from the form stored in the computer to the form transmitted or received on the cable (Fig. 6.2.4).

A network adapter receives data to be transmitted from the motherboard of a computer into an area of memory called a buffer. The data in the buffer is then passed through some electronics that calculates a checksum value for the block of data and adds address information, which indicates the address of the destination card and its own address, which indicates where the data is from. Each network adapter card is assigned a permanent unique address at the time of manufacture. The block is now known as a frame.

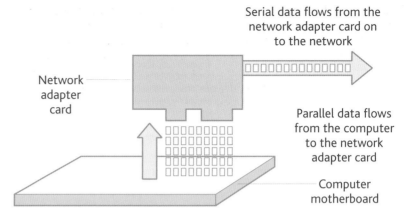

Serial data flows from the network adapter card on to the network

Network adapter card

Parallel data flows from the computer to the network adapter card

Computer motherboard

Fig. 6.2.4 *Network adapter*

The network adapter then transmits the frame one bit at a time onto the network cable. The address information is sent first, followed by the data and then the checksum. In the Ethernet protocol, each network card is assigned a unique address called its MAC address. MAC stands for media access control. A MAC address is a 48-bit address expressed in hexadecimal and separated into 6 bytes, e.g. 00-02-22-C9-54-13. Part of the MAC address identifies the manufacturer. Each network card manufacturer has been allocated a block of MAC addresses to assign to their cards.

Bus

In a physically wired bus topology, all computers are attached through a network interface card to a linear transmission medium or bus (Fig. 6.2.5). Fig. 6.2.6 shows a wired bus network that uses coaxial cable.

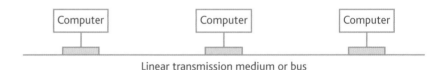

Computer   Computer   Computer

Linear transmission medium or bus

Fig. 6.2.5 *Bus topology*

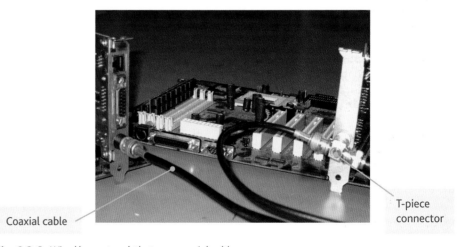

Coaxial cable

T-piece connector

Fig. 6.2.6 *Wired bus network that uses coaxial cable*

Each connected computer has its own unique hardware address provided by the network interface card. In this way, each computer attached to the bus can be uniquely identified. In baseband bus systems a transmission from any computer consists of voltage pulses that propagate the length of the transmission medium in both directions and can be received by all other computers connected to the bus (Fig. 6.2.7). The voltage pulses cease to exist when they reach the end of the bus.

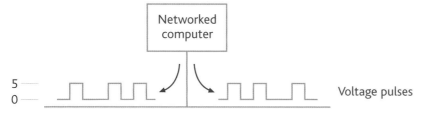

Fig. 6.2.7 *Data transmission from a computer connected to the bus*

A problem arises when two computers transmit onto the bus at the same time. The voltage pulses from each computer will eventually collide, resulting in higher voltage swings. A computer attempting to read these pulses will fail to read them correctly. When this happens, it is called a collision and the bus becomes unusable for the duration of the transmissions from both computers. To reduce the effect of this, the transmission duration is limited to one frame of pulses. A frame consists of a number of pulses up to some maximum. The frame must also have a minimum number of pulses so that a transmitting computer can detect a collision by a rise in pulse voltage. Frames transmitted from two computers situated at opposite ends of a bus must overlap before each stops transmitting.

Even though collisions sometimes occur, it is possible to operate this bus system successfully if each connected computer follows a protocol when transmitting. A commonly used bus protocol is Carrier Sense Multiple Access with Collision Detection (CSMA/CD). Here are the rules for CSMA/CD:

1 If the bus is quiet, transmit a frame.

2 If the bus is busy, continue to listen until the bus is idle then transmit immediately.

3 While transmitting, monitor the bus for a collision. If a collision is detected, transmit a brief jamming signal to let all computers know that there has been a collision then stop transmitting.

4 After transmitting the jamming signal, wait a random amount of time, then attempt to transmit again, starting from step 1.

> ### Did you know?
>
> Ethernet uses CSMA/CD. Ethernet is a very popular bus system and generally refers to a standard published in 1982 by Digital Equipment Corporation, Intel Corporation and Xerox Corporation. It is the predominant form of local area technology used with TCP/IP today. It operates at three speeds: 10 Mbps (standard Ethernet), 100 Mbps (fast Ethernet) and 1000 Mbps (gigabit Ethernet). It uses 48-bit addresses. Data to be transmitted is broken into variable-sized packets called frames (Fig. 6.2.8).

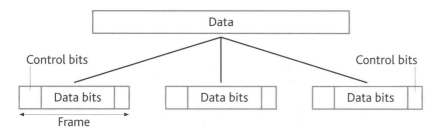

Fig. 6.2.8 *Ethernet frames*

Switched Ethernet

In switched Ethernet the LAN is wired in star topology with the nodes (computers or workstations) connected to a central switch (Fig. 6.2.9). Even though the physical layout or topology is a star, the LAN still behaves as a bus. The central switch queues frames until each frame can be placed onto the backbone. The switch ensures that collisions do

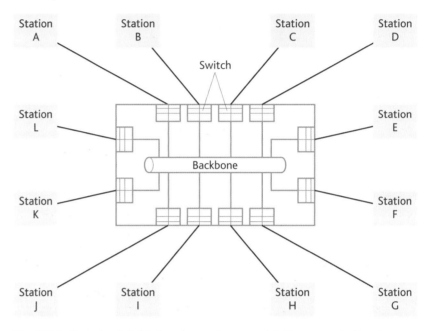

Fig. 6.2.9 *Central switch details and computers or workstations connected in a star configuration to this central switch*

not occur. For example, if computer A launches an Ethernet frame for computer F, the switch creates a temporary exclusive connection from computer A to computer F. If computer B simultaneously launches an Ethernet frame for computer D, the switch will buffer the frame until the backbone becomes free. Switched Ethernet eliminates collisions, so its performance is superior to Ethernet LANs based on coaxial cable.

A separate cable is run from a central switch to each workstation. If there are *n* workstations, there are *n* separate cables. At the switch end, a cable is connected to a line card. Therefore, for *n* cables there are *n* line cards. Fig. 6.2.10 shows a cable connected to a line card. To enable bidirectional data transfer, the cable consists of two independent pairs of wires. One pair of wires forms the input circuit and the other the output circuit. The wires in each pair are twisted together, hence the name twisted pair. A workstation may be a workstation computer, a server, a dumb terminal or some other device. A workstation transmits a packet of data to the line card along the input pair. The packet is stored in the input buffer of the line card. The switching electronics reads the destination address contained in the packet then routes the packet along a backbone in the switch to the line card connected to the destination. A backbone is a high-speed bus.

PC activity

Use the World Wide Web to research Ethernet switches.

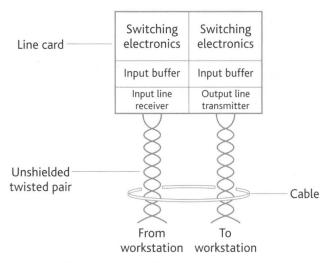

Line card

Unshielded twisted pair

Cable

From workstation

To workstation

Fig. 6.2.10 *A line card connected to a cable containing two unshielded twisted pairs*

Segmentation

Non-switched Ethernet bus networks are often split into smaller parts to improve their performance. These smaller parts are called **network segments**. A segment refers to one physical string of computers. Performance in a non-switched Ethernet network can drop significantly as more stations are added to it. This is because in Ethernet the cable along which data travels is shared by all stations connected to it. If lots of stations have data to transmit, the network gets congested and many collisions occur.

Segmentation is one solution to congestion on an Ethernet network. Segmentation is a process of splitting a larger non-switched Ethernet network into two or more segments linked by bridges or routers. The resulting segments have fewer stations contending for access to the network; this should produce fewer collisions. The bridges and routers ensure that communication is possible between two computers on different segments. A bridge holds a table of addresses, one for each machine connected to the segments joined by the bridge. They are actual Ethernet interface card addresses.

A router also holds a table of addresses. These addresses are Internet Protocol (IP) addresses, which are more flexible than interface card addresses. They can be assigned to user accounts so two users on different segments can communicate, whichever machine they are logged onto.

Star

Fig. 6.2.11 shows a star-wired **thin-client network** that behaves as a star network. In a thin-client network, all processing takes place in a central server; the workstations connected to the central server have very little processing power and no hard disk storage. They do little more than communicate keystrokes and mouse clicks to the central server then display the results of processing on a video monitor. Thin-client workstations are often called dumb terminals because of their lack of processing power and lack of permanent storage capability.

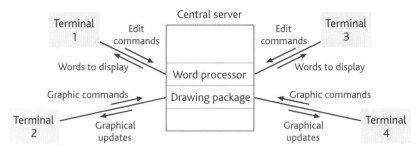

Fig. 6.2.11 *Thin-client star network of terminals*

The central server is an application server, a file server and a domain controller all rolled into one. The domain controller validates users when they initiate a login session. The central file server stores users' files. The central application server runs applications programs such as wordprocessor and drawing package, whatever is required by the users. The applications launch and run in the central server and users share the code of each application. The commands travel along the network spurs from each terminal to the centrally running applications. The results from running the application code on the commands are returned for display on the users' terminals. An example of a thin-client system is the Linux Terminal Server Project (LTSP).

Comparing bus and star networks

Bus and star topologies appear very similar in the way that they are physically wired using the current switch-based hardware. Even thin-client systems, which can be considered to resemble a traditional star network, use an Ethernet bus switch to connect a central server to nodes. In a traditional star network, each link from node to central computer is an independent link. Each link is therefore secure from eavesdropping by other nodes. If a link to a node goes down, the other links and nodes are unaffected. However, if the central computer goes down, the whole network will fail. In a true star-based network, the speed of each link to the central computer should remain high, because the links are not shared.

Traffic between nodes in a switch-based bus network will not be adversely affected if a node goes down, unless the traffic involves the broken node or the node is a domain server that validates users when they attempt to log in. Unplugging a network cable in a switch-based bus network will not affect the rest of the network.

In a coaxial cable bus network, a break in the cable stops the whole network from working. All connected nodes are able to read the frames travelling on the coaxial cable bus network. Therefore coaxial cable bus networks are not secure against eavesdropping. The frames in a coaxial cable Ethernet bus network can collide when multiple nodes send at the same time, causing a noticeable slowdown. Although collisions between frames in switch-based Ethernet bus networks cannot occur, performance can be affected when traffic volumes are high, because the buffers in the switches suffer overflow.

A wireless network is a broadcast network, so it is less secure than a cabled switch-based Ethernet network unless wireless encryption is enabled. In a wireless network without encryption, it is possible to eavesdrop on traffic intended for other computers. A wireless network can also suffer congestion because the channels are shared.

Questions

4 Draw a diagram that illustrates the essentials of a bus network.

5 Draw a diagram that illustrates the essentials of a star network.

6 What is a network adapter?

7 What is a MAC address?

8 Explain the collision problem in the context of a bus network.

9 Why are coaxial cable bus networks segmented?

10 How does switched Ethernet overcome the collision problem?

11 What is a thin-client network?

12 What is a thick-client network?

13 Compare and contrast bus and star networks.

■ Peer-to-peer networks

In a **peer-to-peer network** there are no dedicated servers. All computers are equal and are known as peers. Normally, each computer functions as a client and a server. There is no central control and normally there is no administrator responsible for the entire network. The user at each computer acts as a user and an administrator, determining what data, disk space and peripherals on their computer get shared on the network. Security control is limited because it has to be set on the computer to which it applies. The computer user typically sets the computer's security and they may choose to have none.

It is possible to give password protection to a resource on the computer, e.g. a directory, but there is no central login process where a user's access level is protected by a single password. It is not possible to specify which users are allowed to access a particular resource. A user logged in at one peer computer is able to use resources on any other peer computer if the resources are unprotected by passwords or if the user knows the relevant password. Peer networks are organised into workgroups and a workgroup typically contains fewer than 10 computers. Each computer must support the local user and each remote user. Fig. 6.2.12 shows a peer-to-peer network.

Peer-to-peer LANs

A peer-to-peer LAN is a good choice for environments where:

- there are fewer than 10 users;
- the users are all located in the same area and the computers will be located at user desks;
- security is not an issue, so users may act as their own administrators to plan their own security;
- the organisation and the network will have limited growth over the foreseeable future.

Key terms

Peer-to-peer network: a network that has no dedicated servers. All computers are equal, so they are called peers.

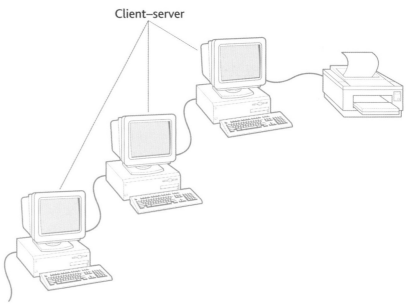

Fig. 6.2.12 *Peer-to-peer network*

Peer-to-peer WANs

Peer-to-peer (P2P) operation in WANs such as the Internet is used to share files among a large number of users connected temporarily (Fig. 6.2.13). Networks such as the file-sharing network Gnutella or the data-sharing network Freenet use a P2P structure for all purposes and are sometimes called true P2P networks.

P2P protocols such as BitTorrent are used on the Internet to distribute large files. In the BitTorrent protocol, a large file is sent out only once, from the source to a group of clients requesting the file, after first splitting it into smaller pieces. Each client in the group receives a piece directly from the source. Each client then becomes a source to the other clients for the piece of the file that it has received. In this way, each client gets the rest of the file from other clients.

The source of the large file only needs to send out one copy of the file for all the clients to receive a copy. The bandwidth demand placed on the source by the group of clients is lower than the bandwidth demand for the source to send each client the complete file. Using the BitTorrent P2P protocol, each client is capable of preparing, requesting and transmitting any type of computer file over a network. A peer is any computer running an instance of the client P2P software for transferring large files.

Another P2P Internet protocol is Skype. Skype is a P2P voice-over-IP (VoIP) client developed by Kazaa that allows its users to place voice calls and send text messages to other users of the Skype client application. Skype grew from Kazaa's file-sharing application Kazaa Media Desktop. Kazaa Media Desktop is a P2P file-sharing application using the FastTrack protocol and owned by Sharman Networks. Kazaa Media Desktop is commonly used to exchange MP3 music files over the Internet, but it can also be used to exchange other file types, such as videos, applications and documents.

■ Key point

A pure P2P network does not have the notion of clients or servers but only equal peer nodes that simultaneously function as clients and servers to the other nodes on the network.

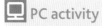 PC activity

Investigate P2P networks, protocols and applications such as Gnutella, Freenet, BitTorrent, Skype and Kazaa Media Desktop.

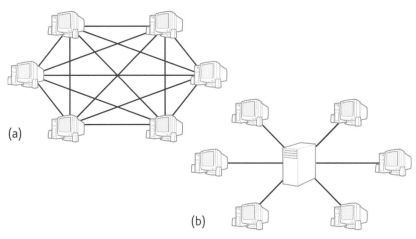

Fig. 6.2.13 *(a) A P2P network, (b) a server-based network*

Server-based networks

A P2P network, with computers acting as both **client** and **server**, is seldom adequate for a system with more than 10 users. Therefore most networks use dedicated servers. A **server-based network** is a network in which resources, security, administration and other functions are provided by dedicated servers.

A dedicated server is one that functions solely as a server and is not used as a client or workstation. Servers are usually optimised to quickly service requests from network clients and to ensure the security of files and directories. Larger networks with a higher volume of traffic employ more than one server.

Clients use servers for services such as file storage and printing. Client computers are usually less powerful than server computers. A server can also authenticate users attempting to log on at client workstations; it stores the client users' IDs and passwords for this purpose. Typically, school networks are server-based networks (thick-client networks): a central domain controller stores user accounts and a central file server stores users' work and some applications that users download into the client machines they work at. Web servers and FTP servers are examples of server-based systems.

Web 2.0

Web 2.0 is a set of principles and practices that tie together a different approach to the use of the World Wide Web and the Internet. In Web 2.0, software becomes a service that is accessed over the Internet. Google's search engine is an example of Web 2.0. Google began its life as a native web application and was not sold or packaged for its customers. The web application, Google's search engine, is delivered as a service and customers pay directly or indirectly to use that service. None of the trappings of the old software industry are present. There are no scheduled software releases, just continuous improvement.

There is no licensing or sale, just usage. There is no porting to different platforms so that customers can run the software on their own equipment, just a massively scalable collection of commodity PCs running open source operating systems plus Google-written applications and utilities that no one outside the company ever gets to see. Google's data centres where it all happens are closely guarded and visitors are not

Key terms

Client: a computer that uses the services provided by a server.

Server: a computer that provides shared resources to network users.

Server-based network: a network in which resources security and administration and other functions are provided by dedicated servers.

Web 2.0: software that becomes a service accessed over the Internet.

welcome. The software never needs to be distributed but only performed. Google's service is not a server but it is delivered by a massive collection of Internet servers. Neither is it a browser, yet it is experienced by the user within the browser. Nor does its flagship search service even host the content it enables users to find. This content is located on the Web in the web pages. Google's software finds the links in these web pages and, using a very clever algorithm, arrives at a page rank index for pages on the Web.

Yet as with many areas of Web 2.0, the label 2.0 is not something new, but a fuller realisation of the true potential of the Web platform. To date, iTunes is the best example. iTunes seamlessly reaches from the hand-held device to a massive Web backend; the PC acts as a local cache and control station.

Web services

Web services are at the heart of Web 2.0. Web services are self-contained, modular applications that can be described, published, located and invoked over a network, generally the Web. Fundamental to web services is the notion that everything is a service. An application programming interface (API) is published for use by other services on the network that encapsulates implementation details.

Software as a service, or **SaaS** (typically pronounced 'sass'), is a model of software deployment where an application is hosted as a service provided to customers across the Internet. SaaS eliminates the need to install and run the application on the customer's own computer. This releases the customer from having to maintain the application software, e.g. from having to update the software, and from having to provide the hardware on which to run the application and to get and keep the application functioning on this hardware. Conversely, customers relinquish control over software versions or changing requirements. In addition, costs to use the service become an ongoing expense rather than a one-off purchase.

However, using SaaS can conceivably reduce the upfront expense of software purchases as the customer now pays only when the software is used. From the software vendor's standpoint, SaaS has the attraction of providing stronger protection of its intellectual property and establishing an ongoing revenue stream. The SaaS software vendor may host the application on its own web server, or this function may be handled by a third-party application service provider (ASP). This way, end users may reduce their investment on server hardware too.

Web services architecture

Traditional systems architectures incorporate relatively brittle coupling between various components in the system. The bulk of IT systems, including web-oriented systems, can be characterised as tightly coupled applications and subsystems. Monolithic systems like these are sensitive to change. Redesigning one of the subsystems will often cause the whole system to break. Hence the term 'brittle'. This situation is manageable to some extent through skills and numbers of people. This brittleness will be exposed by increases in scale, demand, volume and rate of business change. Any significant change in any one of these aspects will cause the brittleness of the systems to become fully exposed: unavailable or unresponsive web sites, lack of speed to market with new products and services, inability to rapidly shift to new business opportunities, or competitive threats. IT organisations will not be able to cope with changes because of the coupling; the dynamics of the Web makes it untenable to manage these brittle architectures.

These problems have been solved by changing to **web services architecture**, a more flexible architecture that yields systems which are more amenable to change. Web services systems promote significant decoupling and dynamic binding of components. All components in a system are services, in that they encapsulate behaviour and publish a messaging API to other collaborating components on the network. Services are marshalled by applications using service discovery for dynamic binding of collaborations. Web services reflect a new service-oriented architectural approach, based on the notion of building applications by discovering and orchestrating network-available services, or just-in-time integration of applications.

Ajax

Ajax is a group of interrelated web development techniques used for creating interactive web applications which can retrieve data from the web server asynchronously in the background, without requiring a complete reload of a web page.

Using Ajax only, the part of a web page that needs updating is fetched from the web server. The HTTP protocol is a very simple protocol used for fetching web pages and resources located in web pages. When a web browser fetches a web page from a web server it sends the command `GET/NameOfWebPage.html`. If the web page contains dynamic data, e.g. oil prices, then the browser must repeatedly send `GET/NameOfWebPage.html` to get the web page to display the current oil price.

The `GET` command fetches the entire web page even though only part of this web page needs to change. With Ajax support, the web browser may repeatedly request just the oil price data after the web page has loaded. This significantly reduces the number of bytes that need to be transferred from web server to web browser and leads to a smoother display in the web browser.

■ Wireless networking

Before **wireless networks**, setting up a computer network in a business, home or school often required running many cables through walls and ceilings in order to deliver network access to all the network-enabled devices in the building. A wireless access point (WAP) allows devices operating wirelessly to connect to a wired network. It allows data to be relayed between the wireless devices (such as computers or printers) and wired devices on the network. The consequence is that network users are now able to add devices that access the network with few or no new cables. Today's WAPs are built to support a standard for sending and receiving data using radio frequencies. These standards and the frequencies they use are defined by the Institute of Electrical and Electronics Engineers (IEEE). Most WAPs use IEEE 802.11 standards.

Wi-Fi

Wireless networking has been around for a very long time. In the Second World War, British agents sent into occupied Europe communicated with England by using radio transmitters and receivers, or transceivers. The network of overseas agents and their controllers back in England formed a wireless network for communication purposes. More recently, mobile phone networks have extended the principle to allow wireless communication across a mobile phone network. It was not long before a standard was drawn up for connecting computers together wirelessly

Wi-Fi: trademarked IEEE 802.11 technologies that support wireless networking of home and business networks.

Bluetooth: a wireless protocol for exchanging data over short distances from fixed and mobile devices.

Router: a device that receives packets or datagrams from one host (computer) or router and uses the destination IP address the packets contain to pass them, correctly formatted, to another host (computer) or router.

 PC activity

Use the World Wide Web to research WEP and WPA.

 PC activity

Use the World Wide Web to research the Bluetooth protocol.

in a LAN. This standard is called **Wi-Fi**. Wi-Fi is the trademark for the popular wireless technology used in home and business networks, mobile phones and other electronic devices that require some form of wireless networking capability. In particular, it covers the various IEEE 802.11 technologies (including 802.11a, 802.11b, 802.11g and 802.11n).

Wireless networks are typically slower than networks connected using Ethernet cable. Wireless networks are more vulnerable, because anyone can intercept the radio broadcasts that carry the data between wirelessly networked computers. Wired Equivalent Privacy (WEP) was introduced in 1997 to give wireless LANs an equivalent level of security to wired LANs. But in 2001 several serious weaknesses were identified in WEP, and a WEP connection can now be cracked in minutes using readily available software.

Following the failure of WEP to reliably secure wireless networks, the Wi-Fi Alliance introduced Wi-Fi Protected Access (WPA), which provides more security to wireless networks than a WEP security set-up. In WEP each user must enter a passphrase into their wireless-networked computer to access the network and other computers on the network, although most operating systems allow the passphrase to be stored on the user's computer at the user's discretion to avoid the inconvenience of entering it for each connection. The passphrase must also be stored in the wireless access point.

Bluetooth

Bluetooth is a wireless protocol for exchanging data over short distances from fixed and mobile devices, creating personal area networks (PANs). It was originally conceived as a wireless alternative to RS232 data cables used in serial data transmission between the serial ports of personal computers and devices. Bluetooth uses a radio technology called frequency-hopping spread spectrum (FHSS) which can achieve a gross data rate of 1 Mbps. The data is chopped into chunks and the chunks are transmitted on up to 79 frequencies. Bluetooth provides a way to connect and exchange information between devices such as mobile phones, laptops, personal computers, telephones, printers, GPS receivers, digital cameras and video game consoles. It uses a secure, unlicensed short-range ISM band at 2.4 GHz. ISM bands are radio bands that are reserved for industrial, scientific and medical use.

■ Questions

14 Give the meaning of these terms in the context of networking: (a) peer-to-peer network, (b) server, (c) client, (d) server-based networking.

15 Give the meaning of these terms in the context of the Internet: (a) Web 2.0, (b) web services, (c) software as a service, (d) web services architecture, (e) Ajax.

16 Give the meaning of these terms: (a) wireless networking, (b) Wi-Fi, (c) Bluetooth.

17 Explain why Google's search engine is considered a Web 2.0 technology.

■ Routers

A **router** is a device that receives packets or datagrams from one host (computer) or router and uses the destination IP address the packets contain to pass them, correctly formatted, to another host (computer) or router. It is vitally important that hosts and routers are able to identify the network part of the destination IP address, because this part features largely in routing. The route chosen is determined by the destination IP address. A router is usually connected to a network of other routers. A datagram may pass through several routers before reaching its destination. Each router maintains a table of routes to various destinations; for example, a router in England will know which router to send a datagram to next if the destination IP address indicates a destination in Malaysia. This router will know which router it should pass the datagram to, and so on. A router can only pass a datagram to a router it is directly connected to. By relaying the datagram from router to router, the datagram eventually reaches its destination.

Fig. 6.2.14 shows the hierarchy of routers for a single country. Each router in this hierarchy maintains a table of other routers, computers and networks it is directly connected to and enough information about the hierarchical structure of the Internet to route a packet onto a path that will lead to the desired destination.

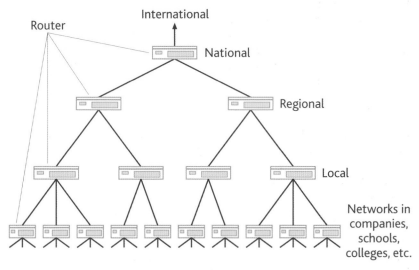

Fig. 6.2.14 *Routing hierarchy for one country*

For example, the IP address range 202.0.0.0 to 203.255.255.255 has been allocated to the Asia-Pacific region. Suppose a host on a school network in England wishes to communicate with a host on a network in Malaysia. It will send packets to the gateway router on the school network. This router will pass the packets on to the local router it is connected to. The local router will pass these packets on to the regional router it is connected to. The regional router will pass packets on to the national router it is connected to, and so on, until the gateway router of the destination network is reached. Each router in the path uses the NetID part of the IP address to make the routing decision. In this example the decision is to route packets up the national hierarchy, because 202/203 addresses are outside England.

 PC activity

Use the World Wide Web to research the structure and organisation of Internet routing.

Routable and non-routable IP addresses

IP addresses

An IP address defines where a host is on the Internet. It can be a public address or a private address set aside for use on home, office or school networks. The Internet Assigned Numbers Authority (IANA) is responsible for global coordination of the IP addressing systems and for routing Internet traffic.

Currently there are two versions of IP addresses in active use: version 4 (IPv4) and version 6 (IPv6). IPv4 was initially deployed on 1 January 1983 and is still the most commonly used version. IPv4 addresses are 32-bit numbers often expressed as 4 octets in dotted decimal notation (e.g. 210.25.0.48). Deployment of IPv6 began in 1999. IPv6 addresses are 128-bit numbers and are conventionally expressed using hexadecimal strings (e.g. 2001:0cd8:56a7:0000:0000:3d8a:0170:7554).

Both IPv4 and IPv6 addresses are generally assigned in a hierarchical manner. Users are assigned IP addresses by ISPs. ISPs obtain allocations of IP addresses from a Local Internet Registry (LIR) or National Internet Registry (NIR), or from their appropriate Regional Internet Registry (RIR) as shown in Fig. 6.2.15.

Fig. 6.2.15 *Regional Internet Registries: see Table 1 for key*

Table 1 *Key to Fig. 6.2.15*

Registry	Region covered
AfriNIC	Africa
APNIC	Asia-Pacific
ARIN	North America
LACNIC	Latin America and some Caribbean islands
RIPE NCC	Europe, Middle East and Central Asia

IANA's role is to allocate IP addresses from the pools of unallocated addresses to the RIRs responsible for overseeing the allocation and registration of Internet numbers within a particular region of the world.

Routable (public) IP addresses

Public or routable IP addresses are assigned by RIPE NCC in Europe. RIPE carefully manages the allocation of IP addresses and there is a WHOIS feature to look up the owners of IP addresses.

Non-routable (private) IP addresses

Non-routable IP addresses are used for home, office, school and college networks. These IP addresses are set aside to be used when it isn't necessary (or even desirable) to have a public IP address. They are especially useful where multiple computers are connected to a single proxy server, firewall or router. These machines communicate with other machines connected to the Internet through proxy servers and firewalls. They use network address translation to route traffic to the machines with private IP addresses. The following IP address ranges are for private or non-routable addresses:

10.0.0.0 to 10.255.255.255

172.16.0.0 to 172.31.255.255

192.168.0.0 to 192.168.255.255

Connecting two LANs by routers

Fig. 6.2.16 shows LANs interconnected by two routers. A packet or datagram (part of a message) is sent from a computer with IP address 195.168.0.37 to a computer with IP address 210.5.0.67. The sending computer is located in a LAN with network ID 195.168.0.0 and the destination computer is located in a LAN with network ID 210.5.0.0. The packet has to pass through two routers, one with IP addresses 195.168.0.1 and 195.168.0.121 and the other with IP addresses 210.5.0.1 and 210.5.0.110. Each router has two IP addresses because each router has two network cards. One network card of a router connects the router to the LAN, and the other network card connects the router to the other router.

Fig. 6.2.17 shows how the packet is assembled as it moves from source computer to destination computer. Note that at each intermediate location, the source and destination MAC addresses are changed so that the packet can travel the next link but the source and destination IP addresses remain the same. Table 2 shows the details of the three hops that make up the transmission in Fig. 6.2.17.

PC activity

Use the World Wide Web to research routers.

Fig. 6.2.16 *Two LANs connected through two routers*

Table 2 *Details for the three hops in Fig. 6.2.17*

Hop	Source IP address	Destination IP address	Source Link Layer address	Destination Link Layer address
1	195.168.0.37	210.5.0.67	00-03-47-C9-69-52	00-02-22-C9-54-13
2	195.168.0.37	210.5.0.67	00-02-22-C9-54-44	00-62-77-C9-A1-88
3	195.168.0.37	210.5.0.67	00-62-77-A1-12-40	01-32-07-D6-55-46

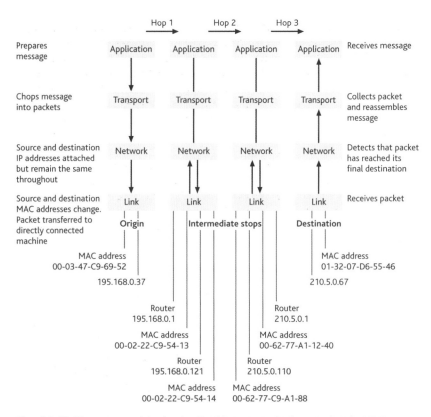

Fig. 6.2.17 *The source and destination IP addresses remain the same but the MAC addresses change (see Table 2)*

Gateways

A **gateway** is a device used to connect networks using different protocols so that information can be passed from one system to another.

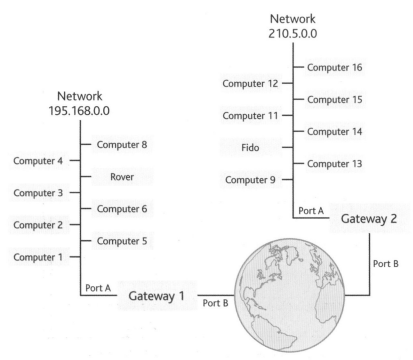

Fig. 6.2.18 *Gateway connections to the Internet*

A LAN is connected to the Internet through a gateway, gateway 1 in Fig. 6.2.18. Another LAN is connected through another gateway, gateway 2 in Fig. 6.2.18. The LANs use a protocol that is very different from the protocols used on the Internet, which is a WAN. The gateway does the job of translating the LAN frame into its equivalent WAN frame or datagram, and vice versa. When a computer such as Rover in network 195.168.0.0 wishes to send to computer Fido in network 210.5.0.0, it knows immediately that Fido is on a different network. It therefore sends to port A of the gateway that it is directly connected to. This gateway then reforms the frame so it is compatible with the Internet and sends this frame on port B to the Internet. When the frame eventually arrives at port B of the gateway for network 210.5.0.0, the gateway reforms the frame before sending it into the LAN via port A. Both gateways have two network cards, one for port A and one for port B. Each card is assigned an IP address.

Setting up a computer on a LAN

Fig. 6.2.19 shows the network control panel dialog box for setting a computer's IP address, gateway address and DNS server IP addresses. Internet Protocol allows computers to send and receive data over the Internet. Each computer (also called a host) with a public presence on the Internet has a unique IP address, much like each home on a street has a unique postal address. When you request web pages or send e-mail, the request is split into smaller pieces called packets that contain your IP address and the IP address of their destination. Internet Protocol directs them to their intended destination. Each computer on the Internet has to have these items set in its networking or TCP/IP settings: IP address, subnet mask, gateway or router address, DNS servers.

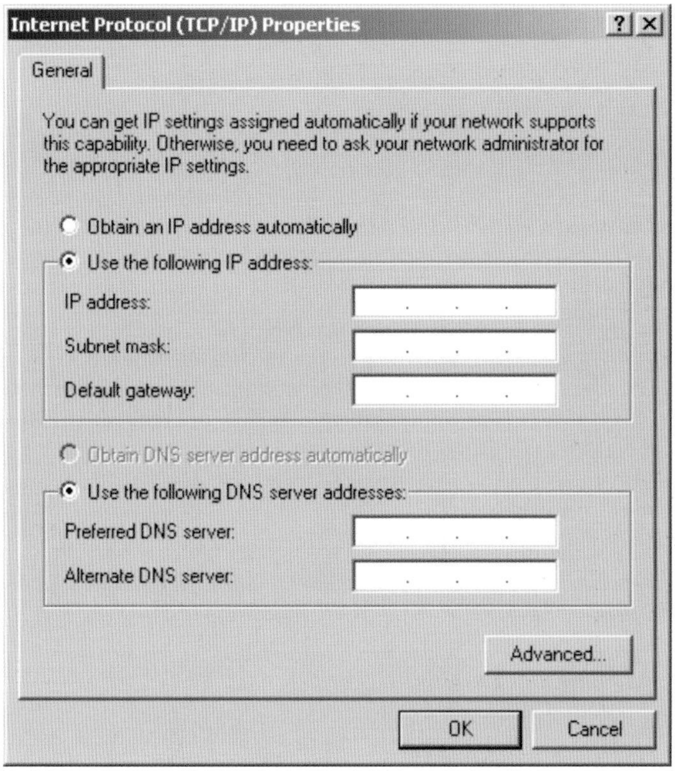

Fig. 6.2.19 *Network control panel dialog box for Microsoft Windows OS*

Subnet mask

The subnet mask defines the size of the network. The subnet mask helps tell a computer which LAN it is connected to, hence the addresses to which it can send packets directly. The subnet mask also tells a computer which addresses it cannot reach directly; to reach these addresses, it must send the packets to the gateway, which forwards them to the next hop on the Internet. The subnet mask for most computers on small LANs is 255.255.255.0.

Gateway

The gateway, or router address, is the IP address of the machine that connects a computer to the next hop on the Internet. If you are using private addresses on a LAN, the gateway is the internal IP address of the machine that directs traffic between the LAN and the connection to the Internet. Each gateway checks the packets coming into it. If it knows where to send a packet, it will send the packet to that network or computer directly. If it doesn't know where to send the packet, it forwards the packet to the router attached to it (another gateway). The next gateway does the same thing, and that is how packets are sent through the Internet.

DNS servers

A network of Domain Name System (DNS) servers keep track of the association between domain names, e.g. educational-computing.co.uk, and which IP addresses are used by that domain name. DNS allows a user to type www.educational-computing.co.uk into a web browser and view the website of Educational Computing Services Ltd, or send e-mail to sales@educational-computing.co.uk.

The DNS servers for educational-computing.co.uk are 212.139.132.228 and 212.139.132.229.

Questions

18 What is a router?

19 What is a gateway?

20 A computer on a LAN in England needs to communicate with a computer on a LAN in Australia. Explain the role of gateways and routers in transferring a message from the computer in England to the computer in Australia.

21 The LAN is connected via router 1 and router 2 to another LAN (Fig. 6.2.20). A web server is running on machine G. Machine A is running a web browser. Draw completed Ethernet frames for a web page request `http://10.7.24.67` from machine A. You are not required to include the web server's response frames.

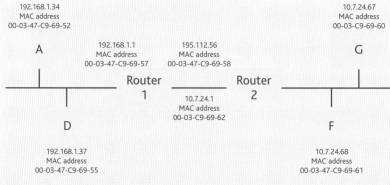

Fig. 6.2.20 *Diagram for Question 21*

6.3 Server-side scripting

Common Gateway Interface

▓ Key terms

Web server extension: a program written in native code, i.e. an executable or a script that is interpreted by an interpreter running on the web server, that extends the functionality of the web server and allows it to generate content at the time of the HTTP request.

Common Gateway Interface: a gateway between a web server and a web server extension that tells the server how to send information to a web server extension, and what the server should do after receiving information from a web server extension.

A web browser uses the HTTP application protocol to fetch web pages from a web server by sending a request message. A web server listens on port 80 for such requests. A web server uses the HTTP protocol to respond with a response message containing a web page or a resource for a web page, e.g. an image. The response message finds its way back to the web browser via the corresponding port that sent the request message (Fig. 6.3.1). A web server is designed to simply transfer a file of bytes. The file of bytes represents a web page or an image or a sound file. However, if the web browser requires information that has the potential to change with time, e.g. the time at the server, then the web server needs to have its functionality extended as shown in Fig. 6.3.2. The extension is called a **web server extension**. The web server extension is a program written in native code, i.e. an executable or a script that is interpreted by an interpreter running on the web server computer. The web server extension generates the web page to be returned to the web browser.

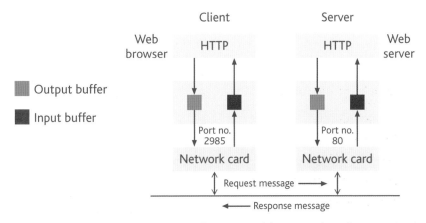

Fig. 6.3.1 *Request–response messaging between a web browser and a web server*

The **Common Gateway Interface** (CGI) is a gateway between the web server and a web server extension. The CGI specification tells the server how to send information to a web server extension, and what the server should do after receiving information from a web server extension. In its simplest form, the gateway consists of two objects, the Request object and the Response object (Fig. 6.3.3).

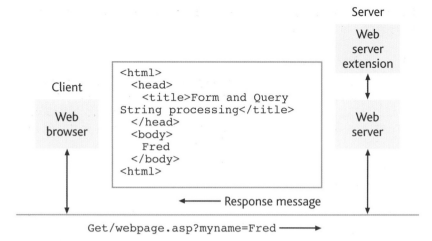

Fig. 6.3.2 *Web server extension to a web server*

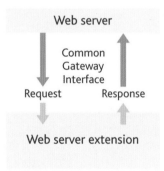

Fig. 6.3.3 *CGI Request object and Response object*

An HTTP client, i.e. a web browser, opens a connection and sends a request message to an HTTP server, i.e. a web server. Table 1 shows the structure of the request message.

Table 1 *Structure of the request message*

Item	Examples or notes
An initial line	`Get /webpage.html HTTP/1.0` `Post /webpage.asp HTTP/1.0`

Zero or more header lines followed by a blank line (CRLF)	`From: fred@somewhere.co.uk`
	`UserAgent = Mozilla/6.0`
	`(compatible; MSIE 7.0; Windows`
	`XP; DigExt`
	`[blank line here]`

An optional message body	If `Post` is used, the body can contain data entered into text boxes in the browser window, e.g. `myname=fred` appears in message body

The data part of the request message is created in one of two ways: as a query string or in the message body.

Query string

Consider the example `Get /webpage.asp?myname=Fred`. The query string consists of a name, my name, separated from a value, Fred, by =. The query string is separated from the `Get` command by a ? symbol. If there is a need to send more than one name–value pair to the server, then the name–value pairs are separated by the & symbol:

```
Get /webpage.asp?myname=Fred&age=6
```

Post method

If the Post method is used by the browser or an HTTP application, then the data (e.g. `myname=Fred&age=6`) is passed in the message body and the command is simply `Post /webpage.asp`, for example. The server then returns a response message. This response message has the same structure as a request message (Table 2).

Table 2 *Structure of the response message*

Item	Example
An initial line	`HTTP/1.0 200 OK`

Zero or more header lines followed by a blank line (CRLF)	`Date: Fri, 31 Dec 1999 23:59:59 GMT`
	`Content-Type: text/html`
	`Content-Length: 1354`
	`[blank line here]`

An optional message body (e.g. a file, query data or query output)	`<html>`
	`<body>`
	`<h1>Hello World!</h1>`
	`[more file contents]`
	`     .`
	`     .`
	`     .`
	`</body>`
	`</html>`

Questions

1 What is the Common Gateway Interface?

2 What is a web server extension?

3 Explain the role of the Request object and the Response object in the CGI.

4 Give an example of a query string.

5 How does the Post method differ from the Get method?

▦ Server-side scripting

The body of a response message contains the HTML web page requested by the client:

```
<html>
  <head>
    <title>Form and Query String processing</title>
  </head>
  <body>
    Fred
  </body>
</html>
```

The web server extension in this instance simply extracts the value part of the name–value pair `myname=Fred` and returns this to the web server embedded in HTML. This is an example of **dynamic web page content**.

▦ Key terms

Dynamic web page content: content that is generated when the web browser request is received.

The full content of the web page is not determined until a request is received. A script is executed on the server to determine the parts of the web page that are dynamically created at the time the request is received.

Fig. 6.3.4 shows how this web page is rendered in the browser. The browser address bar shows that the requested web server extension is `process.asp` and the query string is `myname=Fred`. The ? symbol is used to separate the web server extension from the name–value pair.

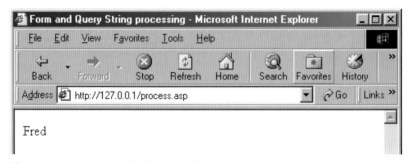

Fig. 6.3.4 *Response rendered in the web browser*

The script `process.asp` is located at the server, hence it is called a server-side script:

```
<html>
  <head>
    <title>Form and Query String processing</title>
    <%@ Language ="VBScript" %>
  </head>
  <body>
    <%
      AVariable = Request("myname")
      Response.Write(AVariable)
    %>
  </body>
</html>
```

PC activity

Run Internet Information Server (IIS), which comes with Windows 2000, XP and Vista. You may have to install it from the Windows installation disk. Place a copy of process.asp in the cgi-bin folder of IIS. Launch a web browser and enter http://127.0.0.1/process.asp?myname=Fred into the address bar. Press Return and see the result.

The value `Fred` sent to the web server is passed to the web server extension in the request object. Script `process.asp` recovers this value from the request object and assigns it to `AVariable`. The web server extension then writes this variable's value to the Response object. The web server replaces the section between `<%` and `%>` by the response object's value, `Fred`, before returning the entire web page to the web browser.

Using the Post method

Fig. 6.3.5 shows a web page that contains a hyperlink, an edit box and a button. Here is the HTML that created it:

```
<html>
  <head>
    <title>Two ways of sending data</title>
  </head>
  <body>
    <a href="process.asp?myname=fred&age=6">Click here</a>
    <p>
    <form method="post" action="process.asp">
      Please enter your name:
      <input type="text" name="myname" size"10">
      <p>
```

Form uses the post method

```
          <input type="submit" value="send">
        </p>
      </form>
    </p>
  </body>
</html>
```

The hyperlink demonstrates the use of the Get method of sending data in a query string, and the rest of the page demonstrates the Post method with the data sent in the message body. The Post method is set up using an HTML form.

Fig. 6.3.5 *Get and Post using a hyperlink for Get and a form for Post*

When `Fred` is entered into the edit box on the form and the Send button is pressed, the address bar in the web browser changes as shown in Fig. 6.3.6. The data item `Fred` does not appear in the address bar, because the data is sent by the Post method.

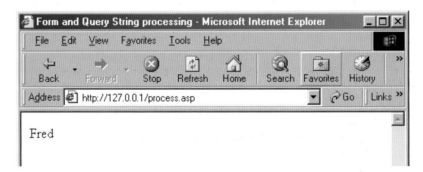

Fig. 6.3.6 *Post: result of clicking the Send button after entering fred in the edit box*

Using the Get method in a form

It is possible to use the Get method in a form:

```
<html>
  <head>
    <title>Two ways of sending data</title>
  </head>
  <body>
    <a href="process.asp?myname=fred&age=6">Click here</a>
    <p>
    <form method="get" action="process.asp">
      Please enter your name:
      <input type="text" name="myname" size="10">
      <p>
        <input type="submit" value="send">
      </p>
    </form>
    </p>
  </body>
</html>
```

Form uses the Get method

Now, if `fred` is entered in the edit box and the Send button is pressed, the address bar of the web browser reveals `fred` in a query string, because the form sends the data using the Get method (see script above). The Get method of sending data is limited to 2048 bytes minus the number of bytes for the path information. The Post method is not as restricted and can send many more bytes of data.

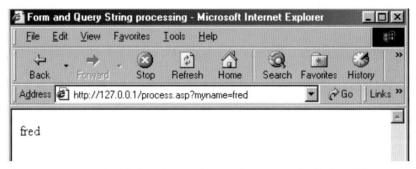

Fig. 6.3.7 *Get: result of clicking the Send button after entering fred in the edit box*

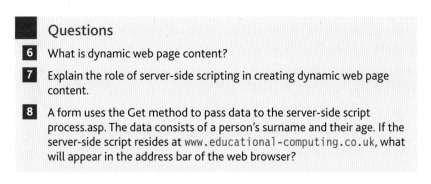

Questions

6 What is dynamic web page content?

7 Explain the role of server-side scripting in creating dynamic web page content.

8 A form uses the Get method to pass data to the server-side script process.asp. The data consists of a person's surname and their age. If the server-side script resides at `www.educational-computing.co.uk`, what will appear in the address bar of the web browser?

AQA **Examiner's tip**

You will not be required to write scripts for the COMP3 examination, but you should have sufficient experience to answer simple questions based on the Response and Request objects.

■ Writing server-side scripts

There are several languages for writing server-side scripts. In each case, access to a Request object and a Response object is the key to understanding how the server-side script communicates with the web browser. Some server-side scripting languages are interpreted, e.g. VBScript, PHP and Perl, whereas others are compiled to produce executables, e.g. Delphi web server applications.

There are two reasons why ISPs prefer to host web sites that use interpreted server-side scripting languages. The first is that the scripts can be read to assess what they do. This is important to prevent hosting scripts that could bring down the web server. The second is that it is much more difficult to bring down a web server that is running interpreted scripts, even when the scripts contain errors.

Server-side scripts that are compiled executables pose a greater threat to web servers. The executable may contain malicious code such as viruses that are intended to do harm to the web server and to computers running web browsers that access the web server. It is much harder to decode a server-side script that is a compiled executable, because it is in machine code. Also, when executables contain errors, they can bring down the web server when a run-time error occurs. Server-side scripts which are compiled executables are often called server-side executables.

Active Server Pages

Active Server Pages (ASP) use VBScript to script the generation of the dynamic part of the web page. ASP scripts have the extension `.asp` and require an ASP interpreter to be present on the server. This interpreter is found in Microsoft's Internet Information Server (IIS), which is provided on the Windows operating system disk. It was called Personal Web Server in Windows 98. The PC activity shows alternative syntax to declare the use of VBScript and to write a simple response message such as "Hello World!" The data is written to the web browser using the notation = for writing to the Response object.

PHP

PHP is a recursive acronym for PHP Hypertext Preprocessor. It began life as PHP/FI in 1995, which its creator Rasmus Lerdorf developed as a simple set of Perl scripts for tracking accesses to his online CV. He named this set of scripts Personal Home Page Tools. PHP 3.0 was the first version that closely resembled PHP as it is today. It was created by Andi Gutmans and Zeev Suraski in 1997 as a complete rewrite of PHP/FI 2.0. They initially used PHP/FI to develop an e-commerce application they were working on for a university project but found that it could not cope with the task. The PC activity shows helloworld.php, a simple PHP script that outputs Hello World! using two different ways and the number 7 (Fig. 6.3.8) when submitted to the PHP interpreter running on web server as a web server extension.

PC activity

Install IIS, then use the following ASP script to test that your server is interpreting the script. Now use the World Wide Web to find other ASP scripts to try.

```html
<html>
  <head>
    <script
    Language="VBScript" >
    </script>
  </head>
  <body>
    <%
    ="Hello, World!" %>
  </body>
</html>
```

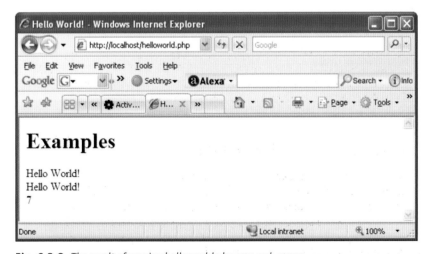

Fig. 6.3.8 *The result of running helloworld.php on a web server*

PC activity

Download and install WAMP.
This runs an Apache web server, a
PHP interpreter and the MySQL
database system. Try the script
shown here. Find other PHP scripts
to run by searching the World Wide
Web.

```
<html>
  <head>
    <title>Hello World!</
    title>
  </head>
  <body>
    <?php
// single-line comments
can be like this
# or even like this
/* multi-line comments
can
be like this */
?>
<h1>Examples</h1>
<?php
echo "Hello World!";
?>
<br />
<?php
// The semicolon at the
end of the statement is
important!
?>
<?php
// print works like echo
print "Hello World!";
?>
<br />
<?php
// simple math
echo 5 + 2;
?>
<br />
  </body>
</html>
```

Variables are created in PHP using the $ symbol. The following script produces Fig. 6.3.9 when submitted to the PHP interpreter running on the web server.

```
<html>
  <head>
    <title>Variables</title>
  </head>
  <body>
    <?php
      /*
    variables start with a $, followed by letter or
    underscore
    variables can contain letters, numbers, underscores, or
    dashes, but no spaces
    variables are case-sensitive
      */
    ?>
    <?php
      $variable1 = 15;
      echo $variable1, "<br />";
      // $myVariable and $myvariable are different
      $myvariable = "Hello World myvariable <br />";
      $myVariable = "Hello World myVariable";
      echo $myvariable;
      echo $myVariable."<br />";
    ?>
    <?php
      // values in variables are variable;
      // $variable1 can be assigned a new value
      $variable1 = 200;
      echo $variable1;
    ?>
  </body>
</html>
```

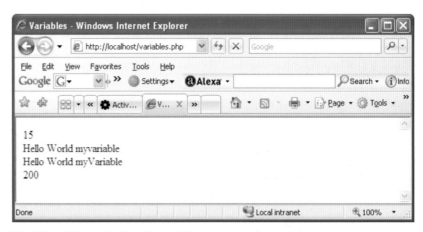

Fig. 6.3.9 *The result of running variables.php on a web server*

Perl

Perl is a high-level, general-purpose, interpreted programming language originally developed as a general-purpose UNIX scripting language to make report processing easier. It is used for writing many different applications, including database access and CGI programming on the

Web. Here is a Perl script that receives data posted to the web server by a web browser. The name–value pairs are parsed and the values extracted are sent back to the web browser via the Response object and the web server.

```perl
if ($ENV{REQUEST_METHOD} eq POST)
{
  read(STDIN, $buffer, $ENV{CONTENT_LENGTH});
  @pairs = split(/&/, $buffer);
  foreach $pair (@pairs)
  {
    ($name, $value) = split(/=/, $pair);
    $value =~ tr/+/ /;
    $value =~ s/%([a-fA-F0-9][a=fA-F0-9])/pack("C", hex($1))/eg;
    $form{$name} = $value;
  }
}
print "Content-type: text/html\n\n";
print "<html>";
print "<head>";
print "<title>Results from Example 1 </title>";
print "</head>";
print "<body>";
print "<h1> Example 1 results </h1>";
print "This is the string that you entered, \"$form{forename}\" ";
print "</body>";
print "</html>";
exit;
```

Delphi

Delphi supports the creation of web server applications. It produces executable files that must be placed in the CGI bin of a web server; the directory is often named cgi-bin. Here is a simple web server application that writes an entire dynamically created HTML web page to the web browser. The web application reads the date and current time at the web server while constructing the web page and puts them in the web page. If the web browser is constantly refreshed, the current time repeatedly updates and once a day the date changes. Fig. 6.3.10 shows the result after one refresh.

```delphi
Program ConsoleProject1;
{$APPTYPE CONSOLE}
Uses
  SysUtils;
Begin
  Writeln('content-type: text/html');
  Writeln;
  Writeln('<html><head>');
  Writeln('<title></title>');
  Writeln('</head>');
  Writeln('<body>');
  Writeln('<h1>The time at the server is</h1>');
  Writeln('<hr />');
  Writeln('<h3>');
  Writeln(FormatDateTime('dd mmm, yyyy hh:mm:ss', Now));
  Writeln('</h3>');
  Writeln('<hr />');
  Writeln('</body></html>');
End.
```

Questions

9 Name three interpreted programming languages for server-side scripting.

10 Why do ISPs prefer to support interpreted server-side scripts rather than server-side executables?

Fig. 6.3.10 *The result after one browser refresh when running ConsoleProject1.exe on a web server*

Accessing data from a DBMS using server-side scripts

The web server extension can use database connection components to connect to a database management system (DBMS), which in turn accesses data in a database (Fig. 6.3.11). There are five steps to make a connection to a database:

1 Create a connection.

2 Select a database.

3 Perform a database query.

4 Use the returned data, if any.

5 Close the connection.

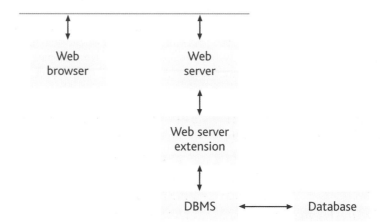

Fig. 6.3.11 *Using a server-side script to access a database via a DBMS*

Active Server Pages

The ASP file Select.asp connects to the Microsoft Access database AgsAltTest.mdb, applies the SQL statement "Select * From TestDB" to extract all records from the table TestDB (Fig. 6.3.12) and displays the fields EmpID and Name for these records.

```
<%@ Language = VBScript %>
<%
```

```
      Dim ObjConnect, ObjResultsSet
      Set ObjConnect = Server.CreateObject("ADODB.Connection")
      ObjConnect.Open("AgsAltTest")
      SQLString = "Select * From TestDB"
      Set ObjResultsSet = ObjConnect.Execute(SQLString)
%>
<html>
  <head>
    <title>All Records </title>
  </head>
  <body>
    <%
    While Not ObjResultsSet.Eof
    %>
    Record: 
    <%=ObjResultsSet("EmpId") %> 
    <%=ObjResultsSet ("Name") %> 
    <br />
    <%
    ObjResultsSet.MoveNext
    WEnd
    %>
  </body>
</html>
<% Set ObjConnect = Nothing %>
```

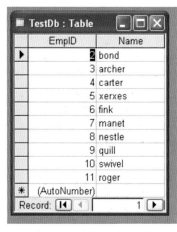

Fig. 6.3.12 *Database table TestDB*

Delphi

Delphi has good support for connecting to databases such as Microsoft Access, MySQL and Interbase.

To connect to an Interbase database called LibraryDB6, launch Delphi and from the file pull-down menu select **New** and then **Web Server Application**. Choose **CGI standalone executable** from the radio button options. Drop a TIBDatabase (IBDatabase) component from the **Interbase** tab onto the web module. Set the **DatabaseName** property of IBDatabase1 to LibraryDB6.gdb. Set the **Params** property in the TString editor to:

```
user_name=sysdba
password=masterkey
```

It is very important that you enter an exact copy of the text shown here. If you don't, your program will not connect to the database.

▨ Change the login prompt of IBDatabase1 to **False**.
▨ Change the connected property to **True**.
▨ Drop a TIBTable component onto the web module.
▨ Drop a TIBTransaction component onto the web module.
▨ Set **DefaultDatabase** to IBDatabase1 for IBTransaction1.
▨ Set the **Database** property of IBTable1 to IBDatabase1.
▨ If it is not already set, set the **Transaction** property of IBTable1 to IBTransaction1.
▨ Select the BOOK table in the **TableName** property of IBTable1.
▨ Drop a TDataSetTableProducer from the **Internet** tab onto the web module.
▨ Set the **DataSet** property of DataSetTableProducer1 to IBTable1.
▨ Set the **MaxRows** property of TDataSetTableProducer1 to 200.

The TDataSetTableProducer object produces the result set which will be based on data stored in IBTable1. Setting MaxRows to 200 limits the result set to 200 rows. We are going to select some fields from IBTable1 and copy data from these fields to table DataSetTableProducer1.

In the following steps, hold down the CTRL key while clicking the mouse with the mouse cursor pointing at the field to be selected.

▓ Right click the IBTable1 component and choose **Fields Editor**.

▓ Right click within the Fields Editor and choose **Add Fields**.

▓ Select the only fields available, BOOKIDNO, TITLE, ISBN.

▓ Select the DataSetTableProducer1 component.

▓ Select the **Columns** property and click its ... button to enter its editor.

▓ Change table properties **Align field** to haCenter and **Border** to 1.

▓ Select the **RowAttributes** property of DataSetTableProducer1

▓ Change **Align** to haCenter.

▓ To add header and footer details to the returned data set which the browser will handle, use the Header and Footer property fields of TDataSetTableProducer1.

▓ Select the **Header** property field of DataSetTableProducer1 in the **Object Inspector**.

▓ Click the ... symbol to open the editor.

▓ You are going to add the first half of an HTML page; the Footer property will contain the rest of this HTML page. The data set returned will appear between this HTML header and the HTML footer.

Insert the following into the header:

```
<html>
  <body>
```

Insert the following into the footer:

```
<hr>
<p>Report any problems to</p>
<a href=mailto:sales@educational-computing.co.uk>Sales</a>
</body>
</html>
```

Double-click the web module (Fig. 6.3.13). The Action Editor should pop up. Click the **Add** icon to add an ActionItem.

Add
icon

Fig. 6.3.13 *Web module window*

▓ Click the ActionItem **WebActionItem1** in the Action Editor to highlight it. Its properties become available to edit in the Object Inspector.

- Change the name of the ActionItem from WebActionItem1 to InterbaseLib1.
- Change its default field to True.
- Click the **Event** tab for the web module. Double-click the **OnAction** event handler.
- Add the following code to the body of the procedure template:

```
Procedure TWebModule1.WebModule1Actions0Action(Sender:TObject;
                              Request : TWebRequest;
                              Response : TWebResponse;
                              Var Handled : Boolean);

  Begin
    With DataSetTableProducer1
      Do
        Begin
          Caption := '<h1>Interbase BOOK Table</h1>';
          CaptionAlignment := caTop;
          DataSet.Open;
          Response.Content := DataSetTableProducer1.Content;
          DataSet.Close;
        End;
  End;
```

Save the project as WebInterbase1.dpr and the unit as Unit1.pas; create a folder named WebInterbase1. Select **Build Project** from the **Project** pull-down menu. Copy WebInterbase1.exe to the cgi-bin folder of the web server. Launch Internet Explorer and enter the following URL into the address bar: `http://localhost/cgi-bin/WebInterbase1.exe`. The browser window should look like Fig. 6.3.14.

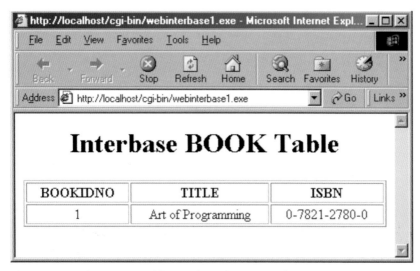

Fig. 6.3.14 *Web page returned from WebInterbase1.exe web server extension*

PHP

Here is a PHP script that connects to database A2Book and selects data from a table Topics within this database. The results of applying this query are returned to the web browser using the command echo.

```
<?php
  // Five steps to PHP database connections:
  // 1. Create a database connection
  // $connection allows the connection to be referenced after
```

```
//                                          it is established
$connection = mysql_connect("localhost","KRB","mypassword");
if (!$connection)
  {
    die("Database connection failed: " . mysql_error());
  }
// 2. Select a database to use
$db_select = mysql_select_db("A2Book",$connection);
if (!$db_select)
  {
    die("Database selection failed: " . mysql_error());
  }
?>
<html>
  <head>
    <title>Databases</title>
  </head>
  <body>
    <?php
      // 3. Perform database query
      $result = mysql_query("SELECT * FROM Topics", $connection);
      if (!$result)
        {
          die("Database query failed: " . mysql_error());
        }
      // 4. Use returned data
      while ($row = mysql_fetch_array($result))
        {
          echo $row["menu_name"]." ".$row["position"]."<br />";
        }
    ?>
  </body>
</html>
<?php
  // 5. Close connection
  mysql_close($connection);
?>
```

In this topic you have covered:

- the Common Gateway Interface (CGI) is the interface between a web server and a web server extension

- the Request object and the Response object are used to communicate data to and from the web server extensions

- the Get and Post HTTP methods are used for sending data from a web browser to a web server

- sending data as a query string and in the message body

- name–value pairs

- server-side scripting in PHP, VBScript, Perl and Delphi

- using web server extensions to access data from a DBMS using server-side scripts written in VBScript, PHP and Delphi.

Questions

11 Draw a diagram that shows how a web browser can retrieve data from a remote database.

12 Name the five steps that are followed when using a DBMS with server-side scripting.

13 Name three languages that support server-side scripts that can connect to a DBMS located on a web server.

6.4 Internet security

Key terms

Virus: a small program attached to another program or data file. It replicates itself by attaching itself to other programs. It usually attacks the computer.

Spam: unsolicited junk e-mails.

Worm: a small program that exploits a network security weakness (security hole) to replicate itself through computer networks. It may attack computers.

Remote login: when someone connects to a computer via the Internet.

Trojan: a program that hides in or masquerades as desirable software, such as a utility or a game, but attacks computers it infects.

Phishing: when someone tries to get you to give them your personal information.

Pharming: when a phisher changes DNS server information so that customers are directed to another site.

Types of security issues

Before the use of the Internet was widespread, the main threat to computer systems came from **viruses** spread by floppy disks used to move files between different computer systems. A virus program will execute when the program it is attached to is running, or the document it is attached to is opened. A virus program can attach itself to, or infect, other programs or data files. When any infected file is opened, the virus program executes. Virus programs also attack computers, usually triggered by some other event or special data, such as a specific date. They can create havoc on infected computers; they may give unwanted messages or destroy data files or erase the whole hard disk.

Connecting an unprotected computer to the Internet is like leaving the front door of your home wide open. You are giving people with malicious intent easy access. Viruses may be attached to downloaded software or e-mail messages. An e-mail virus may replicate itself by mailing itself to the e-mail addresses in the host computer's e-mail contacts list.

Someone can send unwanted e-mails, known as **spam**, to thousands of e-mail addresses by redirecting the e-mail messages through the SMTP server of an unsuspecting host; this is called SMTP session hijacking. It makes the real originator of the e-mails difficult to trace. A **worm** is a malicious computer program that replicates itself through networks. It uses up computer time and drastically increases network traffic. It may also attack the computers and servers of the networks it moves through. While an unprotected computer is connected to the Internet, someone could connect to it through **remote login** and then remotely access files, execute programs, or even control the computer remotely.

In Greek mythology, Odysseus presented a huge wooden horse as a gift to the city of Troy. Once the horse was inside the city walls, the Greek warriors hidden inside emerged and slaughtered the inhabitants of Troy. Named after this myth, a **Trojan** is a malicious payload in a desirable program such as a game or that masquerades as a desirable program. When the desirable program is installed, the Trojan can cause huge damage to a computer's software or data files. Trojans are also distributed through e-mail attachments.

In **phishing** scams, the attacker e-mails customers of a business pretending it is a legitimate enquiry, but then stores the gathered data to commit fraud or even identity theft. This is also known as social engineering. Many e-mail programs allow the 'From' or 'Reply to' fields to be set to any address; this aids the phishing scam as the spoof e-mail is easily set up to appear to come from a legitimate source. For example, it may appear that your bank has e-mailed and asked you to confirm your account details and PIN. Another method is to provide a URL in the e-mail which may look legitimate but directs the victim to the phisher's website. Instead of e-mailing a spoof URL, the phisher may use Trojans containing keyloggers or screen-capture programs.

A malicious attacker can change DNS server information that will direct customers to another site rather than the site they intend to access. This is known as **pharming**. Spyware is a computer program that tracks and records a user's actions, such as which websites are visited, which a phisher may find useful. Spyware is also known to redirect a user's browser to unwanted websites or change computer settings.

How can users protect their computer systems from these attacks? The best line of defence is to run a secure operating system that protects applications from attack. Programmers with malicious intentions exploit software defects. When software producers become aware of a security hole, they produce patches or service packs (programs) to fix the problem. Some programming languages are more prone to coding defects than others. For example, C and C++ are known to be vulnerable to coding defects, whereas Java is more likely to produce robust code. Firewalls, virus detection software and spyware scanners play an important role in protecting low-security operating systems.

Questions

1 Research how some of the famous viruses were distributed and what their attack consisted of. What damage did they do and how many computers were affected?

2 Research the precautions recommended by e-commerce organisations such as banks to help you avoid becoming a victim of phishing or virus attacks.

3 Why do some systems require passwords to be a mixture of upper and lower case letters, digits and other symbols?

Did you know?

UNIX is a secure operating system with security features that don't allow viruses to get to your hard disk.

Firewalls

A firewall can be a hardware device or a program that controls traffic between the Internet and a private network (such as a school network) or computer system (such as a home computer). Firewalls can be customised and rules can be set up that control which data packets should be allowed through and which should not be allowed through. Traffic can be blocked from specific IP addresses, domain names or port numbers. Firewalls can also be set up to search data packets for exact matches of text. Two important methods are packet filtering and proxy server.

Packet filtering

In packet filtering, the firewall analyses the packets that are sent against a set of filters (firewall rules). Packets are either allowed through or blocked.

Proxy server

Using a proxy server, when a user of a private network requests information from the Internet, the proxy server retrieves the information and then passes it on to the requesting computer. This means the computer that hosts the information (web page) does not come into direct contact with the user's computer, only the proxy server.

Encryption

Encryption has been used for over 2000 years by governments and the military. Now that the Internet has become a popular way to communicate and do business, issues of data confidentiality affect many more people. The main uses of **encryption** are to store information securely and to transmit messages so that only the sender and the legitimate recipient can read them.

Encryption is the process of using an encryption algorithm and an encryption key to convert message data into a form that is not understandable without the key to decrypt the text. A message before encryption is called **plain text**. When the message is encrypted, it is called **cipher text**. To convert cipher text back into plain text, **decryption** is used. Decryption is the process of using a decryption algorithm and a decryption key to convert cipher text into the original message data. **Cryptography** is the science of designing cipher systems. **Cryptanalysis** is the act of trying to find the plain text from the cipher text without the decryption key. The aim of cryptanalysis is to **break the code** – to arrive at the original message by guessing or deducing the key.

Symmetric encryption

Encryption is symmetric if the cipher text can be decrypted by knowing the encryption algorithm and the encryption key. Here are some simple examples.

Worked example

Substitution cipher

Each letter of the alphabet is substituted with a different letter. Shift the alphabet right four places.

A	B	C	D	E	F	G	H	I	J	K	L	M	N	O	P	Q	R	S	T	U	V	W	X	Y	Z
W	X	Y	Z	A	B	C	D	E	F	G	H	I	J	K	L	M	N	O	P	Q	R	S	T	U	V

Decrypt the message OAYNAP.

Answer: SECRET.

Worked example

Substitution cipher

Each letter of the alphabet is substituted with a different letter. Each letter has its own key).

A	B	C	D	E	F	G	H	I	J	K	L	M	N	O	P	Q	R	S	T	U	V	W	X	Y	Z
R	G	I	E	J	L	C	M	O	A	P	S	B	T	U	H	V	D	W	F	X	K	Y	N	Z	Q

Decrypt the message JRWZ.

Answer: EASY.

These ciphers are easy to break if the language they are written in is known and relative frequencies of letters in that language's text are analysed. If some words of the text are known, this aids the breaking of the cipher. For example, during the Second World War, intercepted radio messages transmitted at the same time each day contained the word *Wetterbericht* 'weather report' at the beginning of a message.

Later in the war, the Germans developed a more elaborate substitution cipher where the substitutions changed during the message. This was

Key terms

Encryption: using an algorithm and a key to convert message data into a form that is not understandable without the key to decrypt the text.

Plain text: message data before it is encrypted.

Cipher text: message data after it has been encrypted.

Decryption: using an algorithm and a key to convert encrypted message data into its plain text equivalent.

Cryptography: the science of designing cipher systems.

Cryptanalysis: trying to find the plain text from the cipher text without the decryption key.

Break the code: find the plain text from the cipher text by guessing or deducing the key.

achieved using the Enigma machine. The code breakers at Bletchley Park were successful because they knew the way the machine was built and had other detailed knowledge. By using Colossus, the world's first digital computer, the code breakers eliminated possible keys until they found keys that produced messages which made sense. The Germans changed the key settings every day, so this was a daily challenge for the code breakers at Bletchley Park.

Worked example

Transposition cipher

The plain text is written into a grid, row by row. Any remaining spaces are filled with Z. The cipher text is produced by reading the table contents column by column. The key is the number of columns used. Here the key is 5. The message COMPUTING IS GREAT FUN becomes CTSTOIGFMNRUPGENUIAZ.

C	O	M	P	U
T	I	N	G	I
S	G	R	E	A
T	F	U	N	Z

Decrypt the message YAOOVTUEIHGT using the key 4.

Y	O	U	H
A	V	E	G
O	T	I	T

Answer: YOU HAVE GOT IT.

The problem with symmetric keys is that they are difficult to distribute to the other party without the possibility of the key being intercepted. Anyone who obtains the key can decrypt the intercepted message.

Asymmetric encryption

In asymmetric encryption, or public key encryption, both parties who want to communicate securely have a pair of keys, a private key and a public key. The private key is kept secret and the public key is freely available to anyone. The encryption algorithm is also publicly available. A message encrypted with a private key can only be decrypted with the corresponding public key. Conversely, a message encrypted with a public key can only be decrypted with the corresponding private key.

If A encrypts a message with A's private key, then B (and anyone else who intercepts the message) can decrypt the message with A's public key (Fig.6.4.1).

If A encrypts a message with A's public key, only A can decrypt the message with A's private key.

If A encrypts a message with B's public key, only B can decrypt the message with B's private key.

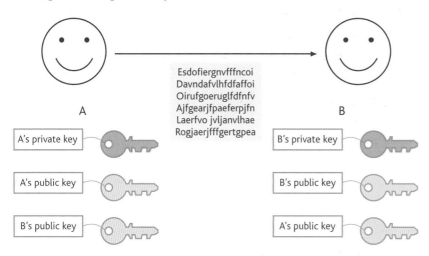

Fig. 6.4.1 *A and B each have one private key and two public keys*

The best-known public key system is RSA, invented by Ron Rivest, Adi Shamir and Len Adleman in 1978. Software is used to generate large prime numbers, p and q. These primes are secret. They are used to calculate the private key. The number N is the product of p and q. N is used as the public key. The idea is that for a sufficiently large number N, it is not possible to determine p and q because it would take too long to calculate the factorisation of N.

Asymmetric encryption involves complicated calculations, so encryption and decryption are slow. Secure web browsing and e-commerce use a protocol known as Secure Sockets Layer (SSL). The website accessed by the browser will send its public key to the browser. The browser creates a symmetric key (known as a session key) that it sends to the website encrypted by the website's public key. So only the website can decrypt the symmetric key. This symmetric key is then used for the rest of the session.

How can the browser be sure the website's public key is authentic? The website sends its public key certificate (see below) once the secure session has started. This is to avoid 'man in the middle' attacks, where E intercepts the communication between A and B and impersonates B to A and A to B.

Digital signatures and digital certificates

To prove that a message is genuine, sender A can digitally sign the message. This makes it possible to detect whether the message has been tampered with, and the signature is proof that it has been sent by A.

A hash, also known as a digest, is produced from the message. This digest is encrypted using A's private key. Recipient B can decrypt the digest by using A's public key. This proves that the message really came from A, because only A has access to A's private key. Then B produces the

> **Did you know?**
>
> In a browser, the web address of a page protected by SSL begins with `https` instead of `http` and the browser window usually displays a padlock icon.

digest from the received message. If the digest produced by B matches the decrypted digest, then the message has not been tampered with.

Here are the processes required before A's message is sent to B (Fig. 6.4.2):

▨ The message is hashed to produce a message digest.

▨ The message digest is encrypted with A's private key; this becomes the signature.

▨ The signature is appended to the message.

▨ The message is encrypted using B's public key.

▨ The encrypted message is sent to B.

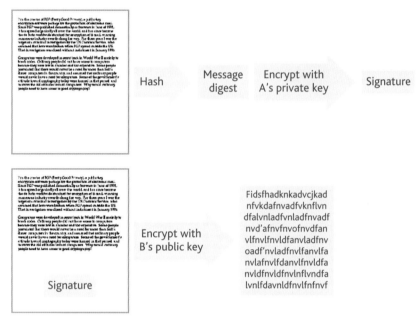

Fig. 6.4.2 *A hashes the message to produce a message digest then encrypts it into a signature*

Here are the processes required to ensure that the message received by B is genuinely from A (Fig. 6.4.3):

▨ B decrypts the message with B's private key.

▨ B decrypts the signature with A's public key to retrieve the original message digest.

▨ The decrypted message is hashed again to reproduce the message digest.

▨ If the decrypted digest equals the reproduced digest, the message has not been tampered with.

Key authentication is vital. How can the recipient be sure that the public key of the sender is genuine? Certification authorities (CAs) can issue a digital certificate, which is encrypted using the CA's private key. If the recipient has access to the CA's public key, the digital certificate can be decrypted and the public key of the sender can be accessed.

For example, when using SSL the browser receives the website's certificate and decrypts it using the CA's public key. The decrypted certificate contains the website's public key, which can now be used by the browser to encrypt the symmetric session key before sending it to the website.

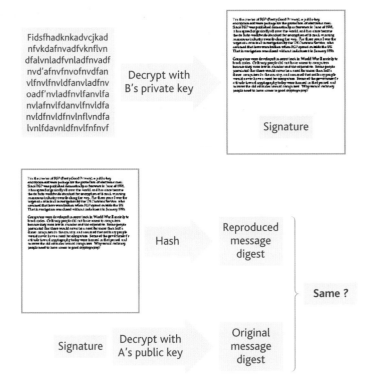

Fig. 6.4.3 *B checks the digest from the decrypted signature against the reproduced digest to see whether anyone has tampered with the message*

■ Virus detection

Virus detection software, often called an antivirus scanner, checks files against a dictionary of known viruses. A newly created virus can appear at any time and will remain undetected by the antivirus scanner until it has been added to the dictionary. Computer users must be vigilant and must regularly update the dictionary on their system so that files are checked against all known viruses. If an infected file is found, the antivirus scanner will try to delete the virus from the file. If this fails, the infected file will be quarantined – kept in a separate area of the hard disk where it can't infect other files. The only way to clean up the system may be to delete the infected file.

■ Computer security procedures

Authentication

To verify that a user of a computer system is a legitimate user, it is possible to use passwords, biometric data, security tokens or digital certificates. For example, phishing attacks are possible if the recipient of an e-mail is not aware that the sender is not who they say they are. To authenticate the identity of the sender, the e-mail must be digitally signed. The digital signature must be authenticated through a digital certificate issued by a trusted third party such as a certification authority.

Authorisation

Authorised users of a computer system are given a user ID and a password. Users may be authorised to use certain resources. This is usually done by the system administrator granting permissions to users or groups of users. Passwords and encryption are used to keep data secret from unauthorised persons.

Accounting

It is vital to detect any security breach as soon as possible and to identify any parts that may have been compromised. That is why systems generate activity logs to create audit trails. In the case of Internet access, a system may log every IP address to show what websites have been visited.

☑ *In this topic you have covered:*

- the types of security issues that may affect Internet users
- how firewalls are used to keep systems secure
- symmetric encryption and asymmetric encryption
- how digital signatures and digital certificates are created and used
- virus detection
- authorisation, authentication and accounting for computer security.

Introduction

This section is designed to help you produce a Computing project that lets you demonstrate your understanding of the different areas of computing.

Choosing the right topic can be a difficult decision. Accept the help of your teacher, who has probably seen the development of many projects, good and bad, and knows the pitfalls and what your strengths and weaknesses are. Discuss your ideas with as many people as possible. Hopefully, during your year of studying AS Computing, you have come across some problem for which you would like to produce a computer solution. If not, where do you start? Maybe a member of your family has a need for a computerised solution to a problem; maybe a hobby or a 'Saturday' job provide an initial idea. There are endless possibilities, but as a starting point you might consider:

- a data-processing problem of an organisation, such as your school or a small business
- a scientific or mathematical problem such as plotting fractals
- a simulation of a real-life situation, such as modelling queues at the school cafeteria checkouts
- a computer-aided learning system, such as teaching young children simple arithmetic skills
- a control system such as a getting a robot buggy to find its way around a room.

A good project has a real end user. However much you think you can imagine what a user might want, there is no substitute for investigating a real problem and taking into account the realistic needs of a user. Remember you are trying to demonstrate your problem-solving and programming skills that you have been practising during the AS year. Your teacher should be able to advise you in deciding on a project topic that is neither too simple nor too complex. You should aim at developing a complete working solution to the problem you have chosen. Be realistic, you will not be able to produce a stock control system for a national supermarket chain. However, cataloguing your music collection might be too simple a task, as it could be completed in a weekend.

The skills you need to demonstrate include analysing the problem, designing and implementing a solution, as well as thoroughly testing that your solution is robust, and evaluating your solution to check how well it solves the original problem. You should work through each stage of the system life cycle so that at the end of each stage the outcome should be detailed enough so someone else could continue with the project and produce the intended solution.

The work must be your own work, but you can ask friends or your teacher to check that your analysis is thorough enough to give all the information required to produce a design, and that your designs are detailed enough to produce the solution your user is expecting. You should also involve your end user and ask for their feedback to ensure you are producing what they asked for.

You may find that you do not have all the programming skills you need to produce your planned solution. There are many good resources online to help you develop your expertise. You can join discussion forums where you can ask questions or explore specific techniques, such as writing your own classes for graphic tools.

Remember to keep a notebook or diary where you can jot down your ideas, questions, designs and solutions you found. It is very important that you note down straight away where you found information. If the source was on the Internet, copy the URL into a page that can become your bibliographic appendix. When you come to write up your technical documentation and bibliography you will be very pleased that you kept a record during all those months of planning and development work.

7.1 Analysis

▦ Feasibility study

Fig. 7.1.1 *Humber Bridge*

The Humber Bridge near Kingston upon Hull in England is the fifth-largest single-span suspension bridge in the world. It spans the River Humber and connects the East Riding of Yorkshire to North Lincolnshire. The road distance between Hull and Grimsby was reduced by nearly 50 miles (80 km) as a consequence of the bridge. The building of this bridge solved a clearly identified problem. A problem presented daily to all the commuters between Hull and Grimsby. The builders of the bridge delivered a product to a specification. The bridge's consulting engineers, Freeman Fox & Partners, now Hyder Consulting, started with a set of product requirements obtained from the customer, Kingston upon Hull Corporation, and the Labour government at the time, such as:

▦ The solution must cope with a volume of traffic crossing the river per hour up to ...

▦ The solution must cover a distance across water of ...

▦ The solution must be capable of supporting a total weight of ...

▦ The solution must connect to the existing road network in the area.

The consulting engineers then turned these requirements into a set of specific objectives that the bridge builders, Sir William Arrol & Co., could understand:

▦ The bridge must have dual carriageways in both directions.

▦ The bridge must span the points between grid reference 1 and grid reference 2.

The bridge must be illuminated at night with lighting operating at 300 lumens per square metre.

And so on.

Questions to be answered

This example shows that a series of questions need to be answered before proceeding with any particular solution:

1 What is the current system?
2 What is the problem with the current system?
3 What are the possible solutions?
4 What are the problems with implementing each of the possible solutions?

What is the problem with the current system?

Commuters between Hull and Grimsby have to travel further than they want to, wasting time and fuel.

What are the possible solutions?

- a ferry between the south and north shores, and vice versa
- a hovercraft between the south and north shores
- a bridge between the south and north shores.

All three solutions have existed; the bridge is the surviving solution.

What are the problems with implementing each of the possible solutions?

- **Ferry**: limited capacity, have to wait, slow to embark, disembark and cross, may not be possible to operate in rough seas.
- **Hovercraft**: limited capacity, less than ferry's capacity, have to wait to cross, slow to embark and disembark, faster crossing speed than ferry but slower than a bridge, may not be possible to operate in rough seas.
- **Bridge**: higher capacity than ferry and hovercraft, always there so no waiting, faster crossing speed but expensive to design and build.

This is what may be described as a preliminary investigation or **feasibility study**.

This is a very important phase of project working. It is followed by the analysis phase, but first a decision is made about which of the possible solutions will be analysed. In the case of the Humber river crossing, the project team decided to analyse the bridge.

Questions

1 What was the problem that the Humber Bridge solved?
2 Give three examples of product requirements for the Humber Bridge project.
3 What were the possible solutions for crossing the Humber?
4 Why do you think that the requirements had to be turned into a set of specific objectives for the bridge designers?

Analysis

Analysis is the phase that follows the initial investigation or feasibility study. The objective of analysis is to answer the question, "Exactly what must the system do?" What the system must do has to be decided before considering how the system should do it. In the traditional approach, a systems analyst works with the customer and users to establish what the system that solves the problem must do, e.g. allow 120,000 cars per week to cross the River Humber in both directions. The systems analyst must then communicate what the system must do to the developer. The job of the developer is to work out how to solve the problem and then to solve it, e.g. build a dual carriageway bridge, with a centre span of 1,410 metres and a total length of 2,220 metres, across the River Humber joining the A15 and using a suspension bridge design consisting of two towers.

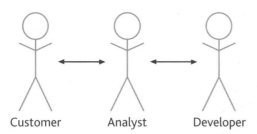

Fig. 7.1.2 *Communication pathways in a project*

The analysis phase involves gathering information about the customer's needs and defining, in the clearest possible terms, the problem that is expected to be solved. This analysis includes understanding the customer's business context and constraints, the functions the product must perform, the performance levels it must adhere to, and the external systems it must be compatible with.

Analysis involves a big commitment of funds in a real-world scenario. The consulting engineers' fee for the Humber Bridge project was £20 million in 1972.

What must the system do?

This is answered in two ways: business or customer requirements that the customer can understand; a requirements specification consisting of a set of specific objectives that the developer can use to develop a solution.

Business requirements

Establishing business or customer requirements is known as requirements analysis. It is the phase of analysis where the customer and users are interviewed to find out what they want, the constraints that the customer will impose, e.g. the project must cost no more than x pounds and must be delivered no later than date y. It is also an information-gathering phase. For example, the Humber Bridge project needed to know the anticipated maximum volume of traffic per unit time on the bridge, and what roads to connect with.

Information may be gathered by interviewing individuals or small groups, by research into the paperwork, past studies, by survey (i.e. questionnaire) and by observation of workflow. In the Humber Bridge project, observations could be traffic flow observations. Also, the opinions of commuters between Hull and Grimsby could be surveyed by questionnaire, and groups of commuters could be interviewed.

The business requirements need to be documented and expressed in language that the customer can understand.

Key point

Fact-finding uses these techniques: interview, examination of paperwork, survey by questionnaire, observation.

Key point

There are several stakeholders: the customers who pay for the solution in a real-world situation, and the people who end up using the system, often called the end users. The end users may include the customers.

Requirements specification

The outcome of analysis must also be a set of general and specific objectives that developers can understand. These objectives need to be documented and expressed concisely and unambiguously and in a language that developers can understand. Developers are technical people and they understand technical language; if the objectives can be misinterpreted, they will be. Unfortunately, any misinterpretation will be costly. The design will fail to meet the customer's requirements and might fail, full stop, which would be a disaster in the case of the Humber Bridge.

Activities

The difficulty of specifying precisely

1. Draw a diagonal line.
2. Draw another diagonal line connected to the top of the first one.
3. Draw a straight line from the point where the diagonal lines meet.
4. Draw a horizontal line over the straight line.
5. At the bottom of the straight line, draw a curvy line.
6. Draw a diagonal line from the bottom of the first diagonal to the straight line.
7. Draw a diagonal line from the bottom of the second diagonal to the straight line.
8. What object have you drawn?

Software development and analysis

Most developers like to follow the 'just do it' creed. The customer has a business need, so the developers immediately move into problem-solving mode and start writing code. There is no more rewarding feeling than completing an application and showing the customer. Until, of course, the customer informs the developers that this is not quite what he or she had in mind.

Developers can sometimes forget that the first phase of any development project is gathering business requirements to understand what the customer wants. It is only when the business needs are agreed on that it is possible to move on to the fun stuff – design and construction.

Software development models

Just as bridge builders need to follow a project pathway from conception to delivery, so do software developers, but which pathway?

Waterfall model

The waterfall model was devised in the early days of software development. It gets its name because once a phase is finished, it cannot be revisited, just as water always flows naturally downhill, never uphill, so the progress through the phases is always one way.

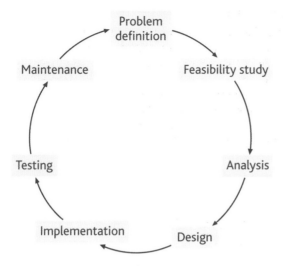

Fig. 7.1.3 *Systems development life cycle: waterfall model*

Here are the phases of the waterfall model:

1 problem definition
2 feasibility study
3 analysis
4 high-level design
5 low-level design
6 implementation and testing
7 maintenance.

Once a phase is complete, it is not revisited. In the waterfall model, mistakes in analysis or design discovered during analysis or early in design can be rectified at a fraction of the cost of fixing analysis or design errors discovered during implementation. Implementation is the phase when the product is built and installed.

Unfortunately, this model has several other shortcomings caused by its forward-working nature:

▓ Customers have only a vague idea of what they need. It is up to the analyst to ask the right questions and to turn the answers into a formally documented software requirements specification that can be used for a project plan and to inform design. Failure to ask the right questions or to interpret the customer's answers correctly will lead to an incomplete analysis.

▓ The requirements defined in analysis may change as the project progresses. This may occur because, as development progresses, customers are able to see problems with the original plan more clearly and may require changes. Changes to requirements may also be needed because the business changes during the lifetime of the project, so the original problem may change.

▓ The communication path between the customer and the developers is very long, i.e. indirect, because developers talk to analysts, who talk to customers.

▓ No analyst in the world can express the requirements that they know about 100% completely and correctly through writing.

▓ Customers express themselves in everyday English, whereas developers use technical language. A gulf can develop, which may lead to imperfect communication.

Spiral model

In the spiral model, water is allowed to 'flow uphill', i.e. the analysis, design and implementation phases can be revisited. The model works like this:

1 Perform preliminary problem definition and analysis.
2 Design and develop a basic solution or specific aspects; the specific aspects could be a set of user interfaces.
3 Show the basic solution to the customer, obtain feedback and refine the problem definition and analysis.

Steps 1, 2 and 3 are repeated (iterated) until a clear set of specific objectives can be generated for a solution. This model tends to overcome several of the problems with the waterfall model, but it does not fully address the problem of changing requirements.

Agile development model

Agile methods rely on face-to-face communication rather than written documents. Most agile teams are located in a single open office to facilitate such communication. The agile development approach is to use small teams. Instead of creating large functional requirements documents, an agile project begins by having the end users or customers of the software create user stories describing what the new applications need to do.

Most agile development methods minimise risk by developing software in short amounts of time. Software developed during one unit of time is called an iteration; an iteration typically takes 2–4 weeks. Each iteration passes through a full software development cycle, including requirements analysis, planning, design, writing unit tests, then coding until the unit tests pass and a working product is finally demonstrated to customers.

The goal of agile development is to have a working product, without bugs, for the customer to evaluate after each iteration. This addresses several of the problems associated with the waterfall model. The claim is that the agile development model leads to a development process that is more responsive to customer needs – more agile – than traditional methods, while creating software of better quality. However, it requires a team of people and it tends not to produce much of the documentation needed for maintenance.

A Level project

The A Level project provides an opportunity to test your understanding of the connections between the different areas of computing. It allows you to demonstrate your knowledge and understanding of the systems development life cycle. The skills to be demonstrated include analysis, design, construction and implementation, testing and evaluation of a substantial computer-based task undertaken over an extended period. The report should summarise the work carried out by you.

The project topic could involve a computer solution to:

- a data-processing problem of an organisation
- a scientific or mathematical problem
- a simulation of a real-life situation
- a computer-aided learning system
- a control system or robotics.

Systems development life cycle

Different models for developing software systems have been described: waterfall model, spiral model, agile development model. These models fit into the systems development life cycle. It runs from the problem identification stage through analysis, design, implementation and maintenance stages until, after a period in service, the solution itself becomes a problem that needs a solution. Software is just one aspect of a solution. Software needs hardware on which to run. People are required to operate it, configure it, install updates, and so on. Therefore, people are needed to work with the solution.

These people will need to use documentation produced for the solution. The solution will output paper reports. The solution may need to scan in data from paper forms, etc. A solution is more than just software, it is a system. A **system** is a collection of people, machines, methods, software, reports, input paper forms and documents organised to accomplish a set of specific functions. Thus the life cycle of a solution is more appropriately described as the systems development life cycle, or simply the systems life cycle (Fig. 7.1.3).

The most appropriate model to use for your A Level project is a combination of the waterfall model and the spiral model. This is appropriate because you are not yet a professional software developer and you will be working on your own. In this approach, you will gather preliminary requirements that you will use to build an initial version of the solution – a prototype. You show this to the customer or end user, who then gives you additional requirements. You change the application and go round the cycle again with the customer. This process continues for the an agreed number of iterations until you are able to specify precisely what the customer requires.

Prototyping

To ensure that a design is what the customer wants, the customer must see an early implementation of the proposed system. This early version is a **prototype**. For example, you can test the usability of the user interface very early in the design process and take account of the customer's evaluation. To ensure that the functional requirements of the system are covered, a prototype is shown to the customer to discover if analysis omitted any requirements or did not specify them with sufficient clarity.

Showing the prototype to the customer can help them clarify what they want the system to do. Often a customer is unable to give a complete specification of everything they want until they see a prototype of the proposed system. Until they see a prototype, the customer may have a limited perception of what a computerised solution can do. The developer can use the prototype to improve their understanding of what is required. The developer uses **prototyping** to see if a particular design is feasible or to discover a method of solving a problem.

What must my project do?

The problem that you choose to solve must lead to a computer-based solution in which the system that has been produced collects an input, processes this input then generates some output every time it is used. The project cannot, for example, consist solely of using a word processor to produce some report.

Key terms

System: a collection of people, machines, methods, software, reports, input paper forms and documents organised to accomplish a set of specific functions.

Prototype: an early or trial working version of the proposed system developed to test possible solutions.

Prototyping: building a working model, demonstration system, simplified version, rough copy or trial piece of software to help the analyst.

Key point

Prototyping
- Clarify requirements.
- Perform risk analysis.
- Find solutions to a particular problem.
- Check whether a solution can handle the workload.
- Test a solution within the proposed environment.
- Through a process of refinement and in conjunction with users, progress to a final working system; this is called evolutionary, iterative development.
- Discover errors in design.
- Discover problems.

Defining the problem

You should not begin to solve a problem until you have defined the problem you are going to solve. This may seem a rather obvious statement, but a surprising number of unsuccessful projects have begun with a student not having a clear idea of what it is they are tackling. Therefore, every project should begin with a clear statement that specifies the problem to be solved. Here is an example of a problem definition:

Membership database for Princes Risborough Tennis Club

The current system identifies members of the tennis club for whom a subscription renewal is due in the following month. It generates and sends renewal notices specifying the correct category of renewal fee followed by overdue subscription reminders if necessary. The current system is entirely paper-based and operated manually by the club's secretary. This was a manageable task when the membership was low (20 members) and there was only one fee category but now that the membership has grown to over 200 with four different categories of membership subscription, it has become an excessive time burden for the secretary maintaining the paperwork. Further, complaints have been received from some members that they have received a demand for payment which has not been applicable.

This definition is sufficiently clear for your project supervisor to understand the problem that you intend to solve, to assess whether it will satisfy the criteria of the examining board and to assess whether you are likely to succeed.

The problem is not how to produce a comsuter-based subscription system. That is just one possible solution to the problem. The real problem is that the secretary is finding it difficult to keep track of membership subscriptions payments with the current manual system.

Your supervisor will want to know the proposed end user. In the above example, it should be the club secretary. The problem definition should be shown to the end user in order to check that the end user agrees with your understanding of the problem to be solved.

What are you expected to do next?

In the commercial world, after you have defined a problem, the next stage is a low-cost, brief, mini investigation to consider how best to solve the problem before a company or an organisation commits significant funds. This is known as a feasibility study. Its objective is to investigate the potential for a new system. The outcome of this study could be:

- to reject a computer-based solution, perhaps on cost grounds or because no significant benefit would be gained
- to recommend purchasing a special-purpose application package that exists already and was designed to solve a similar problem
- to recommend committing funds to developing a software and hardware solution to the problem.

In your case, your supervisor will have assessed the feasibility of your project and given you feedback. Assuming that you have received approval to develop the project, you may now begin the next stage, analysis.

The project analysis

The objective of analysis is to answer the question: Exactly what must the system do?

The main purpose of analysis is to gather requirements. Requirements are statements that describe what the customer needs and wants. If you are automating a manual process, the requirements describe the way the process should work. If you are building a house, they describe the size, room layout, plot size, room colour, and so on. Requirements may be classified into product requirements and process requirements. Between them, they should identify everything the customer or end user needs.

Product requirements

Product requirements describe the needs in terms of the main deliverables or products that are created. For example, the deliverable product for a computer-controlled lighting system for a school's drama studio would be the application software, the computer, the lighting controllers and the lights. The product requirements would be such things as the number of lights to be controlled, the electrical power that each controller must control, and so on.

Process requirements

Process requirements describe how people interact with a product and how a product interacts with other products. Here are some possible process requirements for the lighting control system:

- The user must be able to set up and save a lighting sequence.
- The system must load a pre-recorded lighting sequence and execute the sequence.
- The system must display a visual representation of the progress through the loaded lighting sequence.

Putting it into practice

A significant percentage of the marks for the project are awarded for an analysis of the customer or end-user requirements. This will include finding out and documenting how the current system works, if there is a current system, and what the inputs and outputs are. Most importantly, it will include finding out what the customer or end user would like the new system to do. Analysis, or systems analysis to give it its full name, must establish the requirements for the new system. The person who does the analysis is known as a systems analyst. This is a highly demanding task and is well paid in the commercial world.

The analyst may use one or more of the following fact-finding methods in performing analysis:

- interviewing staff
- examining existing paperwork, documentation, records and procedure manuals for the current system
- using a questionnaire to survey opinions of staff
- observation of how the current system operates.

Interviewing

Interviewing is useful because facts can be gathered directly from the people who have direct experience of the present system. Full and detailed answers can be obtained by pursuing particular lines of questioning.

Examination of existing paperwork

Examination of the existing paperwork, documentation, records and procedure manuals can be used to identify the data that is used in the current system, the information that is produced by the current system and the procedures that are carried out.

■ **Key point**

What a system must do is not the same as how it does it. For example, a bouncing ball must bounce if it is to live up to its description. How it bounces is not the same thing. For example, a solid rubber ball bounces because of the elastic energy stored in its rubber when the rubber is compressed on contact with the ground. On the other hand, an inflated ball bounces primarily because of the rise in pressure of the air it contains when the ball is compressed on contact with the ground.

Survey

Questionnaires enable the same set of questions to be asked to many people. A carefully designed questionnaire can be a very quick and cheap way to obtain specific answers to specific questions from a large number of people.

Observation

Observation of the current practice enables current methods of working to be examined and necessary exceptions to the normal pattern of working to be noted.

Building models

One or more fact-finding methods are used by the analyst to obtain a full and detailed understanding of the requirements of the proposed system. The analyst will then use this understanding to build models that represent this understanding. These models may then be shown to the customer or end user to check that the analyst has understood the requirements of the end user. For your project, you will find it helpful to use the following modelling techniques.

- Use data flow diagrams to model the processing requirements.
- Use Entity–Relationship (E–R) diagrams to model the data requirements and entity descriptions recorded.
- Use a data dictionary to capture descriptions of the facts, such as the maximum length of surnames.
- Use object analysis diagrams to represent the relationships between objects in the project and to create an abstraction hierarchy.
- Use other forms of data representation such as graphs.

The interview

Before requirements can be specified and models produced, it is necessary to plan for an interview with the end user. You will have made contact with the end user when you drew up the problem definition. Now it is time to arrange a meeting to establish the detailed requirements of the end user. Several meetings may be required. Between each meeting, try to summarise the information you have gathered on the proposed system. Summarise the information and draw data flow diagrams, E–R diagrams, object analysis diagrams and data representations such as graphs. Create a dictionary that contains an entry for every item of data that will feature in the proposed system. Each entry should clearly explain the purpose of the data item, its type and range of permitted values. This is the project's **analysis data dictionary**.

Preparing for an Interview

The key to a successful interview is preparation. Try to prepare questions in advance of an interview so that you can focus on what information is needed. This should avoid the interview being conducted as a vague chat resulting in many questions remaining unanswered.

Here is a checklist of points you may want to cover in an interview:

1 Objectives: what is the proposed system to do?
2 What are the problems with the current way of doing things?
3 What data or information is recorded in the current system? How much data is recorded at present? What data or information is to be recorded in the proposed system? How much data will the proposed

---

Key terms

Analysis data dictionary: a dictionary of the data that an end user will encounter. It should record the data item's name, its purpose, its type, its range of values and examples.

Key point

Analysis should be logical, not connected with anything physical such as magnetic hard drives; physical aspects come under design. Obtain or produce a specification which is agreed with the end user – a shopping list of things that must be done. Collect any algorithms that the business uses, such as algorithms to calculate profit and loss. Produce diagrams of what needs to be done, such as data flow diagrams and object analysis diagrams The analysis data dictionary is filled in by the customer so the customer can understand it.

Key point

Business requirements are statements that describe the needs of the customer. Gathering business requirements is the most important aspect of analysis. After the requirements are gathered, they should be formally approved by the customer.

system record? How frequently will the data need to be updated? Will new records need to be added or old ones deleted? How often? Will the changes come in batches or in ones and twos? How important is the data or information that is recorded?

4 Functions or processes: what processes or functions are performed by the current system? What processes or functions are to be performed by the new system? When should they be done and where? What special algorithms do these processes use, such as calculation of compound interest? Which processes should be executed manually?

5 Inputs: what are the inputs to the current system and what inputs will be required for the proposed system? Ask to see any input documents that are used in the current system.

6 Outputs: what are the outputs from the current system and what outputs will be required from the proposed system? Establish whether hard-copy output is required. How often will outputs be required? Ask to see some output from the current system.

7 Existing hardware and software: what computing resources does the end user possess?

8 Funding: is the end user prepared to purchase software or hardware resources?

9 Security: is security an issue? Should there be limited access to some or all parts of the proposed system?

10 Exceptions: how are exceptions and errors handled in the current system? What errors and exceptions should be reported in the proposed system? How should they be reported? Should anything else be done?

11 Constraints: are there any constraints on hardware, software, data, methods of working, cost, time, and so on?

12 Suggested solutions: does the user have a particular solution in mind? Do you have some suggestions to make to the user?

The purpose of the interview is not design

A word of caution is appropriate. The user's view of how the data should be structured when stored in the proposed system is heavily influenced by:

- the structure of the data in the current system
- the structure of the data that is input into the system
- the structure of the information that is output.

The most appropriate structure for storing the data in the proposed system should not be decided by the end user. This is a matter for the designer of the proposed system. As systems analyst for the project, you must ensure that the end user's requirements on inputs, processing and outputs are established and recorded, but how these requirements are satisfied is not the purpose of analysis. In any interview, good systems analysts should be able to help an end user clarify what information is needed for the design stage. Design will attempt to solve the end user's problem. Many end users will not be aware of what a computer-based system can offer, so it is the job of the analyst to enlighten and guide them.

Summarising the objectives

The objectives, or requirements, of the proposed new system need to be formally identified and stated. Objectives are usually at two levels of detail. Higher-level objectives state the purpose or overall objective of the system. Naturally, they are in broad, general terms and are usually qualitative. Lower-level objectives are somewhat more detailed. They are qualitative and quantitative. The quantitative objectives are measurable and can therefore be used to evaluate the effectiveness of your solution.

Where possible, include qualitative and quantitative objectives. Here is an example of a qualitative objective:

> It should be easy to locate details of a particular member of the tennis club.

Here are some examples of quantitative objectives:

> It should be possible to locate any member's details in under 5 seconds.

> The system must be capable of storing 10 000 carer records.

> The system must ring an alarm if the temperature rises above 30°C.

> The system must print the surname, first initial, address and telephone number with STD code of the selected customer.

State the objectives as clearly as possible. The clearer the objectives, the easier it is for the end user to check that you understand their requirements. It will also be easier to evaluate how closely your final solution satisfies the objectives.

Here are some possible objectives for a proposed new membership subscription system for Princes Risborough Tennis Club.

Overall objectives

To create a system that will automate the process of identifying, notifying and reminding members whose subscriptions are due.

Specific objectives

The specific objectives may be classified into the input requirements, output requirements, processing requirements, data storage requirements and performance requirements. The input, output and processing requirements are often grouped together.

Input, processing and output requirements

1 The system to be created must automatically produce a list of members whose subscriptions are due.

2 The system to be created must automatically print a standard letter (contents specified by the club secretary) with forename, surname, address, membership number, category of membership, subscription and date due inserted into the letter for each member one month in advance of the date when the subscription is due unless the subscription has been paid (mail-merge application). The member's record must store that a letter has been generated and the date it was generated.

3 The system to be created must allow a subscription payment to be recorded. The club secretary is to enter the member's membership number, the date of payment and the amount paid. The system should locate the correct member's record and check the subscription fee due against amount paid then, if correct, record the date of payment and increment the number of years of membership. If incorrect, the system should display an appropriate error message.

4 The system to be created must automatically print one standard letter (contents specified by the club secretary) with the name,

address, subscription, date when it is due and the date of the previous notification for each member whose subscription is overdue by two weeks. The member's record must record that a letter has been generated and the date it was generated.

5   The system to be created must automatically generate one more reminder letter (contents specified by the club secretary) for each member whose subscription is four weeks overdue. The member's record must store that a letter has been generated and the date it was generated.

6   The system to be created must automatically cancel membership for each member whose subscription is eight weeks overdue and print a standard letter (contents specified by the club secretary) of notification of termination of club membership with name, address and dates of the previous three letters inserted. The cancelled member's record should not be deleted.

And so on.

Data requirements

1   The system should record the following information about a member: membership number, surname, forename, address, home telephone number, work telephone number, membership category code, number of years of membership, date of payment of subscription, date next subscription falls due, subscription renewal notice sent, date subscription renewal notice sent, first overdue reminder sent, date first overdue reminder sent, second overdue reminder sent, date second overdue reminder sent, membership cancelled, date membership cancelled.

2   The system should record the following information about membership categories: membership category code, category description, subscription fee.

The following objectives are on **volumetrics**. Developers need volumetric information to take appropriate design decisions:

1   The system should be able to store 200 member records initially and to cater for an expansion of up to 1 000 members.

2   The system should cater for 10 categories of membership initially and to allow expansion up to 20 categories. Table 1 shows the 10 categories to be recorded and their current subscription fees.

> ### ▥ Key terms
>
> **Volumetrics:** measurement or assessment of the volume of data that a system will be required to process and store.

Table 1 *Membership categories and subscription fees for Princes Risborough Tennis Club*

	Membership category code	Subscription fee (£)
(i)	full adult	200
(ii)	weekend adult	100
(iii)	evening only adult	100
(iv)	morning adult	50
(v)	afternoon adult	50
(vi)	full junior	100
(vii)	weekend junior	50
(viii)	evening junior	50
(ix)	novice	30
(x)	trial	10

Key point

A picture is worth a thousand words.

Performance requirements

Here are some examples of performance requirements, the first for the tennis club, the others for different projects:

> It should be possible to locate any member's details in under 5 seconds.

> The graphical output must update smoothly and without flicker when nodes and edges are dragged to new positions on the screen.

> The population growth of bacteria must update smoothly and be without flicker.

Most database projects will easily meet their performance requirements, but it can sometimes be a real challenge for non-database projects to meet a performance requirement. They tend to be projects involving graphics or a calculation that requires a very efficient algorithm so the calculation does not take too long, such as an algorithm for calculating very large prime numbers.

Agreeing the objectives with the end user

It is important that the set of objectives are agreed with the customer or end users. However, it is very easy for you and the end users to overlook something important that should be included. A list is not always the best way of visualising what needs to be done. Analysis must also try to represent pictorially what needs to be done. One way is to use a data flow diagram.

Data flow diagrams

A data flow diagram (DFD) is often a good way of summarising the sources and destinations of data and the processing that takes place. It shows how data is transformed into information as it moves through a system and what data needs to be stored in the system along the way. A data flow diagram is a good way to show the end user what you think the existing system does and what you think the new system should do, and a good way to check that you have included every objective that the user wants the new system to satisfy.

Data flow diagrams can also work in control projects. The data becomes signals that represent events that trigger some process. Fig. 7.1.6 shows the symbols used in data flow diagrams.

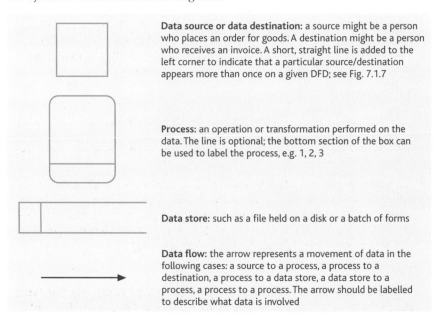

Data source or data destination: a source might be a person who places an order for goods. A destination might be a person who receives an invoice. A short, straight line is added to the left corner to indicate that a particular source/destination appears more than once on a given DFD; see Fig. 7.1.7

Process: an operation or transformation performed on the data. The line is optional; the bottom section of the box can be used to label the process, e.g. 1, 2, 3

Data store: such as a file held on a disk or a batch of forms

Data flow: the arrow represents a movement of data in the following cases: a source to a process, a process to a destination, a process to a data store, a data store to a process, a process to a process. The arrow should be labelled to describe what data is involved

Fig. 7.1.6 *Symbols used in data flow diagrams*

Context diagram

The analyst should start with a context diagram before drawing a full data flow diagram. The context diagram will only use the source/destination and data flow symbols in Fig. 7.1.6 . A blank circle is drawn where the rest of the data flow diagram should appear. This blank circle will enclose the system. The sources and destinations and the data flows to and from the system will appear in the rest of the diagram. The context diagram identifies the system's users and their interactions with the system.

Why draw this very high level diagram?

The reason for drawing a context diagram is that it focuses on the inputs and outputs of the system. It can be used to design the user interface. It should also clarify what is outside the system and therefore not part of the system. It is very easy to think that a printer is outside the system because a printer is physically separate from a computer when, in fact, a printer is part of the system. Therefore, printers cannot be a source or destination. Data flows in this instance should be labelled 'printed . . . report'.

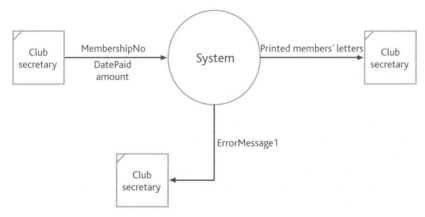

Fig. 7.1.7 *Context diagram*

Fig. 7.1.7 is a simplified context diagram. It shows one input and two outputs. The diagram has one source and two destinations; all of them are Club Secretary. The data flows are labelled. In order for this context diagram to be useful to a designer, the data flows must be defined, so the diagram must be accompanied by a data dictionary. The data flow labelled ErrorMessage1 should have the entry given in Table 2.

Table 2 *Analysis data dictionary*

Name	Alias	Description	Data Type	Size or range
ErrorMessage1	An error message	No such member	String	14 characters

The context diagram plus its analysis data dictionary should contain enough information for a user interface designer to work with this information to produce a user interface that could be shown to the end user. The analysis data dictionary is the place to write any descriptions or definitions of terms that the customer has specified.

Level 1 DFD

The next stage is to add the high-level processes, data stores and data flows inside the system (Fig. 7.1.8). The blank circle is replaced by a high-level

> **Key point**
>
> An analysis data dictionary captures the facts discovered during analysis.

representation of the proposed system. To be useful, this data flow diagram must be backed up with a data dictionary that contains the details of all the input and output messages. A description of each process, data flow and data store may also be included if it is not self-evident.

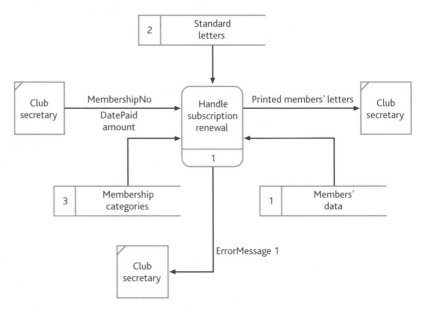

Fig. 7.1.8 *Level 1 DFD*

Level 2 DFD

Finally, a level 2 DFD is drawn. Fig. 7.1.9 shows a sample. It is necessarily detailed and is probably the most useful DFD for the designer. You are not required to put a level 2 DFD in your project write-up. However, it is useful to draw one before you begin to design. It will help you to clarify precisely what needs to be done in a way that a level 1 DFD will not.

Business algorithms

Sometimes a project will need to use algorithms supplied by the end user. These are algorithms used by the existing system or would be used if a system existed. An example from another scenario is an algorithm for calculating interest on an investment. Suppose a customer invests £100, how much interest would be earned in the first year of the investment and in subsequent years? Here is an algorithm to calculate it:

```
APR := 0.05;
Year := 0;
Repeat
   Year := Year + 1;
   Interest := SumInvested * APR;
   SumInvested := SumInvested + Interest;
Until Year = NoOfYearsRequested;
```

Data modelling involves representing the data and relationships between the data. In some scenarios, the relevant model is an entity data model consisting of E–R diagrams and entity descriptions; see Topic 5.1 on conceptual data modelling.

E–R diagram

Before drawing the data flow diagrams, you may wish to identify the entities in the system – the things for which your project will store data.

Next you need to identify, or spot, the relationships between the entities: one-to-one, one-to-many, many-to-many. Finally, you need to draw a diagram that shows the entities and the relationships between them, the E–R diagram.

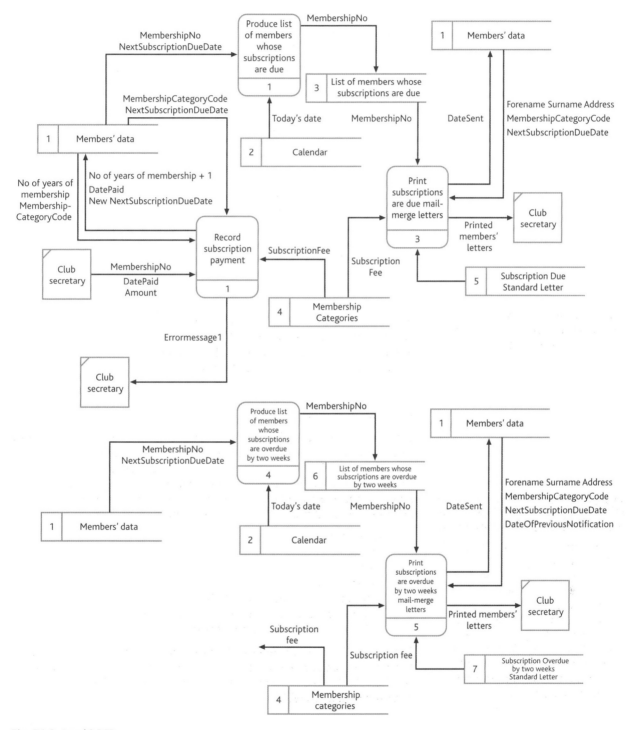

Fig. 7.1.9 *Level 2 DFD*

Fig. 7.1.10 *E–R diagram*

Questions

1. State the stages of the waterfall model for the systems life cycle.

2. What documents could you ask to look at?

3. What fact-finding techniques could be used when analysing this problem? Explain why each technique is used.

4. What is prototyping? State three reasons why prototyping is used.

5. What are the limitations of the waterfall model?

6. How does the spiral model differ from the waterfall model?

7. Why is the spiral model a more appropriate model for you to use in your A Level project?

8. What is volumetrics? Why is analysis concerned with volumetrics?

9. Why are data flow diagrams used? State the three kinds of data flow diagram that are used.

10. What is meant by a business algorithm? Give one example.

Entity description

Each entity must be described, where 'described' has a specific meaning. In this context it means writing the entity name followed by its attributes enclosed in brackets. The entity identifier must be clearly indicated by an underline. Here is the description for the entities in this project:

> **Member**(MembershipNo, Surname, Forename, Address, HomeTelephoneNumber, WorkTelephoneNumber, MembershipCategoryCode, NumberOfYearsOfMembership, DateOfPaymentOfSubscription, NextSubscriptionDueDate, SubscriptionRenewalNoticeSent, DateSubscriptionRenewalNoticeSent, FirstOverdueReminderSent, DateFirstOverdueReminderSent, SecondOverdueReminderSent, DateSecondOverdueReminderSent, MembershipCancelled, DateMembershipCancelled)

> **MembershipCategory**(MembershipCategoryCode, CategoryDescription, SubscriptionFee)

The data requirements section of the analysis was used to construct the entity descriptions.

Princes Risborough Tennis Club's membership database system is one type of problem that could be solved at A Level. However, there are many more problems to solve that do not involve databases. Simulations and search problems are other possible areas for A Level projects. In simulations, it is very important to separate the modelling from the graphical output. Imagine a biological simulation that models the response of bacteria when attacked by white blood cells and antibiotics. There are two major aspects to consider:

- the mathematical model for the interaction between the bacteria, white blood cells and antibiotics

- the graphical output which presents the outcome over time of the mix of bacteria, white blood cells and antibiotics.

In this scenario, an object-oriented solution is advisable, therefore analysis should include an object analysis of the scenario (page 280).

Object analysis

Object analysis has three stages:

1 Determine the objects in the problem domain, the nouns.

2 Determine the relationships between the objects: **association**, **aggregation** and **inheritance** diagrams.

3 Determine the **attributes** and the **behaviours** of each object.

For more about object-oriented theory and practice, see Section 2.1 on programming paradigms.

Fig. 7.1.11 shows how an electronic book would be represented in an object analysis diagram. The diagram is shorthand for 'a book with a specific bookID has one or more pages with each page identified by a pageRef'. In an object-oriented programming approach, the design would be programmed in a particular way based on this diagram.

Fig. 7.1.11 *Composition or aggregation class diagram*

Fig. 7.1.12 shows an inheritance diagram for types of bank account. The diagram is shorthand for 'an ordinary account is a kind of bank account' and 'a gold account is a kind of bank account'. GoldAccount differs from OrdinaryAccount in the rate of interest offered but both share features abstracted to BankAccount.

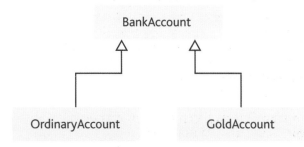

Fig. 7.1.12 *Inheritance class diagram*

Fig. 7.1.13 shows a third kind of relationship, association. If a relationship isn't aggregation – 'has a' or 'is composed of' – and it isn't inheritance – 'is a kind of' – then the relationship is association. Let's put this to the test. Teacher is not a kind of Course and Teacher is not composed of Course, so 'a teacher teaches a course' is association. Fig. 7.1.13 also shows that a class has a name, attributes and operations. The second row of each class rectangle is for attributes, the third row for operations. Omitting the detail for these is optional. Fig. 7.1.14 shows the detail of these two rows for the Teacher class.

Fig. 7.1.13 can be read as follows:

- A teacher teaches one or more courses.
- One or more courses are studied by zero or more students and a student studies one or more courses.
- A course is composed of one or more lessons, zero or more tutorials and one or more assessments.
- Coursework is a kind of assessment and an exam is a kind of assessment.

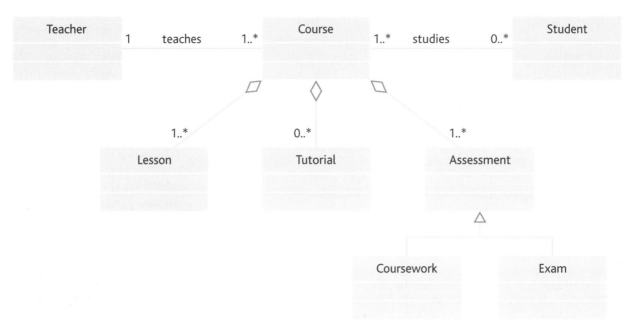

Fig. 7.1.13 *A class diagram that shows aggregation and inheritance, and association*

Fig. 7.1.14 shows the definition of a class from Fig. 7.1.13 appropriate for analysis. The Teacher class has attributes Surname, Title and Subject. This class has operations AddSurname, EditSurname, and so on.

Teacher
Surname
Title
Subject
AddSurname
EditSurname
AddTitle
EditTitle
AddSubject
EditSubject

Fig. 7.1.14 *Class definitions of attributes and operations*

Other abstractions

Analysis may throw up scenarios that require a transformation into a well-known representation. Consider the following scenario. A mobile phone company has to site five mobile phone masts in Aylesbury so that mobile phone users have continuous coverage. In mobile systems, each mobile mast has a short range and frequencies have to be reused

The problem is to allocate mobile phone frequencies so that reuse of frequencies does not cause interference. The company wants to know the minimum number of frequencies it must buy. How could you represent the information in Fig. 7.1.15 to make it easier to understand?

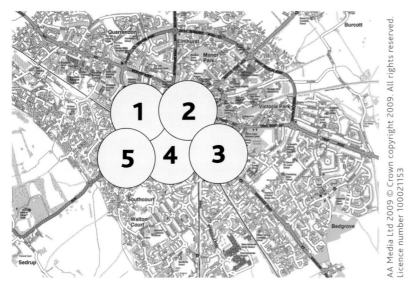

Fig. 7.1.15 *Situation and range of mobile phone masts 1, 2, 3, 4, 5*

The solution is to use a graph like Fig. 7.1.16. This is an abstraction of the scenario that is much easier to understand and design with when automating the solution. The connections between the nodes represent potential for interference: mast 1 could interfere with the transmissions from masts 2, 4 and 5. So masts 2, 4 and 5 must not use the same frequency as mast 1. This is a version of a map-colouring problem that goes back to 1852. The problem was to colour a map so that no two countries that share a boundary use the same colour.

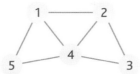

Fig. 7.1.16 *A graph that represents the mobile phone mast locations and the overlap of frequencies*

Constraints

The solution to be developed will be subject to hardware, software and time constraints and must be tailored to the IT ability of the prospective users. The developed system must also consider constraints imposed by the need to provide a particular level of security. We may specify the following constraints for the membership database system at Princes Risborough Tennis Club.

Software

The club secretary already has MS Access 2007 and is keen to see it used for this project because he has some experience with it already. However,

AQA Examiner's tip

You are more or less limited to the hardware that your end user has, as this is a significant cost factor. However, you may demonstrate a solution on your school's hardware if there is no alternative, provided the project objectives are realistic and the end user has the potential to use your solution.

Do not commit yourself to a particular software approach at this stage, unless the end user insists. The choice of software should be a design issue, but an end user's resources and requests must be taken into account.

he is prepared to accept a well-reasoned case for an alternative approach that requires no additional expenditure.

Hardware

In order to run Access 2007 and to be able to perform a mail merge using Word, a Pentium 4 PC with a minimum of 500 MB of RAM is required. A fast processor such as a 3.2 GHz Pentium 4 is needed if the system is not to appear slow. The user has a Pentium P4 with 1 GB of RAM, which will be perfectly suitable, and similar machines are available for development work at the school.

Users

Access to the system is to be restricted to the club secretary, Mr Smith.

Time

The project should be completed and fully documented by April 15th 2011.

User's IT skills

Mr Smith, the club secretary, is familiar with Microsoft Word and has good keyboard skills, so he should have no problem entering data and learning how to use the system. Mr Smith is keen to learn how to use Access 2007.

Limitations

The system to be developed is to focus solely on dealing with subscription renewals. It will not include keeping the accounts of the tennis club or any other aspect of running the club. However, the design of the subscription renewals system must allow it to incorporate accounting in the future.

Research possible methods of solution

With requirements analysis done, documentation now exists that specifies in detail what the customer requires, what processing must be done and a model of the data that can be used by design. The analysts must now consider in outline how the requirements may be met. The analysts may already have been involved with the customer in roughing out user interface designs, drafting report layouts, and so on, as a prototyping exercise to clarify user requirements. This involvement should become a part of the appraisal of the feasibility of potential solutions.

You may be considering a solution based on a set of files, a database or database management system, or a particular algorithm that you have identified from reference sources. Your project may involve graphics or animations, so you will need to select an appropriate development system following an evaluation. Will your solution need to be networked? If so, this will influence your choice of development system. Here are some summaries of appraisals. The A Level project requires you to come up with more than one potential solution and summarise the appraisal of each solution. But here, for brevity, we summarise just one appraisal for each project.

Simulation of the growth of bacteria

▇ Consider using object-oriented approach because essentially the entities are particles which can be bacteria, anti-resistant bacteria, white blood cells, antibiotics.

▇ These particles can be modelled in separate classes that inherit from a particle class.

■ Their behaviour is independent of any user interface; object-oriented programming supports information hiding.

■ Environment class can then contain any number of different particles.

■ Method of graphical output can then be changed easily if first choice proves not to update without flicker.

3D graphics tutorial

■ Consider using OpenGL because it is platform-independent.

■ It has a high-level API that supports all user's requirements.

■ It supports 3D transformations, translations and rotations, solid filling, hidden line removal.

■ There is good library support in Delphi for OpenGL that hides the complexity normally associated with OpenGL in other languages, e.g. C.

Portal for an after-school maths club

■ Solution must be web-based, so could use an Apache web server.

■ Database solution would be best because there are several different record types; MySQL is readily available on most public web servers.

■ Scripting language PHP is an option because it is readily available on most public servers and there is good support for working with MySQL.

Justification of chosen solution

It is important to offer a choice of potential solutions that include some genuine alternatives. Strong reasons must now be advanced in support of the chosen solution. In the bacteria simulation, an alternative solution could be a non-object-oriented approach. Here are some arguments against this:

■ Using a separate record for each type of particle will lead to repetitive coding whereas in the object-oriented approach all common operations can be placed in a particle class and then shared.

■ It will be easier to make changes to an entity's properties or operations if the design of the entity can be hidden. Hiding such detail is not fully supported in a non object-oriented approach.

■ It is much easier to separate roles in an object-oriented approach than in a non-object-oriented approach, the graphical output will have a clear boundary from the biological modelling.

Possible framework for writing up the analysis

1 Introduction

1.1 Background

1.2 Problem definition

2 Investigation

2.1 The current system (including summary of main points of interview if appropriate)

2.2 Data flow diagram of existing system

2.3 Discussion of problems with the current system

2.4 Data flow diagram of proposed new system

2.5 Description of processes, data flows and data stores

2.6 Data dictionary

2.7 Input forms, output forms, report formats from existing system

2.8 Algorithms used by current system that must be applied to the data in the new system

3 Objectives of the new system

3.1 General objectives

3.2 to 3.n Specific objectives

4 Entity–relationship diagram and entity descriptions

4.1 E–R diagram

4.2 Entity descriptions

5 Object analysis diagrams

5.1 Inheritance diagrams

5.2 Aggregation diagrams

6 Other models of abstraction

6.1 Graphs

7 Constraints

7.1 Hardware constraints

7.2 Software constraints

7.3 Time constraints

7.4 User's knowledge of information technology

7.5 Who will be allowed to use the various parts of the system

8 Limitations

8.1 Areas which will not be included in computerisation

8.2 Areas considered for future computerisation

9 Consideration of alternative solutions

10 Justification of chosen solution

Questions

11 A specification describes what the system to be built should do. A design describes how the system should do it. In practice, things are more complicated: the specification provides a partial description of the system to be built, the design completes this description by adding the missing details. Given a specification S, how many designs can we construct that will satisfy S? S = Sort into ascending order a set of integers with values in the range 0 to 1000. (Hint: think sorting algorithms, use the web to research an answer.)

12 A specification describes what the system to be built should do. Design describes how the system should do it. It is not always obvious whether something is specification or design, e.g. the number will be redialled every 20 seconds until a connection is obtained. In practice, a specification consists of those decisions the user or customer makes for themselves (user requirements). Design consists of those decisions that are made by the developer. Are these statements part of a specification or a design?

a When a sensor event is recognised, the system should invoke an audible alarm.

b The set of currently selected products should be sorted into alphabetical order using the Quicksort algorithm

c The system should be accessible through Internet Explorer and Mozilla.

d The system first reads details of all available products into an array.

e The number will be redialled every 20 seconds until a connection is obtained.

13 Name three types of object analysis diagram. Explain each.

14 State four ways to get the analysis wrong. Explain the consequences in each case.

In this topic you have covered:

- the software and systems life cycle
- the waterfall, spiral and agile software development models
- the purpose of analysis
- feasibility study: research into potential solutions
- fact-finding techniques: observation, survey, examination of paperwork, interview
- requirements analysis
- producing an analysis data dictionary
- the A Level project
- how to prepare for the interview
- how to derive the user, data and processing requirements of a system, including consideration of the human aspects and physical environment
- how to specify and document the data, processing and performance requirements for a computer-based solution to a problem
- context diagrams, level 1 and level 2 data flow diagrams
- the usefulness of prototyping
- producing an appropriate data model or representation suitable for automation
- documenting any constraints, assumptions and limitations
- object analysis diagrams covering association diagrams, inheritance diagrams, aggregation diagrams, class definitions of class attributes and operations
- data volumes and volumetrics
- consideration of alternative solutions
- how to structure the write-up of the project analysis.

7.2 Design

The result of the analysis stage was the requirements specification, or objectives. During the design stage, this specification must be translated from the logical model of the system into the physical model. This should be done in two stages:

- system design, also known as high-level design
- detailed design, also known as low-level design.

High-level design

The key question now is: How, in general, is the problem to be solved? The result of this stage is the production of an outline solution consisting of:

- the components of the system
- the user interface, also known as a human–computer interface
- test cases.

Systems can be broken down into three basic stages: input, process and output (Fig. 7.2.1). What components are required for the input stage? What components (programs) are required for the processing? What components are required for the output stage?

$$Input \longrightarrow Process \longrightarrow Output$$

Fig. 7.2.1 *Systems can be broken down into three basic stages*

Fig. 7.2.2 *Why does Tanya suggest they should make a drawing first?*

System flowcharts

The components of the system can be represented diagrammatically using a system flowchart. A system flowchart is a high-level picture of a physical system. When a system flowchart is drawn, each discrete component of the system is represented with a separate symbol (Table 1).

Table 1 *Flow chart symbols*

Process	Input/output	Online storage	Flow line
(rectangle symbol)	*(parallelogram symbol)* Device	*(cylinder symbol)* Device	←→ —→
This could be a program or a manual process	This could be data keyed in at a keyboard, a bar code read with a bar code reader, an error report output on a printer, a graph shown on a monitor	This could be a database on magnetic disk, a data file on CD-RW	Links the symbols to define sequence and direction of flow

Fig. 7.2.3 shows the hardware and software components of a system that is used to produce monthly statements for account customers of a builder's merchant. A computer program reads transactions from a keyboard and updates the customer file on magnetic disk. The program sends the monthly statements to the printer. Any errors are sent to an error log file on magnetic tape.

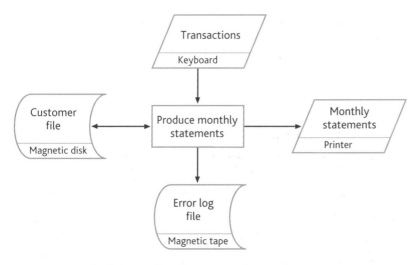

Fig. 7.2.3 *Example of a system flowchart*

Questions

1 Draw a systems flowchart to represent the following system. Orders are keyed in and validated before the valid data is written to magnetic disk. An invalid order report is printed.

2 A computer program is used to extract details of members whose subscriptions are overdue. The program reads a members file held on magnetic disk and writes names and addresses to a new file on magnetic disk. A mail-merge program is then used to produce reminder letters from the overdue subscriptions file and a standard letter stored on magnetic disk. The letters are printed out.

User interface

The input and output of systems may be through user interfaces. The computer program presents the user with textual, graphical or auditory information and the user can respond using an input device such as a keyboard, mouse or microphone to control the program.

Here are some things to consider for good user interface design:

- the type of user, such as expert, novice, frequent, occasional, young child, technical
- user needs and accessibility issues such as sight impairment, limited hand mobility
- choice of appropriate input/output devices, including size of screen
- use of colour, perhaps to alert or to present a house style
- use of icons, symbols or text
- type of interface, such as command line or graphical
- type of menu, such as drop-down, full-screen or pop-up
- consistency of design, such as keeping to conventional menu groupings.

Good user interface design provides:

- feedback to the user, such as when a record has been saved successfully
- confirmation, perhaps before deleting a record
- clearly marked exits, such as going back to a previous screen or the main menu
- online help, such as using the F1 key, menu options, call-outs on rollover
- helpful error messages at a level appropriate for the prospective user
- optional keyboard shortcuts.

How to present user interface designs

Fig 7.2.4 shows a hand-drawn sketch of a user interface and Fig. 7.2.5 shows a user interface prototype produced in Delphi. A prototype is an ideal means of communicating with the end user to check that the design meets the user's needs. Show the prototype to the user and discuss issues of design. For example, the user may suggest that terminology used in the interface is not what they are accustomed to, or that not enough space or too much space is allocated to a data entry. Maybe a menu option is missing.

Book Loan System-User Interface-Flow of Control

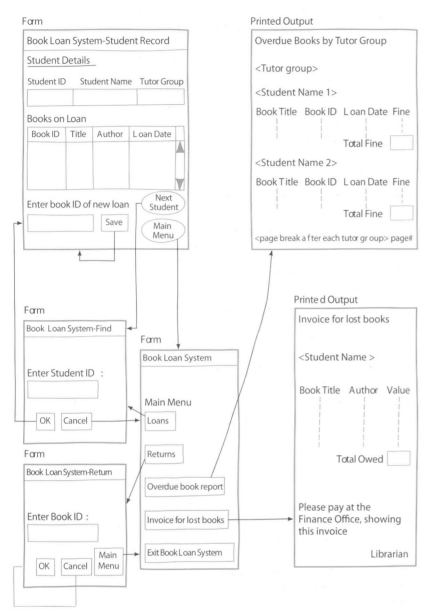

Fig. 7.2.4 *Hand-drawn sketch of a user interface and flow of control diagram*

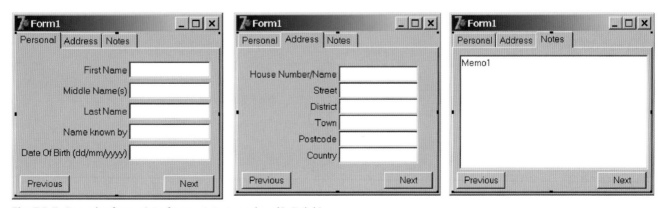

Fig. 7.2.5 *Example of a user interface prototype produced in Delphi*

Low-level design

The key question now is, "How is the problem to be solved in detail?" The result of this stage is a detailed design consisting of:

- hardware specification (sufficient to purchase the required components)
- hierarchy charts and structure charts (*AQA Computing AS*, pages 84–89)
- design data dictionary, including data types and validation of input data
- object diagrams and class definitions (Topic 2.1)
- data structures such as arrays or records (*AQA Computing AS*, Topics 2.6 and 2.7)
- file organisation
- Entity–Relationship diagrams (Topic 5.1)
- normalised database tables (Topic 5.2)
- algorithms using structured English or pseudocode (*AQA Computing AS*, Topic 1.4)
- queries using SQL (Topic 5.3)
- detailed design of printed output
- preliminary test plan
- detailed test data.

Depending on the type of problem to be solved, not all the above parts will be relevant. For example, when designing a house, the outline plans, sufficient for planning permission (Fig. 7.2.6) must be developed further (Fig. 7.2.7) so that a builder can build a house that will meet the building regulations, as well as the home owner's expectations. Each component of a computer system must be defined to a level of detail sufficient for the implementation (programming) step.

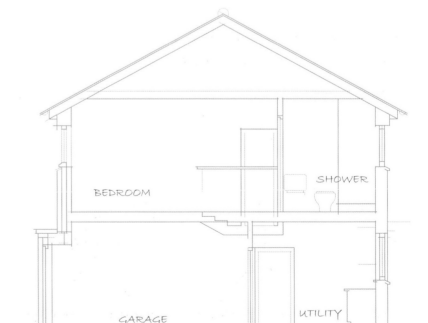

Fig. 7.2.6 *Drawing for outline planning permission*

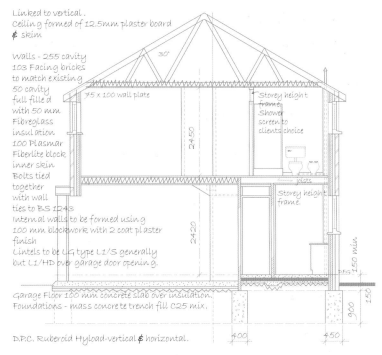

Fig. 7.2.7 *An architect's blueprint for a house extension*

Hardware specification

What is the minimum specification for input and output devices, online storage, main memory requirements, back-up storage?

Worked example _____

> Keyboard and mouse required for input screen display should be at least 400 pixels × 800 pixels. Hard drive required for online file storage. Main memory 512 MB, Back-up possible onto USB memory stick, 128 MB minimum.

Hierarchy charts and structure charts

See pages 84–89 in the *AQA Computing AS*.

Worked example _____

> Figure 7.2.8 shows an example of a hierarchy chart.

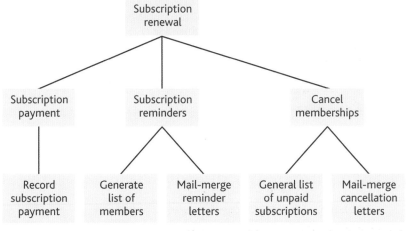

Fig. 7.2.8 *A hierarchy chart*

Design data dictionary

The design data dictionary should include data types and validation of input data appropriate for chosen implementation e.g. Delphi and MySQL. Use the analysis data dictionary and amend and add entries for variables you need for processing purposes. Decide on data types for all data items; this could include data structures such as arrays or records. Add validation rules with reasons why they are required and what they are testing. How are the values to be stored while the program is running and what data needs to be stored long-term? Is data to be stored in database tables or files?

File organisation

Choose between simple text files, CSV files or typed files (see AS book, pages 74–82). If the data structures to be used are records, typed files would be appropriate. If data is stored in arrays while the program is running, but needs to be stored long-term, then serial or sequential file organisation should be considered. If the program is to access data records held on disk as and when required, then a random access file organisation might be more appropriate.

Worked example

A direct access file is to store login details of users. The following record structure is to be used:

UserID: String[12]

Name: String[25]

Password: String[15]

AdminStatus: Boolean

LastLogin: TDateTime

NumberOfAttemptedLogins: Integer

There will be approximately 500 user details stored. The file size is to be 1000 records. Records will be accessed by hashing the userID.

Entity–relationship diagram (see Topic 5.1)

Worked example

The analysis phase identified the entities Student, Course and Lecturer (Fig. 7.2.9). To implement such a system, many-to-many relationships need to be resolved into one-to-many relationships using link entities. This will produce Fig. 7.2.10.

Fig. 7.2.9 *An E-R diagram*

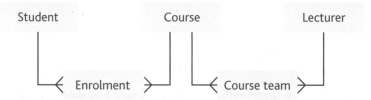

Fig. 7.2.10 *Many-to-many relationships resolved into one-to-many relationships*

Normalised database tables (see Topic 5.2)

Use the entity descriptions (attributes) identified in the analysis stage and organise the attributes into tables so they are fully normalised.

Object diagrams and class definitions (see Topic 2.1)

Worked example

Fig. 7.2.11 shows a class diagram for a lending library loaning books and CDs.

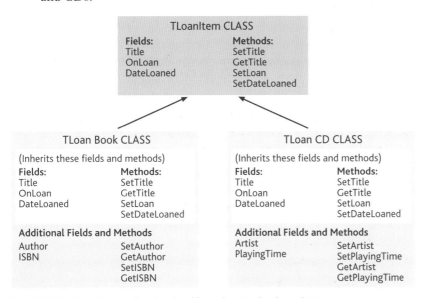

Fig. 7.2.11 *Class diagram for a lending library loaning books and CDs*

Algorithms using structured English or pseudocode

The processes identified for system functionality need to be designed effectively. For example, if a search function is required, which standard algorithm would be appropriate, sequential or binary? What processes need careful planning and therefore should be written as algorithms during this stage?

Worked example

Here is a hashing algorithm for userIDs:

```
Function HashedAddress(UserID): Integer
  NumberOfChars ← Length(UserID)
  For ThisChar ← 1 to NumberOfChars
    Total ← Total + ASCII(UserID[ThisChar]) * ThisChar
                                // weighted ASCII
  EndFor
  HashedAddress ← (Total Mod 1000) + 1
          // ensure address is between 1 and 1000
EndFunction
```

To find a user's record:

```
Get ThisUserID
Seek(HashedAddress(ThisUserID)) // go to hashed address
```

```
Read(UserRecord)
While UserRecord.UserID <> ThisUserID
      AND NOT UserRecord = Empty
  Read(UserRecord) // read next record in file
  If EOF Then Seek(1) // wrap round to start of file
                      // if end of file encountered
EndWhile // when correct record is found
```

Queries using SQL (see Topic 5.3)

If the solution involves a database, then searches can be done using SQL. The required SQL statements should be written during the design stage.

Worked example

Here are some SQL statements to search the database:

```
SELECT Forename, Surname, Address, MembershipNumber,
       MembershipCategoryCode, SubscriptionFee,
       DateNextSubscriptionFallsDue
  FROM Member, MembershipCategory
  WHERE Member.MembershipCategoryCode =
        MembershipCategory.MembershipCategoryCode
    AND DateNextSubscriptionFallsDue > Now
    AND DateNextSubscriptionFallsDue < Now+28
```

Detailed design of printed output

What is the required output on paper? Headings and layouts should be sketched out.

Worked example

Fig. 7.2.12 shows the mail-merge template for a membership subscription letter.

Tennis Club Logo and Address

<Forename> <Surname>
<Address>

<Today's date>

Dear <Forename>
Re: Membership Number: <MembershipNumber>
Membership Category: <MembershipCategoryCode>.

Your membership subscription is due on <DateNextSubscriptionFallsDue>.
The subscription for the next year is <SubscriptionFee>.
Please pay the above fee by sending a cheque to the above address within 28 days.

Best wishes

Membership Secretary

Fig. 7.2.12 *Membership subscription letter*

Preliminary test plan and detailed test data (see Topic 7.3)

Worked example

Table 2 is an example of an outline test plan and Table 3 is part of a detailed test plan.

Table 2 *Example of outline test plan*

Test series	Purpose of test series
1	Test the flow of control: Do the menu choices (menu structure) or user interface options go to correct form, report or option? User can only choose appropriate options (other options disabled) (top-down testing)
2	Validation of input data performed correctly (bottom-up testing)
3	Iterations and decisions performed correctly. Calculations, searches and sorting performed correctly (white box testing and desk checking)
4	Data is saved into correct tables, fields or files (system testing)
5	The system produces the required results as per specification (black box testing)

Table 3 *Part of a detailed test plan*

Test series and number	Purpose	Description	Test data	Expected result	Actual result	Evidence in appendix
2.1	Validate number of seconds input	The input box should accept positive integers and values with one decimal place	15 21.6 −3 'abs'	Accept 15 Accept 21.6 Error Error	Accepted Accepted Error Error	Fig. 2.1a Fig. 2.1b Fig. 2.1c Fig. 2.1d
. . .						
5.1	Count down works correctly, stopping at zero.	Test with integer and fractional values, including a .0 number	15 12.7 0.3 1.0	The time left decreases to zero in steps of 0.1	As expected	Fig. 5.1a Fig. 5.1b

Writing up the design

Worked example

Table 4 shows a possible framework for writing up the design.

Table 4 *A possible framework for writing up the design*

1 Outline system design
   1.1 System flow charts
2 User interface designs
3 Hardware specification
4 Program structure
   4.1 Hierarchy charts
   4.2 Structure charts
5 Design data dictionary
6 Object diagrams and class definitions
7 Data structures
8 File organisation
9 Entity–Relationship diagram
10 Normalised database tables
11 Algorithms
12 Queries
13 Detailed design of printed output
14 Preliminary test plan
15 Detailed test data

In this topic you have covered:

- how to draw system flowcharts
- what to consider when designing user interfaces
- how to present user interface designs
- the purpose of a prototype
- how to choose an appropriate file organisation
- what algorithms should be included
- how to show designs of printed output
- how to design a preliminary test plan and test data
- how to write up the design.

7.3　Testing

AQA Examiner's tip

Ask one of your friends to test your program and give you feedback.

The purpose of testing

You might think that the purpose of testing is to show that the program works correctly. However, your testing will be more successful if you approach it from a different angle.

The purpose of program testing is to discover any errors that might be present in a program. Testing a program can never prove the correctness of the program; it can only reveal the existence of errors. According to Edsger Dijkstra, 'Program testing can be used to show the presence of bugs, but never to show their absence!'

It is impossible to test any application exhaustively, but you must set about it systematically so that as many potential problems as possible can be located and put right. When all the parts of the system have been tested, the system as a whole also needs to be tested, to ensure the integration of the parts has been successful.

Testing strategies

During the design phase, you should identify suitable testing strategies that you are going to use.

Bottom-up testing

The system is developed from the bottom up and the lowest-level modules are tested first. If this is your method of development, this will be your method of testing.

Top-down testing

Top-down testing is also known as interface testing and stub testing. In top-down testing, a skeleton of the complete system is tested. Modules are written as stubs so that interface calling can be tested. The testing starts with the top module and works downwards as more and more modules are added. Each new module is initially created without the actual code its body should contain. Instead, a stub of code is written into the body so that the calling of the module can be tested. This type of testing should be used with top-down design and implementation.

Mixed-level testing

Testing some low-level modules while doing some interface testing may have advantages over both of the above strategies. It is relatively rare that the whole system is implemented in a strict top-down or bottom-up approach. Different approaches are often taken for different parts of the system. This suggests a mixed-level approach to testing.

Dry running

Dry running is sometimes called walkthrough, tracing or desk checking. Code is read through and checked by hand. A trace table is completed to check the values of variables at every stage of execution. Desk checking can reveal possible causes for errors:

- Is every variable declared and initialised?
- Are array subscripts always within range?
- Will every loop terminate?
- What happens the first time or last time through the loop?
- Check each division to see if it is possible to divide by zero.
- Check all expressions and check that precedence rules are followed.
- Are all Boolean expressions correct?
- Are parameters supplied in the correct order?
- Is the end-of-file checked before and during file reading?

White box testing

White box testing is also known as structural testing. Tests are derived from the knowledge of the program code. Test cases are devised that execute every possible route through the code. In this way, each logical path through the code is tested. This can get quite complex, especially if nested selection statements are involved.

Fig. 7.3.1 shows an example. To test every possible path, test data needs to be designed to test the following routes through the system: a, bc, bd. This testing strategy is generally used for individual code modules.

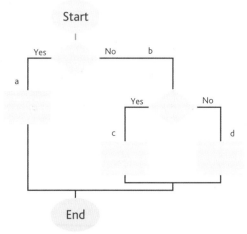

Fig. 7.3.1 *Flow chart with condition boxes showing different paths through a system*

Black box testing

Black box testing is also known as functional testing. The tests are derived from the program specification. Test cases are devised that test a program with inputs. The corresponding outputs produced by a program are examined for correctness. The actual code contained in the program is kept hidden. This type of testing can also be used to test the interface to a module. This testing strategy is usually deployed for system testing.

Unit testing

A system is rarely built in one go. Instead it is broken down into its constituent parts. For the software part of a system this means separate programs. These separate programs are broken down into separately compiled modules, which can be linked by a linker, and these modules are broken down into smaller modules called procedures or functions. Unit testing is about testing these components. You should do this as you write procedures or functions.

Integration testing

Integration testing takes place when the modules of a system are put together. It tests that separately developed modules work together as planned, without error. The integration is usually done incrementally. Two modules are combined and tested together. When the tests don't show up any errors, the next module is added to these two. When the tests don't show up any errors, the next module is added to these three. And so on, until all modules have been integrated.

System testing

The entire system is tested to check that it is working correctly. This is done with reference to the original specification. Black box testing is the most suitable approach for system testing.

Alpha testing

This is the final testing stage carried out in-house.

Beta testing

The software is released to potential users who will use it with real data and report errors to the developers.

Acceptance testing

Acceptance testing is testing specified by the system's customer. The customer checks that the supplied system meets their requirements as specified at the analysis stage. It may be carried out by the customer or by the developer under the scrutiny of the customer using test cases supplied by the customer. Your end user should do this and then feed back to you as the developer.

Test plan

You should produce an outline test plan with test cases (see choice of test data below) during the design stage. Table 1 is an example of an outline test plan.

Table 1 *Example of outline test plan*

Test series	Purpose of test series
1	Test the flow of control: Do the menu choices (menu structure) or user interface options go to correct form, report or option? User can only choose appropriate options (other options disabled) (top-down testing)
2	Validation of input data performed correctly (bottom-up testing)
3	Iterations and decisions performed correctly. Calculations, searches and sorting performed correctly (white box testing and desk checking)
4	Data is saved into correct tables, fields or files (system testing)
5	The system produces the required results as per specification (black box testing)

This outline plan needs to be expanded into a detailed test plan. The first five columns of this test plan should largely be completed during the design phase. Table 2 is part of a detailed test plan.

Table 2 *Part of a detailed test plan*

Test series and number	Purpose	Description	Test data	Expected result	Actual result	Evidence in appendix
2.1	Validate number of seconds input	The input box should accept positive integers and values with one decimal place	15 21.6 −3 'abs'	Accept 15 Accept 21.6 Error Error	Accepted Accepted Error Error	Fig. 2.1a Fig. 2.1b Fig. 2.1c Fig. 2.1d
. . .						
5.1	Count down works correctly, stopping at zero.	Test with integer and fractional values, including a .0 number	15 12.7 0.3 1.0	The time left decreases to zero in steps of 0.1	As expected	Fig. 5.1a Fig. 5.1b

Designing the test cases in Table 2 may highlight the following questions:

▓ **Test 2.1**: should the program accept or reject values over 60 seconds (test 2.1)?

▓ **Test 5.1**: should the program show trailing zeros (test 5.1)?

Thinking about different test cases will help you write robust code, because you will be aware of the type of data your program should be able to handle. Be realistic, you can't test everything, but you should cover a wide range of tests.

Choice of test data

Here are some things that test data must include:

▓ **Normal data**: include some typical examples of the system's data.

▓ **Boundary values**: include values on the boundary, values just below the boundary and values just above the boundary.

▓ **Erroneous data**: include values that lie outside the acceptable ranges.

▓ **Extreme values**: include top and bottom of number ranges, plus text fields that are too long.

▓ **Exceptional data**: include text instead of numbers plus blanks or nulls and unexpected key presses.

▓ **Sufficient records**: include enough records to test page breaks in reports.

▓ **Sufficient variety**: include enough variety to test searches and sorts, especially group sorts.

Choose test data so that a minimal set covers the above categories. Test data needs to be chosen very carefully.

Worked example _____

A routine is to be tested that calculates the charge for boarding a cat at a cattery. The routine's parameters are BookedStartDate,

`BookedEndDate`, `DateCatCollected`. These parameters have been entered through a calendar component, which checks that the input date is a valid date. A booking has an agreed start and end date. Part of a day is charged at the full daily rate of £5. If the cat is collected after the agreed day, the extra days are charged at the higher rate of £7. No cat is accepted before the date booked. If a cat is collected before `BookedEndDate`, a retainer fee of £2 per day is charged for the remaining booked days. The minimum booking is an overnight stay. The longest booking accepted is 28 days. What data should be chosen as test data?

Note that test data chosen just inside a boundary is normal data and test data chosen just outside a boundary is erroneous data. Choosing test cases carefully means that you can use a minimal set of data. Table 3 shows a minimal set of test cases.

Table 3 *A minimal set of test cases for the cattery charging routine*

BookedStartDate	BookedEndDate	DateCatCollected	Expected result	Reason for choice
06/06/09	09/06/09	09/06/09	4 x £5	Normal data
08/06/09	09/06/09	same	2 x £5	Overnight stay; test either side of boundary and on boundary
08/06/09	08/06/09	08/06/09	not accepted	
08/06/09	10/06/09	10/06/09	3 x £5	
08/06/09	05/07/09	same	28 x £5	Extreme values 28 days exactly
08/06/09	10/06/09	12/06/09	3 x £5 +2 x £7	Test higher the charge applied correctly
				Exceptional values BookedEndDate before BookedStartDate

System testing

Refer to your test strategy and test plan. Use the test data that you have chosen during the design stage. Do not make it up as you go along. If problems are located during testing, fix the bug if possible and then retest. If fixing the problem is not possible (e.g. lack of time, normalisation incorrect), leave it but discuss it in the test evaluation section (page 264).

Dealing with bugs

Use built-in debugging facilities. This will allow you to see the contents of variables at every step through your program or at breakpoints you have set up. Another way is to deduce the error from the test cases that produced correct results and the test cases that produced incorrect results. Dry running the suspect parts of your code is sometimes the only way to find the error. When a bug has been found and corrected, the test cases have to be run through again. Often, changing code in one part of the program to correct a mistake can have unwanted side effects elsewhere.

Writing up the testing phase

Here are some suggested headings for writing up the testing:

- test plan
- test data
- test evaluation
- evidence of testing (refer to appendix) cross-referenced to test plan
- evidence of normal working of your system (also refer to user manual).

The testing write-up should demonstrate the functioning of the implementation. It should contain clear, concise and comprehensive evidence that the system as a whole operates as required. You should provide a well-designed test plan that shows expected results supported by selected samples of carefully annotated and cross-referenced screen captures showing test runs that prove the reliability and robustness of your system. The testing evidence in the appendix should consist of annotated screen captures and printed reports, if appropriate, to support the results of your testing. Screen captures must be cross-referenced to the test plan. Give them a reference number and say exactly what they are for: 'This screen capture shows that test 3.7 has discovered the following problems.' Screen captures should show the state before a test is carried out and the state afterwards.

Write a test evaluation section. Explain how you approached the testing, what major problems you discovered and what you did about them. Do a full evaluation of your testing and say what its strengths and weaknesses are.

In this topic you have covered:

- the purpose of testing
- different testing strategies
- how to write a test plan
- how to choose test data
- how to test the developed system
- dealing with bugs
- how to write up the testing phase.

7.4 Implementation

Implementation is the stage when the new system is built and installed. A bricklayer will not rely just on his skills of building walls, incorporating doors and windows wherever he sees fit, but will follow the architect's blueprint so that the house will conform to the plans approved by the customer and the planning department of the local council.

As you build your solution, you should refer frequently to the design you drew up from the requirements specification (objectives). Follow your designs exactly. If you discover a mistake or omission in the design section, such as a missing attribute in a table or an incorrect form layout, go back and correct it in the design section and check through for any unforeseen side effects. You may need to check with your end user to clarify any incomplete or imprecise requirements. Beware of embellishing your implementation with features that were not asked for, even if you think they are fun to do.

When using visual development environments such as Delphi or Access, keep a record of which properties you change from default, which wizards you use and what choices you make while running wizards. This is essential for the documentation section. You may wish to keep a small exercise book handy whenever you are working on your project so you can jot down these details quickly. Don't rely on your memory. There is no absolute order in which to set about building a system, but you must be methodical in your approach.

Selection of hardware and software

During the design stage you selected an appropriate hardware and software configuration. During the implementation phase you need to select the precise versions, bearing in mind how they are going to be used.

For example, if you designed your system to use a bar code reader as a data input device, you need to check which type of bar code reader will be fit for purpose. Can you expect the user to swipe the bar code at close range or should the bar code be readable from a distance of 50 centimetres?

If you planned to write your program using Delphi and store the data in an underlying database, you need to ensure that you have the appropriate components in Delphi to connect to the chosen type of database. You will need ActiveX Data Objects (ADO) components to connect to an MS Access database.

You should also address volumetrics. Do hard drive and back-up media have sufficient capacity to store the forecast file sizes when your system is in full use?

Top-down approach

Start with the user interface prototype. Each menu option should produce just a message that the relevant option has been called. Write the code to implement each option. Test each procedure as you write it.

Key point

There are many tutorials and forums on the Internet to help you with programming techniques. Remember to list your sources of useful hints in the appendix of your report.

AQA Examiner's tip

The marks for the technical solution are awarded for evidence of technical competence. Make sure you demonstrate your programming skills appropriately. Don't rely on wizards that generate code automatically. You will not get credit for code you have not written yourself.

Bottom-up approach

Start with one procedure. After successful testing, add the next procedure, and so on, until the whole system is developed. Here is a suggested order for a Delphi solution incorporating a database:

1 Set up any underlying database tables and ADO connections in a separate data module.
2 Declare global variables and classes in a separate module.
3 Build a form (user interface) and name all objects appropriately.
4 Write the procedures.
5 Repeat steps 3 and 4 for all necessary forms.

Readability of code

Computer programs in the real world go through many revisions in their life cycle. This is known as maintenance. Maintaining a program that has been written by other programmers can be extremely difficult. Making changes to code that is only partly understood can have disastrous consequences. When debugging a program, you need to understand the code you are reading before you can make effective changes.

A good programmer takes programming style seriously. This requires conscious effort, but the reward is easy-to-understand code. You should always write code with maintainability in mind, even if you think the source code will only be seen by you. Maintainability is the ease with which a program or solution can be corrected if an error is encountered, adapted if its environment changes, or enhanced if the customer changes their requirements. Good programming style is self-documenting; see page 89 of the AS book.

Code should be easy to understand and maintainable with:

- meaningful identifiers
- consistent use of uppercase and CamelCaps
- consistent indentation (two columns per indent is ideal)
- good use of standard commenting features (avoid handwritten annotation)
- a comment to explain the purpose of every subprogram
- use of local variables whenever possible
- use of procedures and functions with interfaces (see Topic 2.5 in the AS book)
- structured statements such as selection and iteration or repetition (see Topics 2.3 and 2.4 in the AS book)
- a program structure that reflects the outline algorithm for your solution.

Here is an example algorithm:

```
Repeat
  Show menu
  Get a response
  Case response
    1: enter new order
    2: edit customer details
    3: find unpaid invoices
    4: exit program
  End Case
Until user wants to exit program
Save all data before closing program
```

This algorithm should be reflected in the main program body. Here is a possible Pascal solution:

```
Program Example;
// variable and procedure declarations to go in here
//********main program body ***********
Begin
  Repeat
    ShowMenu;
    Get(Response);
    Case Response Of
      1: EnterNewOrder;
      2: EditCustomerDetails;
      3: FindUnpaidInvoices;
      4: ExitProgram := True;
    End; // of Case
  Until ExitProgram = True;
  SaveData;
End.
```

> These are all procedure calls. Note that the final solution should include procedures with interfaces (parameters)

Writing robust code

You, as the programmer, are responsible for writing reliable, error-free code. The structured programming approach is important in writing reliable code. Object classes and information hiding help to reduce unwanted side effects. Many errors happen because a programmer accidentally assigns an incorrect value to a variable. If you use a programming language which supports strong typing, such as Pascal, then the compiler will detect many of these errors. You can also build exception-handling opportunities into your code (see pages 97–98 in the *AQA Computing AS*). Catching an error and handling it appropriately, rather than the program crashing, results in more **robust code**.

You may wish to include output statements in your code to help you diagnose possible errors, or bugs. They can be removed (or commented out) later when the code is known to be working correctly. It is easier to include extra output statements at the time of writing the code, than later when you are trying to debug your complete program.

Do not rely on one copy of the implementation. Make the necessary back-ups and, if possible, have back-up copies in different places. Get a flash memory stick. Make big changes on a copy of your last working version, so that you can go back to this working version if your change was unsuccessful.

Did you know?

'The Go To statement as it stands is just too primitive, it is too much an invitation to make a mess of one's program', so said Edsger Dijkstra, a Dutch computer scientist who received the 1972 Turing Award for fundamental contributions in the area of programming languages.

Key terms

Robust code: the program will function reliably and not crash or go into infinite loops, even with incorrect inputs or unpredictable values.

Key point

Things always go wrong at the most critical moment, so be prepared. Save frequently and keep two versions (work on a copy of yesterday's files). Clear out old copies. Do not fill up your hard drive so the system will not allow you to save the latest version.

Key terms

Rollout: setting up a new system and then using it for real for the first time.

Rollout

When the development is finished and all the testing has been successfully completed, your end user should carry out acceptance testing (see Topic 7.3). **Rollout** is the process of setting up the new system and starting to use it for real. After acceptance testing is complete and the customer has accepted the solution, rollout can begin.

Before the new system can be put to work, more tasks may need to be completed:

1   Install new hardware: this might be just a new printer but could be network connections and a server.
2   Set up or convert data files: this may involve keying in large volumes of data.
3   Training: your end users will need to learn to use your system by working through the user guide.
4   Choose a changeover option.

Here are some changeover options:

■ **Direct changeover**: the user stops using the old system and starts using the new system. This option is used if the new system is very different from the old system or there is a shortage of staff time to do a parallel conversion. However, this can be risky.

■ **Parallel conversion**: the new system is used alongside the old system. This means that results can be compared and the new system is only totally relied on when it has proved satisfactory. This can be very expensive on hardware and personnel.

■ **Pilot conversion**: the new system is used in one part of the organisation until it has been proved to work successfully. This is a popular method for organisations where there are several branches or offices. For example, a new checkout system for a supermarket chain might be used in one store only, until it works without glitches. Then the system will be rolled out to the other branches.

■ **Phased conversion**: this method is often used for larger systems when new modules are introduced individually into the existing system. For example, an ordering system may be introduced first, then an invoicing system, and finally a stock-control module when the other modules have been running successfully for some time. Phased conversion is less likely to apply to a system developed as an A Level project.

In this topic you have covered:

■   the order of development of the solution

■   how to write reliable code

■   the meaning and importance of robust code

■   how to roll out the final solution.

AQA Examiner's tip

The marks for your coursework come entirely from your report. It is important you write up all the work you have done and present it in an accessible format.

Here are some hints and tips to help towards completing a successful final project report. It is this report that is submitted to the examination board for marking, so it is important that it reflects the work you have done on the project.

Marks are awarded for three aspects of the written communication:

- The report is set out in a clear and logical way using the sections identified in the specification.
- There is good use of English grammar, punctuation and spelling. There are few errors, so meanings are clear. Information is presented in continuous prose that is easy to follow.
- There is good use of word-processing features that include header, footer with project title, candidate name, and automatically generated page numbers. There are consistent heading styles with a table of contents generated by word processor.

Start by setting up a document template for your report using a word processor. Set up your styles with different levels of heading (Fig. 7.5.1). You may need three or four levels. If you use them consistently, they will help you later to create your table of contents and footers with section titles.

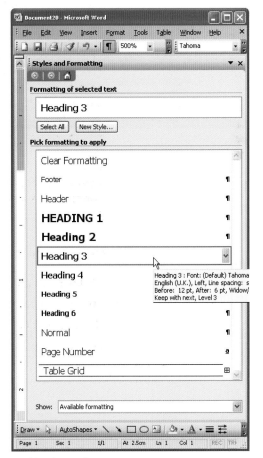

Fig. 7.5.1 *Example of heading styles*

Here are some possible choices: bold size 16 for heading 1, bold size 14 for heading 2 and bold size 12 for heading 3. Body text could be plain size 12. Choose a sensible font such as Tahoma size 12 for normal text. To frame your pages, click **Format > Borders and Shading** then select the tab **Page Border**. To put a border on the header or footer, click into the header or footer, then click **Format > Borders and Shading** and select the tab **Border**. Don't overindulge; this is a computing project, not a piece of art.

Set up the document header and footer to include the following items on every page (Fig. 7.5.2):

- your name
- your centre number
- your candidate number
- the project title
- section title
- the date
- the page number.

Save the template in your templates folder so you can use it for new documents by choosing **File > New**.

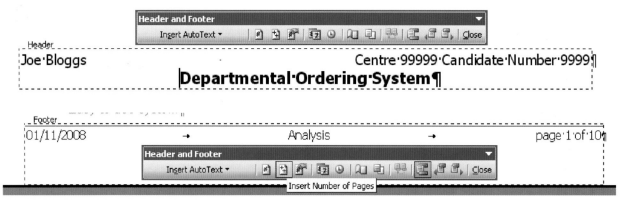

Fig. 7.5.2 *Header and footer examples*

Use page breaks to force a new page to start new sections on a new page (Fig. 7.5.3). Section breaks have several uses:

- Use sections if you want to organise part of your document in several columns.
- Each section can have a different header or footer if required.
- If most of your report is printed in portrait orientation, but some pages would be better shown in landscape orientation, you can do this for different pages using section breaks within a single document. One section can be formatted using portrait layout, another using landscape layout (Fig. 7.5.4).

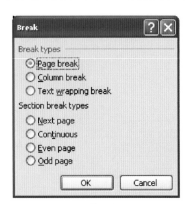

Fig. 7.5.3 *Types of break to insert in a document*

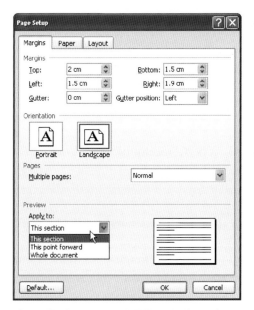

Fig. 7.5.4 *How to choose landscape or portrait for part of your document*

The project report must contain all the following sections:

- title page
- table of contents
- analysis
- design
- system testing
- system maintenance
- user manual
- appraisal
- appendices
- acknowledgement of sources of any third-party material.

The appendices should contain:

- transcripts of interviews
- summary of questionnaire answers (if used)
- original documents of system investigated (e.g. invoice, order form)
- program listing
- test data
- test results.

Organise different appendices for each section as this will assist in referring to individual printouts. Use a reference number system for each section and subsection as well as in the appendices. This is especially helpful in the system testing section as most of the supporting printouts will be in the appendices and will need clear references. Here is an example:

In the command button interface test (see appendix C, test log 3, test 4) it was discovered that ...

Refer to other sections in this book for details of what should go in the different parts of your report: Topic 7.1 for analysis, Topic 7.2 for design, Topic 7.3 for testing and Topic 7.6 for evaluation and appraisal.

AQA Examiner's tip

This part of the project is to demonstrate your technical competence. The examiner will not see your working implementation. All they have to assess your skilled work is the quality of your system maintenance documentation and your user guide.

System maintenance

System maintenance documentation is the technical documentation needed by a programmer who has to maintain your system. Here is what it should include:

- a brief discussion of the environment used to solve the problem, its capabilities and special features and a clear description of the features you have used
- a system overview (a clear technical overall view of the solution)
- an explanation of the modular structure of all the code
- annotated variable lists with reference to the data dictionary in the design section
- screenshots of all tables, forms, queries, relationship windows, etc., in design view
- a discussion of test results with reference to the testing section
- explanation of any parts of the code that are difficult to understand plus samples of detailed algorithms developed by you
- reference to the program listing in the appendix
- a list of system settings and the system configuration
- acknowledgement of any automatically generated code or code incorporated from other sources.

Only final versions need to be included. Copies of documentation showing development are not required.

Key point

Always have several back-ups of your work. Number your versions carefully, so you know which is the most recent work.

User manual

The user manual should be self-contained and have its own contents page. Its purpose is to explain how to use the new system correctly, what help the system may give if the user makes mistakes (such as what error messages are displayed), and how to carry out any back-up and recovery procedures that may be necessary.

Include the following sections:

1 Introduction: say what the application covers and who could use it.
2 Explain how to install, load or start the application
3 In the form of a tutorial, describe all the functions of the application:
   - Lead the user through the application and explain the menu options, dialogue boxes and printed reports.
   - Explain possible error messages from the system and from your own error-trapping routines and what to do about them.
   - Explain how to save the data.
4 Describe any limitations, input validation and things it will not do.
5 Say when and how to use back-up and recovery procedures.

The user manual should consist of a detailed description of how to use the system that you developed for your end user. You should give explanations with actual screen displays at a level appropriate to your end user. If there are two types of user, then there may be more than one type of explanation, such as different instructions for teachers and pupils on how to use a computer-aided learning system. Use the screen-capture utility to capture images from the real application to illustrate the user guide.

If you incorporate online help, you must provide evidence of the content. This means that you need to produce all your online help as hard copy to include in the report. You still need to produce a brief user guide that gives an overview and installation details (see above).

Give the completed user manual to your end user when they test the system. Ask them to give you feedback on how successfully your solution tackled the original problem.

Question

1 Have a look at user manuals written by professionals. What makes them easy to use?

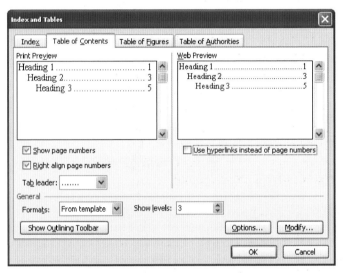

Fig. 7.5.5 *Dialog box for inserting a table of contents*

In this topic you have covered:

- the importance of the report presentation
- the essential sections of the report
- how to set up styles in your document template
- how to add a header and a footer with essential information
- how to document system maintenance
- how to present the user manual.

AQA Examiner's tip

Although you are expected to develop a complete working solution, the project report need only contain carefully selected samples of evidence in order to demonstrate each skill. The report should summarise the work carried out. For example, you may have several input forms of very similar design. Include a detailed design of one rather than several very similar drawings.

Key point

Word-processed documents can behave erratically when they get very large. Don't try to keep the whole of your report as one document. Split it up into sections while you are working on it. Embedded images can get lost if you move your document from one disk drive to another. Keep all your report sections in the same folder and copy the whole folder to another drive or part of a drive. Just before you want to create the table of contents, combine the sections into one document.

AQA Examiner's tip

Do not file your pages in PVC sleeves. Bind the report using treasury tags.

AQA Examiner's tip

Remember to complete all forms, sign the declaration that it is your own work and name any books or websites you have used to help you.

In this topic you will cover:

- evaluation of solutions against the requirements specification

- evaluation of effectiveness, usability and maintainability.

Key terms

Evaluation: systematic assessment of whether something meets its objectives or specifications and how well it meets the specifications in its effectiveness, usability and maintainability.

AQA Examiner's tip

Evaluation is an important part of your COMP4 project. You will report in the appraisal section of your project an evaluation of your solution.

Project evaluation

For COMP4 you are required to generate a solution to a real problem. The problem must be specified by a third party; for convenience, we will call them the end user or customer.

When you have produced a solution to this problem, you must do an **evaluation** of this solution against the specification that you wrote during analysis and that was agreed by the customer when summarising their requirements. Table 1 shows a sample list of specific input, processing and output requirements. The specification that you wrote is a set of specific requirements, also called specific objectives.

Table 1 *A sample list of specific input, processing and output requirements*

Requirement number	Details
1	The system to be created must automatically produce a list of members whose subscriptions are due
2	The system to be created must automatically print a standard letter (contents specified by the club secretary) with forename, surname, address, membership number, category of membership, subscription and date due inserted into the letter for each member one month in advance of the date when the subscription is due unless the subscription has been paid (mail-merge application). The member's record must store that a letter has been generated and the date it was generated
3	The system to be created must allow a subscription payment to be recorded. The club secretary is to enter the member's membership number, the date of payment and the amount paid. The system should locate the correct member's record and check the subscription fee due against amount paid then, if correct, record the date of payment and increment the number of years of membership. If incorrect, the system should display an appropriate error message

Meeting the specific requirements of the customer

Firstly, you should report on whether each specific requirement has been met. For example, you should state that your solution meets specific requirement 1 if it automatically produces a list of members whose subscriptions are overdue. If this has not been achieved, then you should state what has or has not been achieved of this requirement and why. The customer should also have an opportunity to report on whether each specific requirement has been met.

Effectiveness

Just reporting that a specific requirement has been met is not enough. Consider the analogy of a motor car. A customer specified that a four-wheeled vehicle was required that would run on 95 octane petrol, have a top speed of 100 mph (161 kph), accelerate from 0 to 60 mph (97 kph) in under 10 seconds, keep the occupants dry in all weathers, keep the occupants warm in cold weather and cool in hot weather, and so on.

The car produced passed every one of the specific requirements. However, the customer was very disappointed with the end result. The car was noisy, understeered when cornering, suffered from excessive vibration on most surfaces, had instruments that were difficult to read because they were poorly sited, had limited leg room for all occupants and needed Herculean effort to turn the steering wheel. Ticking off specific requirements is not enough. Judging how effectively each specific requirement has been met is also important. Judging the effectiveness of the parts is one aspect of evaluation but it is also important to judge the effectiveness of the solution as a whole.

You will need criteria on which to base your judgement of effectiveness. Imagine you were required to produce an aid to teaching three-dimensional graphics using OpenGL. The user experience will be an important element in assessing the effectiveness of the solution. Fig. 7.6.1 shows an example of a possible user interface. Here are some questions raised in planning the effectiveness evaluation for such a project:

▨ How many users should be involved in using the solution?

▨ What prior knowledge of OpenGL three-dimensional graphics should these users possess?

▨ How long should users spend using the solution?

▨ What form should testing take when assessing users' acquisition of knowledge and skill in OpenGL three-dimensional graphics after using the solution?

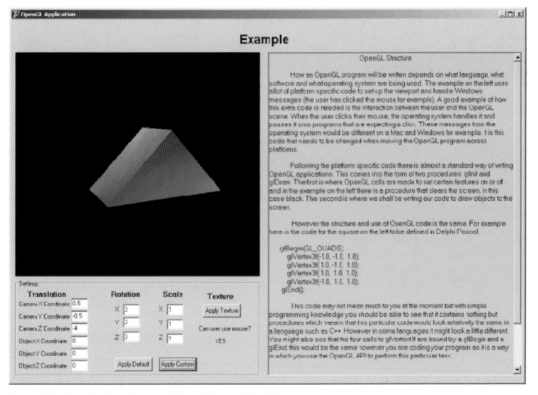

Fig. 7.6.1 *OpenGL three-dimensional graphics teaching aid*

This example shows that evaluation of effectiveness requires four things:

- planning
- planning time
- execution time
- criteria for judging effectiveness.

This also raises an issue regarding the stage or stages at which effectiveness evaluation should be carried out. It may be appropriate to produce several prototypes that can be used by users. The developer, you, can use these prototypes to evaluate the effectiveness of different approaches before committing to one particular design. When the final solution is produced, further effectiveness evaluation is necessary to confirm that the design has achieved what it set out to achieve.

Another example involving graphics illustrates the importance of prototyping. A biological simulation of bacteria, white blood cells, antibiotics and antibiotic-resistant bacteria requires populations of each to be displayed in the same window on the screen (Fig. 7.6.2). Each must be in constant motion and cell division must take place at regular intervals. Cells that collide must interact and some must die. Up to 2000 of each must be displayable simultaneously. The specific requirements impose particular challenges relating to achieving a graphical display that supports smooth motion of a very large number of cell representations. Assessing the effectiveness of the graphical display early in the lifetime of the project is essential. In this instance, a decision was taken to use OpenGL graphics after trying a prototype that used a graphical application programming interface (API) built into the programming language. This prototype was evaluated and proved inadequate.

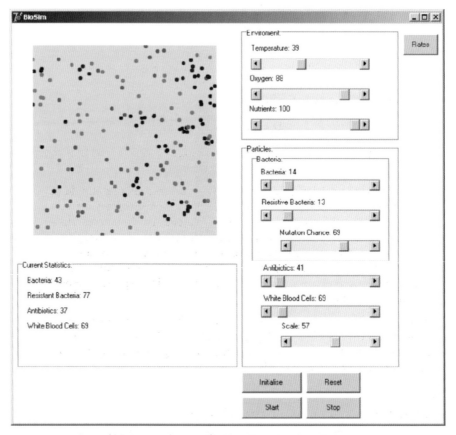

Fig. 7.6.2 *Biological simulation*

The example in Fig. 7.6.2 belongs to a type where effectiveness is judged using response time. Response time is frequently used as a criterion of effectiveness.

Learnability

Ideally, a solution should have no learning curve. Users should acquire instant mastery. In practice, all applications have a learning curve. That is why you need to evaluate how easy it is for users to learn how to use your solution. Learnability is related partly to effectiveness of the design and partly to usability of the user interface.

Usability

If a user finds it easy to use your solution, its **usability** will be high. Your aim is to create a solution with a usability that is high. Usability focuses largely on **human–computer interaction** (HCI) and the human–computer interface. The human–computer interface is often called the user interface (UI).

Usability can be classified by several criteria:

▓ **Target acquisition time**: this could be the time it takes to move the mouse pointer to a position over a button.

▓ **Latency**: how long does a user who has initiated an action have to wait before the action is completed? For example, after they click a button to execute an SQL statement, how long do they have to wait for the data that matches the query?

▓ **Readability**: how easy is it for a user to read commands or guidance?

▓ **Use of metaphors**: are there visual pictures or icons to help users understand what can be done?

▓ **Navigability**: how easy is it to navigate the user interface?

Target acquisition time

Fitts's law is a model of human movement which predicts the time required to rapidly move to a target area, e.g. a button, as a function of the distance to the target and the size of the target:

$$ID = \log_2 (2A/W)$$

where ID is the index of difficulty, A is the distance to move and W is the size of the target.

It predicts that acquisition using Macintosh pull-down menus should be approximately five times faster than acquisition using Windows menus. This has been borne out by numerous user evaluations. It dictates that the Windows task bar will constantly and unnecessarily get in people's way. This has been borne out by numerous user evaluations. And it indicates that the most quickly accessed targets on any computer display are the four corners of the screen, because of their pinning action. How could this be evaluated?

In any usability evaluation of a user interface, always try to answer this question: Has the solution developer applied Fitts's law to their user interface? The evaluator should assess whether large objects have been used for important functions – big buttons are faster.

Latency

Here are some criteria for evaluation of latency:

▓ Are all button clicks acknowledged by visual or aural feedback within 50 milliseconds?

▓ Key terms

Usability: the ease with which a user interface can be used by its intended audience to achieve defined goals.

Human–computer interaction: the study, planning and design of what happens when a human and a computer work together. It consists of three parts: the user, the computer and the ways they work together.

Is an hourglass displayed for any action that will take from 0.5 to 2 seconds?

Is the hourglass animated so they know the system hasn't died?

Is a message displayed to indicate the potential length of the wait for any action that will take longer than 2 seconds?

Is the actual length of the wait shown on a progress indicator?

Is there good use of audible signals to indicate changes of state so that users know when to return to using the system? An example is on return from a lengthy process (longer than 10 seconds).

Are multiple clicks of the same button or object trapped so that multiple instances of an action are not created, causing things to be even slower?

Readability

Here are some criteria for evaluation of readability:

Does text that must be read have high contrast? An example is black text on a white or pale yellow background.

Are grey backgrounds avoided?

Are font sizes large enough to be readable on standard monitors?

Are numbers clearly displayed? Unlike message text, humans are unable to guess character digits, so people need the ability to examine and comprehend every single digit character.

Use of metaphors

Has the designer used metaphors that make it easier for a user to understand how to use the user interface? For example, disk operations can be represented by icons that resemble a floppy disk.

Navigability

Here are some criteria for evaluation of navigability:

Are users given well-marked roads and landmarks to navigate the user interface?

Are users given perceptual cues?

Are actions reversible?

Is there an undo facility?

Is there always a way out?

Is the user offered shortcuts?

Maintainability

In the context of computer software, **maintenance** refers to these three tasks:

Fixing bugs: a common bug is a fence post error, where a count is off by 1. Perhaps For i := 1 To 100 Do should have been For i := 1 To 101 Do.

Changing parameters: it may be necessary to change the rate of VAT.

Responding to new requirements: a system that did not require a bar code reader may now require a bar code reader to input product IDs.

Maintainability of software refers to how easy or difficult it is to carry out these three tasks. The factors that need to be considered when judging whether software will be easy to maintain are very much based on principles of software engineering. When you evaluate the **maintainability of software** you have produced for your COMP4 project,

> ### Key point
>
> Classification of usability: target acquisition time, latency, readability, use of metaphors, navigability.

> ### Key terms
>
> **Maintenance:** fixing bugs, changing parameters and responding to changing requirements.
>
> **Maintainability of software:** how easy or difficult it is to fix bugs, change parameters and respond to changing requirements.

you should consider the following items:

- Is the software modular?
  - Do its procedures and functions perform a single task and are they self-contained?
  - Are collections of related procedures placed in independent units that can be compiled separately?
  - Is information hiding supported by the use of separate units?
- Is the code self-documenting?
  - Are meaningful identifier names used for variable names, procedure names, function names, etc.?
  - Is indentation used to indicate the structure of the code?
- Do blocks of code have one entry point and one exit point?
- Is there minimum use of global variables across units?
- Is there good use of local variables?
- Are parameter values passed in and out of procedures through procedure interfaces?
- Does it use an object-oriented approach to programming?
  - Is inheritance used to allow functionality to be extended?
  - Is polymorphism used to offer different functionality depending on object type?
- Is the database created from a DDL script which itself has been produced using a CASE tool so that the database can be re-engineered using the CASE tool?
- Is the database queried using SQL?
- Is the code commented where clarification is needed?

The documentation that accompanies the software is also essential for software maintenance. Consider the documentation when you evaluate maintainability:

- Is the project supported by analysis and design data dictionaries?
- Are entities and entity relationships documented?
- Is the software accompanied by dataflow diagrams, system flow charts and other relevant diagrams?
- Are algorithms documented?

The maintainability of your solution is evaluated by the person that marks your project. Consider all the above bulleted items from the outset and incorporate them in your solution from the beginning. Fig. 7.6.3 shows part of the analysis of the biological simulation project.

Customer or end-user evaluation

The customer or end user for whom you have developed a solution must contribute to the evaluation of your COMP4 project. They must check that the solution meets their requirements as agreed at the analysis stage. They must comment on how well these requirements have been met, i.e. the effectiveness of the solution. The customer or end user must also evaluate the usability of the solution.

Continuing evaluation

Evaluation doesn't just occur during prototyping and when the solution is ready for the customer. Evaluation continues after the solution is delivered to the customer. The solution should be reviewed periodically to evaluate whether it still meets and satisfies the needs of the customer. At some stage in the future, the solution will fail to meet one or more needs. This can occur for a variety of reasons: the customer's needs change with time, new hardware is developed, new software libraries or services become available that make the solution less optimal, new protocols are developed, new technologies are invented, and so on. A solution that once solved a problem now becomes a new problem.

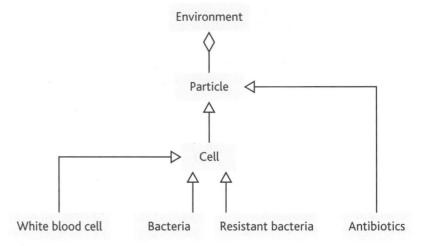

Fig. 7.6.3 *Object analysis diagram of the Biological simulation shown in Fig. 7.6.2*

Question

1. What is evaluation?

2. Name the four types of evaluation that apply to your COMP4 project.

3. The evaluation of software effectiveness requires criteria for judging the effectiveness of a software solution. State three other demands that will be made on the evaluator when evaluating the effectiveness of a software solution.

4. How would you evaluate the effectiveness of a project that provides remote file storage via the Internet for registered users?

5. How would you evaluate the effectiveness of a software solution that allows children aged 7 to practise their knowledge of word spellings?

6. What is meant by usability in the context of software?

7. State five criteria by which usability may be classified. Explain each of your five criteria.

8. What is software maintainability?

9. State four factors that need to be considered when judging if software will be easy to maintain.

10. State when software evaluation may take place.

✅ *In this topic you have covered:*

- evaluation of solutions against the requirements specification
- evaluation of effectiveness, usability and maintainability.

Glossary

Absolute error: the difference between the actual number and the nearest representable value.

Abstract data type (ADT): a data type whose properties are specified independently of any particular programming language.

Abstraction: representation that is arrived at by removing unnecessary details.

Aggregation: relationship between two object types in which one object type has a component which is of the other object type, e.g. a car has an engine or contains an engine.

Ajax: a web technology that allows only the part of a web page that needs updating to be fetched from the web server.

Algorithm: a sequence of unambiguous instructions for solving a problem, i.e. for obtaining a required output for any legitimate input in a finite amount of time. It can be represented as a Turing machine program.

Analysis data dictionary: a dictionary of the data that an end user will encounter. It should record the data item's name, its purpose, its type, its range of values and examples.

Application programming interface: a layer of software that allows application programs to call on the services of the operating system.

Association: if the relationship is not inheritance and it is not aggregation then it is an association, e.g. a snake uses the ground to get from A to B. The relationship is an association because a snake is not a kind of ground and a snake does not contain ground. It is, in fact, a 'uses' association relationship.

Asymptotic behaviour of *f*: is the behaviour of the function *f*(*n*) for very large values of *n*.

Asynchronous serial data transmission: the arrival of data cannot be predicted by the receiver; so a start bit is used to signal the arrival of data and to synchronise the transmitter and receiver temporarily.

Attribute: a property or characteristic of an entity (a named column in a table).

Attributes: the properties of the object, e.g. an object *car* has attributes *make*, *model*, *steering wheel*, *radio*, *engine*, *gearbox*, etc. Some of these attributes are objects themselves.

Automation: turning an abstraction into a form that can be processed by computer.

Backus–Naur Form, (BNF): a notation for expressing the rules for constructing valid strings in a regular language.

Bandwidth: for a transmission medium, e.g. copper wire, this is the range of signal frequencies that it may transmit.

Base case: a value that has a solution which does not involve any reference to the general case solution.

Baseband system: a system that uses a single data channel system in which the whole bandwidth of the transmission medium is dedicated to one data channel at a time.

Basic operation: the operation contributing the most to the total running time.

Baud rate: the rate at which signals on a wire or line may change.

Behaviours: the functions of the object or what the object does, e.g. behaviours of the car include drive forwards, drive backwards.

Bit rate: the number of bits transmitted per second.

Bluetooth: a wireless protocol for exchanging data over short distances from fixed and mobile devices.

Break the code: find the plain text from the cipher text by guessing or deducing the key.

Broadband system: a multiple data channel system in which the bandwidth of the transmission medium carries several data streams at the same time.

Bubble sort: during a pass through the list, neighbouring values are compared and swapped if they are not in the correct order. Several passes are made until one pass does not require any further swaps.

Cipher text: message data after it has been encrypted.

Circular queue: when the array element with the largest possible index has been used, the next element to join the queue reuses the vacated location at the beginning of the array.

Class definition: a pattern or template that can be used to create objects of that class.

Classification of usability: target acquisition time; latency; readability; use of metaphors; navigability.

Client: a computer that uses the services provided by a server.

Client–server system: a system in which some computers, the clients, request services provided by other computers, the servers.

Closed path or circuit: a sequence of edges that start and end at the same vertex and such that any two successive edges in the sequence share a vertex.

Common Gateway Interface: a gateway between web server and a web server extension that tells the server how to send information to a web server extension, and what the server should do after receiving information from a web server extension.

Communication protocol: a set of pre-agreed signals, codes and rules to be used for data and information exchange between computers or a computer and a peripheral device such as a printer that ensure that the communication is successful.

Complexity of a problem: taken to be the worst-case complexity of the most efficient algorithm which solves the problem.

Composite key: a combination of attributes that uniquely identify a tuple.

Computational complexity: of an algorithm, it measures how economical the algorithm is with time and space.

Conceptual model: a representation of the data requirements of an organisation constructed in a way that is independent of any software that is used to construct the database.

Cryptanalysis: trying to find the plain text from the cipher text without the decryption key.

Cryptography: the science of designing cipher systems.

Cycle: a closed path in which all the edges are different and all the intermediate vertices are different.

D

Data model: a method of describing the data, its structure, the way it is interrelated and the constraints that apply to it for a given system or organisation.

Data transmission: movement of data from one place to another.

Database: a structured collection of data.

Database management system: a software system that enables the definition, creation and maintenance of a database and which provides controlled access to this database.

Decidable: describes a decision problem that has a yes/no answer.

Decision problem: a yes/no algorithmic problem.

Decryption: using an algorithm and a key to convert encrypted message data into its plain text equivalent.

Degree: of a vertex the number of neighbours for that vertex.

Degree of relationship: between two entities, it refers to the number of entity occurrences of one entity which are associated with just one entity occurrence of the other and vice versa.

Desktop operating system: an operating system that allows a user to carry out a broad range of general-purpose tasks.

Deterministic finite state machine: an FSM that has just one next state for each pair of state and input symbol.

Directed graph or digraph: a diagram consisting of circles called vertices, joined by directed lines called edges.

Dynamic allocation: memory space is only allocated when required at run time.

Dynamic data structure: the memory taken up by the data structure varies at run time.

Dynamic web page content: content that is generated when the web browser request is received.

E

Embedded computer system: a dedicated computer system with a limited or non-existent user interface and designed to operate completely or largely autonomously from within other machinery.

Encapsulation: combining a record with the procedures and functions that manipulate it to form a new data type: a class.

Encryption: using an algorithm and a key to convert message data into a form that is not understandable without the key to decrypt the text.

Entities: the components that make up a system.

Entity: an object, person, event or thing of interest to an organisation and about which data are recorded.

Entity occurrence: the details of one instance of the entity.

Equivalent Turing machine: all other types of computing machine are reducible to an equivalent Turing machine.

Evaluation: is systematic assessment of whether something meets its objectives or specifications and how well it meets the latter in terms of effectiveness, usability, maintainability.

Explorer's problem: the solution finds a route that traverses each road exactly once before returning to the starting point.

Exponential growth: growth that has the form k^n, e.g. 2^n where $k = 2$ and $n = 1, 2, 3$, etc.

Exponential time algorithm: an algorithm whose execution time grows exponentially with input size.

Feasibility study: a preliminary study investigating the potential of a new system by assessing the problem then evaluating potential solutions and their costs.

Finite state automaton (FSA): that produces no output whilst processing the input but which responds YES or NO when it has finished processing the input. Also called a finite automaton.

Finite state machine (FSM): consists of a set of input symbols (input symbol alphabet) and if it produces output, a set of output symbols (output symbol alphabet), a finite set of states and a transition function that maps a state–symbol pair (current state and input symbol) to a state (next state) and possibly generates an output (output symbol) depending on the type of FSM.

Floating point notation: a real number represented by a sign, some significant digits, and a power of 2.

Foreign key: an attribute in one table that is a primary key in another table.

Gateway: a device used to connect networks using different protocols so that information can be passed from one system to another successfully.

General case: the solution in terms of itself for a value *n*.

Graph: a diagram consisting of circles, called vertices, joined by lines called edges or arcs; each edge joins exactly two vertices.

Halting problem: is it possible in general to write a program that can tell, given any program and its input and without executing this program, whether the given program with its given input will halt?

Halting state: a state that has no outgoing transition.

Handshaking protocol: the sending and receiving devices exchange signals to establish that the receiving device is connected and ready to receive. Then the sending device coordinates the sending of the data, informing the receiver that it is sending. Finally the receiver indicates it has received the data and is ready to receive again.

Heap: the memory locations available to application programs for dynamic allocation.

Heuristic: describes an approach that uses know-how and experience to make informed guesses that assist in finding a polynomial time solution to an intractable algorithmic problem.

Human–computer interaction: the study, planning and design of what happens when a human and a computer work together. It consists of three parts: the user, the computer and the ways they work together.

Inheritance: 1. (first def.) defining a class and then using it to build a hierarchy of descendant classes with each descendant inheriting access to all its ancestors' code and data.

Inheritance: 2. (second def.) relationship between two object types in which one object type is a kind of the other object type, e.g. a car is a kind of vehicle.

Instantiation: an object is defined based on a class.

Interactive operating system: an operating system in which the user and the computer are in direct two-way communication.

Internet: a collection of LANs and computers that are interconnected by a WAN.

Interpreter: an interpreter works its way through a set of source code instructions identifying the next instruction then executing.

Intractable: describes a problem for which no reasonable (polynomial) time solution has yet been found.

Labelled or weighted graph: a graph in which the edges are labelled or given a value called its weight.

Linear queue: elements join the queue at one end and leave the queue at the other end.

Linear search: this search method starts at the beginning of the list and compares each element in turn with the required value until a match is found or the end of the list is reached.

Linear time algorithm: a polynomial time algorithm that executes in $O(n)$ time.

List: a collection of elements with an inherent order.

Local Area Network: linked computers in close proximity.

Maintainability of software: refers to how easy or difficult it is to fix bugs, change parameters and respond to changing requirements.

Maintenance: fixing bugs, changing parameters and responding to changing requirements.

Mealy machine: an FSM that determines its outputs from the present state and from the inputs.

Memory leakage: successive calls to allocate memory space are made, but memory locations no longer required are not released. Eventually no memory is left in the heap.

Model: an abstraction of an entity in the real world or in the problem that enables an automated solution. The abstraction is a representation of the problem that leaves out unnecessary detail.

Moore machine: an FSM that determines its outputs from the present state only.

Neighbours: two vertices are neighbours if they are connected by an edge.

Network operating system: a layer of software is added to the operating system of a computer connected to the network. This layer intercepts commands that reference resources elsewhere on the network, e.g. a file server and then redirects the request to the remote resource in a manner completely transparent to the user.

Network segment: in Ethernet is a run of Ethernet cable to which a number of workstations are attached.

Non-computable: describes an algorithmic problem that admits no algorithm.

Non-deterministic finite state machine: an FSM that may have several possible next states for each pair of state and input symbol.

Normalisation: a technique used to produce a normalised set of entities.

Normalised entities: a set of entities that contain no redundant data.

Null pointer: a pointer that does not point to anything, usually represented by Ø or −1.

O(g), called Big O of g: represents the class of functions that grow no faster than g.

Object: an instance of a class.

One baud: one signal change per second.

Operating system: the most fundamental of all system programs.

Operating system role: this is to manage the hardware resources in order to provide for an orderly and controlled allocation of the processors, memories and I/O devices among the various programs competing for them and manage the storage of data. Also it hides the complexities of the hardware from the user.

Order of complexity: of a problem is its big O complexity.

Order of growth: assesses by what factor execution time increases when the size of the input is increased.

Overflow: the value is too large to be represented using the available number of bits.

Parallel data transmission: bits are sent down several wires simultaneously.

Peer-to-peer network: a network that has no dedicated servers. All computers are equal, so they are called peers.

Pharming: when a phisher changes DNS server information so that customers are directed to another site.

Phishing: when someone tries to get you to give them your personal information.

Plain text: message data before it is encrypted.

Pointer: a variable that contains an address. The pointer points to the memory location with that address.

Pointer type: a variable of pointer type stores an address of a data value.

Polymorphism: giving an action one name that is shared up and down a class hierarchy. Each class in the hierarchy implements the action in a way appropriate to itself.

Polynomial growth: growth that has the form n^k, e.g. n^3 where $k = 3$ and $n = 1, 2, 3, 4$, etc.

Polynomial time algorithm: an algorithm whose execution time grows as a polynomial of input size.

Power of a Turing machine: no physical computing device can be more powerful than a Turing machine. If a Turing machine cannot solve a yes/no problem, nor can any physical computing device.

Precision: the maximum number of significant digits that can be represented.

Primary key: an attribute which uniquely identifies a tuple.

Principle of universality: a universal machine is a machine capable of simulating any other machine.

Priority queue: each element of a priority queue has an associated priority.

Programs and data: can be treated as the same thing.

Prototype: an early or trial working version of the proposed system developed to test possible solutions.

Prototyping: building a working model, demonstration system, simplified version, rough copy or trial piece of software to help the analyst.

Pseudo-random numbers: a series of numbers generated by computer with apparent randomness.

Queue: a first-in-first-out (FIFO) abstract data type.

Real number: a number with a fractional part.

Real time operating system: inputs are processed in a timely manner so that the output can affect the source of the inputs.

Recursive definition: is one that is defined in terms of itself.

Recursive routine: a routine defined in terms of itself.

Referential integrity: if a value appears in a foreign key in one table it must also appear in the primary key in another table.

Regular expression: a notation for defining all the valid strings of a formal language or a special text string for describing a search pattern.

Regular language: any language that an FSM will accept.

Relation: a set of attributes and tuples, modelling an entity (a table).

Relational database: a collection of tables.

Relationship: an association or link between two entities.

Relative error: the absolute error divided by the actual number.

Remote login: when someone connects to a computer via the Internet.

Robust code: the program will function reliably and not crash or go into infinite loops, even with incorrect inputs or unpredictable values.

Rollout: setting up a new system and then using it for real for the first time.

Rooted tree: a tree in which one vertex has been designated as the root and every edge is directed away from the root.

Router: a device that receives packets or datagrams from one host (computer) or router and uses the destination IP address that they contain to pass them, correctly formatted, to another host (computer) or router.

S

Scientific notation: a real number represented by a sign, some significant digits, and a power of 10.

Serial data transmission: single bits are sent one after another along a single wire.

Server: a computer that provides shared resources to network users.

Server operating system: an operating system optimised to provide one or more specialised services to networked clients.

Server-based network: a network in which resource security and administration and other functions are provided by dedicated servers.

Significant digits: are those digits that carry meaning contributing to the accuracy of a number. This includes all digits *except* leading and trailing zeros where they serve merely as placeholders to indicate the scale of the number.

Simple graph: a graph without multiple edges and in which each edge connects two different vertices.

SaaS: software as a service; is a model of software deployment where an application is hosted as a service provided to customers across the Internet.

Space-complexity: of an algorithm indicates how much memory an algorithm needs.

Spam: unsolicited junk e-mails.

Stack: a last-in-first-out (LIFO) abstract data type.

Stack frame: the locations in the stack area used to store the values referring to one invocation of a routine.

Stand-alone computer: a computer that is not networked. It requires its own printer and other peripherals plus its own installation of application software.

State history: consists of state descriptions at each of a chronological succession of instants.

State transition diagram: a directed graph whose nodes represent the states. An edge leading from state s to state t is called a transition and is labelled with a symbolic code, e.g. $a \mid b$. The a part of the label is called the transition's trigger and denotes the input symbol. The b part, which is optional, denotes the output symbol.

Static data structure: the memory required to store the data structure is declared before run time.

System: a collection of people, machines, methods, software, reports, input paper forms and documents organised to accomplish a set of specific functions.

System program: a program that manages the operation of a computer.

T

Task is computable: if and only if it can be computed by a Turing machine.

Thin-client network: a network where all processing takes place in a central server; the clients are dumb terminals with little or no processing power or local hard disk storage.

Time-complexity: of an algorithm, indicates how fast an algorithm runs.

Topology: in the context of networking, the shape, configuration or structure of the connections that connect devices to the network.

Tractable: describes a problem that has a reasonable (polynomial) time solution as the size of the input increases.

Transition function: maps (input symbol, current state) to (output symbol, next state).

Transition table: tabulates the mappings (input symbol, current state) to (output symbol, next state).

Traveller's problem: the solution finds a route that visits each city exactly once before returning to the starting point.

Tree: a connected undirected graph with no cycles.

Trojan: a program that hides in or masquerades as desirable software, such as a utility or a game, but attacks computers it infects.

Tuple: a set of attribute values (a row in a table).

Turing machine (TM): an FSM that controls one or more tapes, where at least one tape is of unbounded length (i.e. infinitely long).

Undecidable: describes a decision-type algorithmic problem that is non-computable.

Underflow: the value is too small to be represented using the available number of bits.

Universal TM, UTM: a UTM, U, is an interpreter that reads the description $<M>$ of any arbitrary Turing machine M and faithfully executes operations on data D precisely as M does. For single-tape Turing machines, it is imagined that $<M>$ is written at the beginning of the tape, followed by D.

Universal Turing machine: a universal Turing machine can simulate any other Turing machine.

Usability: the ease with which a user interface can be used by its intended audience to achieve defined goals.

Virtual machine: the apparent machine that the operating system presents to the user, achieved by hiding the complexities of the hardware behind layers of operating system software.

Virus: a small program attached to another program or data file. It replicates itself by attaching itself to other programs. It usually attacks the computer.

Volumetrics: measurement or assessment of the volume of data that a system will be required to process and store.

Web 2.0: software that becomes a service that is accessed over the Internet.

Web server extension: a program written in native code, i.e. an executable or a script that is interpreted by an interpreter running on the web server that extends the functionality of the web server and allows it to generate content at the time of the HTTP request.

Web services: a self-contained, modular applications that can be described, published, located and invoked over a network, generally the web.

Web services architecture: where all components in the system are services.

Wide area network: a set of links that connect geographically remote computers and local area networks.

Wi-Fi: trademarked IEEE 802.11 technologies that support wireless networking of home and business networks.

Wireless network: any type of LAN in which the nodes (computers or computing devices, often portable devices) are not connected by wires but use radio waves to transmit data between them.

Worm: a small program that exploits a network security weakness (security hole) to replicate itself through computer networks. It may attack computers.

Index